Prisoner Diaries

Prisoner Diaries

Elizabeth M. Schulz

Clear Mind Press

CONTENTS

LEGAL PAGE vii
PRELUDE ix

1
WAYVILLE DETENTION CAMP, ADELAIDE, SOUTH AUSTRALIA

1 | 2

photo insert 17

2 | 19

3 | 33

photo insert 49

4 | 50

photo insert 75

5 | 88

photo insert 112

6 | 116

CONTENTS

2
TATURA INTERNMENT CAMP

7 | 120

8 | 157

9 | 221

10 | 265

11 | 298

photo insert 326

3
LOVEDAY INTERNMENT CAMP

12 | 328

photo insert 392

13 | 402

photo insert 442

ABOUT THE AUTHOR 451
ABOUT THE BOOK 453

LEGAL PAGE

Prisoner Diaries

© Elizabeth M. Schulz

Published by Clear Mind Press
2023 Alice Springs Australia

Print ISBN: 978-0-6459231-0-0
Ebook ISBN: 978-0-6459231-1-7

Cover design by Clear Mind Press
Photos cover: Author's collection
Photo front: 'Schulz - Printing Press'
Photos interior: Author's collection
Portrait of the Author: Maria Ames

All rights reserved. Except as permitted under the Australian Copyright Act 1968 (for example, fair dealing for study, research, criticism or review), no part of this book may be reproduced, stored in a retrieval system, communicated or transmitted in any form or by any means without prior written permission.

All inquiries should be made to the publisher.

info@clearmindpress.com
https://www.clearmindpress.com

PRELUDE

13 December 1940

The episode began with a fire.

A siren sounded across the town of Tanunda, volunteer firemen were alerted to their task, and news of the fire spread throughout the town faster than those flames engulfing Mutton Brothers Store in the neighbouring town of Angaston.

So, with journalistic instinct to the fore, I climbed into my grey Chevrolet sedan and sped off in the direction of Angaston to see what had occurred. It was not so much a conviction that I could be of material help, but the fact that our brigade had been summoned early in the afternoon from a distance of eight miles which suggested that there was more than a rubbish tip ablaze. Knowing how the men of our brigade always raced to their work when summoned by the siren; that they always acquitted themselves with distinction whenever the Chief from Adelaide unexpectedly called them into action, I was eager to see the brigade tackle a man-sized job, and I arrived in Angaston in double quick time.

Mutton Brothers Store resembled an ant heap into which someone had stepped with a heavy boot. The Tanunda and Angaston firemen were struggling to save the building. Axes smashed through walls and jets of water spurted in all directions, while scores of willing hands were salvaging goods to safety across the main street. Despite their efforts the store was gutted, but fortunately the firemen were able to keep the flames within the confines of that business. Driving home later in the day I wonder how I would feel if it were my business in ruins.

PRELUDE

About a mile out from Tanunda a military car comes in my direction, passes me, turns around, and follows me into the town. I stop my car opposite one of the local barber shops to report how valiantly the men of our brigade had worked at Angaston. The other car also stops and one of the occupants walks up to me and asks if it were possible to have a look through my printing office. The man introduces himself as Lieutenant Hill and then joins me in my car for the remainder of the journey.

'Do you have a film of Count von Luckner?' Hill asks.

'Yes, I filmed von Luckner when he visited South Australia,' I reply.

'Where is the film?'

'At my home.'

The two other officers in the visiting car join me and Hill at the printing office and a search of the premises commences. Hill continues his questions.

'Do you know a Dr. Becker?'

'Yes. I have from time to time sought medical advice from him.'

'Have you occasionally received German papers from him?'

'I have.'

'Where are these papers now?'

'They have been returned to the doctor.'

'What did you reprint from these papers?'

'Nothing.'

Lieutenant Hill stares at me in utter disbelief.

The searchers then direct their attention to a shelf containing bound volumes and books published by Auricht's Printing Office. A volume is selected at random and subjected to casual scrutiny with negative result.

'To which Lutheran Church do you belong?' Hill asks.

'I am a member of the Langmeil Church here in Tanunda,' I reply.

'In what respect does this church differ from another Lutheran Church?'

I attempt to explain the differing theological tenets of the two Lutheran Synods: The United Evangelical Lutheran Church of Australia

(U.E.L.C.A.) and the Evangelical Lutheran Church of Australia (ELCA). Hill and I then enter into a superficial discussion on theology as a whole while the other two officers continue their search of the premises.

While in the printing office the plain clothes officer asks for my personal details which he then records in a note book.

'Have you been to Germany?'

'No.'

'Do you have a son?'

'Yes.'

'Has he been to Germany?'

'Yes. I sent Bert to Germany because I wanted him to become proficient in the German language since at that time we were doing quite a lot of printing in that language. I also wanted him to enhance his skills in the new techniques of colour printing.'

The Officer then enquires, 'Do you keep a list of addresses to which you send the paper you print?'

'Yes.'

'Where is it?'

'We print the paper for the Lutheran Book Depot at North Adelaide; they represent the Church. Here is the file from the Book Depot regarding new subscribers, cancellations, and alterations. Stencils are made for each address and the addresses are then printed from the stencils onto wrappers in which the papers go to the Post Office. The papers are forwarded in bulk postings to Adelaide, Suburbs, Country, Victoria, NSW, Queensland, etc.'

'And where are the stencils?'

I open a drawer containing the stencils for Adelaide. The first stencil taken from the drawer gives the address: The Officer in Charge, C.I.B. Adelaide. The second stencil: The Librarian, Public Library, North Terrace, Adelaide.

Lieutenant Hill then requests a search of the Schulz family home. Since my house is situated at the other end of the main street in

PRELUDE

Tanunda, one of the other officers accompanies me as I drive there. While on this short trip he questions me as to my interest in Von Luckner.

'Tell me,' he asks, 'why did you film Von Luckner?'

'I am a showman,' I reply. 'It is my business to get films of universal interest. I might film the local show but beyond one, at most two local screenings and perhaps one in a neighbouring town, the film would arouse no further interest and barely cover the cost of its production. A film of Count Von Luckner, who was instrumental in doing so much harm to our shipping during the Great War, would be a draw card practically anywhere. If Von Luckner were roving the high seas during the present Armageddon and he were again apprehended, and it became known that he was about to be landed on a certain date at Adelaide, or even Melbourne, I would make haste to reach there and film the group.

Upon reaching home, I show the officers my study and produce the film of Von Luckner. A file on my writing table which contains newspaper cuttings, political pamphlets, and information on the last Federal elections, claims the attention of the investigating officers.

'Do you belong to that school of politicians?'

'Not necessarily,' I reply. 'I desire to know about and study the views of political opponents also.'

A copy of Hitler's Mein Kampf is produced from the bookshelf.

'Why have you underlined certain passages in this book?'

'Because these passages give special food for thought and study,' is my reply.

I take down from the bookshelf a copy of Chamberlain's My Struggle for Peace with its many underlined passages. Mein Kampf is impounded; My Struggle for Peace passed by.

'Why do you keep all this?' Hill asks.

'I am endeavouring to keep abreast of things. I do not only read and keep things which please and with which I agree, I also like to see the other person's view of things. As you can see, I have procured Chamberlain's My Struggle for Peace as well as Hitler's Mein Kampf.'

PRELUDE

'Why do you have the German and not the English version of Mein Kampf?'

'Wherever possible, I like to read books in the language in which they are written.'

I am arrested. The officers allow me to change my clothes, pack a few essentials and hurriedly explain to my wife Lena, daughter Else, and son Bert, that I am being detained under the War Precautions Act. After hurriedly discussing business matters with Bert and asking Else to write up a list of all my books as requested by Sergeant Hill, I am quick-marched at bayonet point to the car and driven to Wayville Detention Camp in Adelaide. By 9 p.m. I am in the hands of the Military Authorities.

No accusations were made directly to me in the course of the search, but I know what this arrest means; someone, somewhere, considers me a threat.

WAYVILLE DETENTION CAMP, ADELAIDE, SOUTH AUSTRALIA

13 December, 1940 – 1 June, 1941

1

13 December, 1940

On my arrival at Wayville Camp, Pastor Chris Stolz and Hermann Homburg make me feel welcome. Hermann shakes my hand and offers me a cup of coffee. Hughie Eime introduces me to some of the other inmates: Oscar Johannsen, Arratu Comelli, F Henke, Pastor Lutze, Hoeft, van der Borch, Angus Bohlmann, Ernst Pohl, Schober, Emil Kuhri, Helmut Rothe, W Lebek, M and W Pengelly, Herold, Vini and Vito Caputo, and C. and A. Camporeale.

Pastor Stolz quickly organises a bunk for me, a bed knocked together by the inmates, a straw mattress, and a blanket. Khuri and Lebek are in one adjoining cubicle, two Italians in the other. Lebek points to a mouse racing along the crossbeams.

'I think it would be a good idea if you caught that mouse, Lebek, and had it on toast for breakfast,' advised Khuri.

I was not amused. Just then two guards walk past outside and I hear one ask, 'What date is it?' 'The thirteenth,' came the reply. It sure is, I thought. Friday the thirteenth of December, 1940.

From my bed I can see seven barbed wires.

Reflecting on the events of the day, I must be honest and admit that soon after war had been declared, I did consider myself a likely candidate for arrest, particularly since I had quite openly fraternised with Doctor Becker. I had even discussed the possibility of arrest with my family. But was Becker the only reason? Why had they asked all those questions about my religion, my connections with Germany and Bert's visit there in 1936, about von Luckner, and about my political views?

I am fifty-seven years old, and a respected community leader within the Barossa Valley. What sort of threat do I pose to this country? What has happened in my life which could be construed as detrimental to the safety of our nation?

14 December, 1940

I wake with a start. My back is aching. This straw pallet is nothing like my comfortable bed at home. Slowly I stretch my legs to ease the aches and pains and think about the day ahead. Today is Saturday. Yesterday I was able to move freely around Tanunda, coming and going as I pleased. Today I am surrounded with barbed wire and patrolling guards. I am no longer free.

Hermann Homburg walks into my cubicle and speaking quietly says, 'It is important that you begin to prepare for your defence.'

I must admit I was a little stunned. It's not yet 6 a.m. and I'm still trying to come to terms with the situation I'm in here.

'Don't say too much to anyone here, just start getting your facts together. Write it all down to give to your solicitor so you won't be caught out when they question you,' Homburg continues. 'Tell them about all the work you've done raising money for Red Cross and Comforts Funds. Try to think of every move or statement you have made which could be detrimental to your case, particularly dates and places where they happened, if possible. Then try to find suitable answers for them.'

I continue to stare at him.

'This is very important,' Homburg urges in his subdued voice, 'as this will save you being wiped off your feet by questions suddenly asked of you at the Hearing. You will need to be extremely careful about your association with the Hitler Party and Count von Luckner. This is most important and will require a convincing answer.'

Now I am fully alert.

'I had always considered there was a danger of my being picked up,' I remark, 'also my son, Bert. He was in Germany before the war. I thought that if we put all our efforts into war work then we would be immune from arrest. Actually, I'm surprised that Willie Schulz, your brother Fritz's business partner, hasn't been arrested.'

'Yes, Fritz was jolly lucky too,' Hermann replies. 'The investigating officer was disrated for insufficient investigation before the Court was assembled. Now, getting back to your case. I think you should say what you said to me last night about the fire at Angaston. Don't tell them you went up there for curiosity, tell them you were told a fire had broken out at Mutton's shop in Angaston and you went up to help fight the fire. It all helps to mention Mutton as he is an Englishman. You need to make use of every opportunity. I suggest you have Harford act as your solicitor. He did an excellent job on the Gibbs and Schutze case. And remember you will need to be very careful as your case may affect my brother Fritz, as well as others up there in the Barossa.'

'I will do my best,' I reply.

As Homburg turnes to leave the cubicle, he whispers, 'Be careful what you say while you're in the Camp, you never know who is listening. Stolz said that at his Hearing in Court he was asked questions about what he had been saying in the Camp. Somebody has big ears and an even bigger mouth!'

He left me alone to consider the thought that here too, within these barbed wires, there are spies.

I am finding it difficult trying to adjust to this new environment. Wayville Detention Camp, which had formerly been the Wayville Showgrounds, is in close proximity to Keswick Army Barracks and only a few miles from the business centre of Adelaide. The Camp has been established at Wayville as a holding centre for detainees apprehended for internment who are awaiting notification of their appeal against detention before the National Security Advisory Committee. I'm hoping it will not be too long before I can appeal against my own detention.

Today I signed paperwork for the authorities relating to my 'capture' yesterday and subsequent detention here in Wayville Camp. The spelling of my surname was incorrect as someone had added a 't' to it, but under the circumstances I was not in any frame of mind to point this out to them.

There was also another form to sign notifying me of my right to make objections to this detention. I signed the form and noticed that the person who had filled in the date details prior to my signing had written '14th day of November, 1940.' This is December and it seems I'm not the only one under pressure.

I had slept little during the night from 15th to 16th December. I was pacing my cubicle at about 5 a.m. when Hermann Homburg passed on his way to the lavatory. I asked him to come in and sit down.

'Can you tell me how many people live in South Australia?'

He didn't know.

'There must be more than 600,000, and of this number you and I, British subjects, Australian born have violated the National Security Regulations. As soon as I get the chance I am going to walk out of this damned place.'

'Stay here Monty, my boy,' Hermann replied, 'outside there is just one big lunatic asylum.'

Khuri in the cubicle next to mine is snoring loudly. My bed, made of timber by Camp inmates, is in the habit of creaking loudly whenever I move ever so slightly. It is a wonderful means of waking the snorer. The first time I woke him, he shouted out to me, 'Why the bloody hell don't you grease your bed!'

Now Kuhri is shouting from the cubicle next door. 'You'd better get your soap and towel ready, Schulz!'

Then I remember what day it is. Stolz told me last night that each Saturday and Tuesday morning there is a shower parade. So, I ready myself and join the other internees who are lining up three abreast ready to march to the shower block which is situated at the rear of the open stand at the oval. There in a space approximately 10 yards by 3 yards, a number of hot showers are ready and the entire camp bathes simultaneously, two or three men standing under one shower at a time. Modesty is a thing of the past.

For breakfast in the Mess room we sit six at one table. Each man has his own 'messing gear.' I am given a quart pot, knife, spoon, and fork to use until I can supply my own. The occupants of each table in turn do the washing up and scrub tables, Mess room floor, and the lavatory. Life at Wayville is certainly going to be different.

Morning and afternoon exercises proceed in a lane in the Showgrounds. At 4 p.m. those who wish to do so join in physical drill conducted by Pastor Stolz, who is also the Camp Orderly. It is the Orderly's duty to see that the Camp regulations are complied with. He accompanies the Camp Commandant and the Doctor on their daily rounds of inspection.

Visiting days are Sunday and Wednesday from 2 p.m. till 4 p.m. and I eagerly anticipate visits by my family. On my first Sunday in Camp I attend the Lutheran Service conducted by Pastor Lutze which is held in the Dining Room and during the afternoon my son Bert, daughters Else and Margaret, and son-in-law Ted visit me. They bring with them a mattress, bedding, cake, fruit, and tobacco. There is a sense of unease during this first visit and I feel apprehensive, but they do bring me up-to-date on what is happening in my home town.

During this first week of detention I begin to settle into the routine of Camp life. Mr. Harford, the solicitor from the legal firm Villeneuve Smith, calls on the 16th December to arrange an Appeal for me. Acting on Homburg's advice, I give Harford the details I'd listed regarding my past actions and acquaintances.

Captain Sparks, our Camp Commandant, has given permission for my projector and films to be delivered so I can show movies in the Compound to the others. He is a wonderful man. He treats us all in Camp as being under detention and innocent until heard. He is a missionary among us who fits us to be ready to carry on after our release.

Hermann Homburg is ecstatic. 'See,' he says, 'you will find this is a good move. I told you it would be. This will help your release if they allow you to show films here. They could not object to you showing them outside and you have some quite innocent films.'

On the next day, 17th December, I sign a Statutory Declaration in the presence of Mr. Francis Malone, J.P., objecting to my detention based on the following information previously given to Mr. Harford. The wording is as follows:

I was born at Point Pass in the State of South Australia on the 19th day of March 1883.

I am carrying on business as a printer at Tanunda aforesaid, and have been doing so for 15 years approximately.

I am and have been for one year and six months a Member of the District Council of Tanunda and a Trustee of the Tanunda Orphan's Home, and Chairman of the Tanunda Civil Defence Committee, and President of the Bowling Club of Tanunda, and Vice President of the Tanunda Show and I have served on several committees of other public organisations at Tanunda.

I intended to be a candidate at the next ensuing South Australian State Elections in the interests of the Australian Labor Party.

I am married and have three children, to wit:

Margaret now Mrs. T. Knispel of Nuriootpa residing with her husband and one child of the marriage. The said husband is in business as a Barber at Nuriootpa aforesaid.

A son Wilhelm Berthold Schulz and a daughter Else Schulz.

The respective ages of my children are, 30 years, 29 years, and 23 years approximately.

I reside with my wife and a son and daughter namely Wilhelm Berthold and Else at Tanunda aforesaid.

Since the outbreak of the present War I have devoted much of my time and energy and money to assist Australia in its war effort, and at no time have I been disloyal in word or deed to my allegiance to the Crown.

I have not done anything detrimental to the War effort of Australia or its Allies, nor have I been guilty of any act of disloyalty or otherwise to the Crown by word or deed.

I have done nothing to justify a belief or reasonable suspicion that I am or have been or about to be other than a loyal British subject and I hereby affirm and declare my allegiance and loyalty to the Crown in Great Britain and in Australia.

My financial and family interests are both wholly in South Australia, and I have no interests of any kind in the enemies' territory.

And I make this solemn declaration conscientiously believing the same to be true and by virtue of the provisions of the 'Oaths Act 1936'.

After signing this Notice of Objection, I was handed a copy by Mr. Harford.

Later that day my three-year-old grand-daughter, Marie, visiting me for the first time asks, 'Are you helping the soldiers, Grandpa?' What could I reply?

In cells near our Camp, trainees who offend (in the main A.W.L.= Absent Without Leave) are confined for various length periods. About four o'clock every afternoon we exercise in a lane opposite the yard in which the A.W.L. offenders are confined. On Saturday, 21 December, crowds pass nearby on the way to the Trots. One of the A.W.L. lads mounts an empty garbage tin and offers to lay odds: 'I'll take 6 to 4, I'll take 6 to 4.' His audience consists of two solitary co-offenders: 'I'll have threepence on so and so,' says the one. 'I'll take nothing less than sixpence,' says the bookmaker. 'What! Do you think a fellow is an adjectival millionaire?' is the rejoinder.

***

Christmas week brings a flurry of activity to the Camp and I show some of my films for the first time. A vote of thanks is extended by Hermann Homburg on behalf of all present and Comelli's poster advertising the event is souvenired by Captain Sparks.

On the 24th December, Pastors Stolz and Lutze are released. We are all happy for them but also sad at the thought of not being with our own families for the festive occasion. On the same day, Homburg is called to the Commandant's office during our tea-time and on his return says, 'Gentlemen, I have just been told I am released!'

That leaves us without organisers for the contemplated Christmas Eve celebrations. However, we soon recover our equilibrium and, before darkness sets in, all is ready.

Hughie Eime, Camp Controller, (successor to Pastor Stolz) is now in charge. He opens the evening's proceedings with well-chosen words and the group sings the 'Song of Australia'. I am then asked to say a few words.

'One thousand, nine hundred and forty years ago,' I begin, 'a child was born in a manger whose birthday will be remembered when the birthdays of even the mightiest on this earth are long forgotten. We should all be thankful. Yes, even those of us who are suffering this inconvenience of detention. The reason we should all be thankful is that we are living in that part of the British Empire which has been spared the crucifixion currently being experienced in Europe, where the innocents, the little children and their mothers, are suffering so intensely.'

The group then sings 'Silent Night' and 'O Come All Ye Faithful', and this first part of the programme concludes with songs and vocal items. The lights are then switched off, candles on the Christmas tree are lit and, standing round with Sergeant Link in attendance, we all sing 'O Du Fröliche, O Du Selige', and complete the carol singing with 'O Tannenbaum'.

At this stage Father Christmas arrives in the shape of Franz Drake, who is dressed in a large dressing gown, mask, and flowing beard made from brown paper. In a wheat bag he has a parcel for each inmate of the Camp, which comprises nuts, cigarettes, and tobacco. On the tables stand plates filled with cakes, nuts, streusel kuchen, etc. supplied by relatives and friends, including two dozen bottles of cool drink supplied by our Lutheran Church General President, Stolz. By pooling the entire resources of our little colony, there is enough for everyone, plus a plate of cakes which was sent to the Army lads who have been confined in cells for being Absent Without Leave.

The Christmas tree, candles, and Engelshaar (Angel's Hair, used for decoration) had been brought into the Camp by President Stolz. I saw him struggling through the Camp door, carefully balancing the tree with considerable effort during visiting hours on Sunday.

Father Bede, the Catholic priest who regularly holds Mass in the Camp, had arrived earlier in the day with cigarettes, tobacco, and a card for each person, wishing them the blessings of Christmas and the New Year from Matthew Beovich, Archbishop of Adelaide.

On Christmas Day Hughie begins his role as Camp Controller by letting us know exactly what will happen if there are any sustained complaints. After the usual morning Inspection he surprises us all by announcing he wants a Christmas cake.

'What is Christmas without a cake?' he queries. 'Now that I'm in charge, I'll see what can be done about it.' And off he goes to consult with the authorities.

On his return he announces, 'We can have a cake if we bake it ourselves. Now, who can bake?'

There was no reply. 'Schulz, can you bake?'

'Of course I can bake. Haven't I frequently criticised the baking at home?' I replied.

Then I tell them all that I have only made one mistake in my life when baking at home, when:

'I had measured out the butter with a very solemn air,
The milk and sugar also, and I took the greatest care
To count the eggs correctly and to add a little bit
Of baking powder, which beginners oft omit.
Then I stirred it all together and I baked it quite an hour,
But I never quite forgave myself for leaving out the flour.'

Promising not to forget the flour on this occasion, I ask, 'Who will volunteer to help me?'

'I'll try anything once,' said Hoeft. 'I've watched my wife baking at home,' added Henke, 'so I'm willing to take a chance.'

The magazines 'Woman' and 'The True Magazine', both containing recipes, are handed to me with sympathetic gestures tempered by malicious intent. Passing my cubicle on the way to the Officer's Mess kitchen, I nonchalantly toss the magazines through the doorway and onto my bunk.

'What do you intend to bake?' Hoeft enquires.

'Why the devil ask me?' I reply. I'm only the shanghaied cook.'

'Perhaps we could bake something with raisins in it,' Henke suggests.

'Fine, says Hoeft, 'but who's got raisins?'

They looked blankly at each other.

'I've got some,' I cry out ecstatically. 'I've just remembered that my wife brought me a packet last visiting day.' And I dash off to get them.

On my return I see Captain Sparks is in the kitchen.

'I have a request,' he announces. 'Is it possible for you to bake an extra cake which we can then give to the A.W.L. lads?'

'Certainly,' I reply. 'Why should they live if we die?'

Henke is the driving force and Hoeft the restraining influence. We decide on eighteen cups of flour, two dozen eggs, one packet of seeded raisins, one pound of sugar, some self-raising flour, cream of tartar, and fat. As there is no butter available, we make do with fat.

I work hard, I wanted to work hard rather than give guidance and advice. I sieved a big dishful of flour only to find a small piece of twine. I beat the whites of two dozen eggs until the lot frothed like beer drawn from a keg just tapped. I beat the yolks and melted fat until my arms ached and I was beaten to a standstill. Then the three of us mixed everything together. The mess in the dish resembled a mixture of putty and white lead, and the raisins looked like lumps of soot which had fallen down the chimney.

'Where can we bake it?' Hoeft asks.

'Here you are,' replies the Officers Mess cook. 'This is a fast oven and the other one bakes slowly.'

With the cake finally in the oven, I grab the dishes to wash them at the sink outside, hoping for the best and preparing for the worst. I keep on washing long after the dishes are clean, too afraid to return to the kitchen. When I do return, the cook is pointing to something in a dish on top of the stove. It resembles the crater of an extinct volcano. But it's not our cake. It is something the cook has prepared to wrap around fritzwurst or saveloys which have apparently become ashamed of their appearance. Our cake was still baking.

Some little while later the cook sends a message to the three of us to hurry over as the roof of the oven was lifting. Oh boy! And what a cake it is! Served with a plentiful supply of hot coffee, we all enjoy it for afternoon tea. The Captain receives a piece and I rescue a piece for my family who will visit me tomorrow.

26 December, 1940

My day on Mess Duty in the kitchen entails scrubbing and washing the tables, scrubbing the floor, then hosing it down and applying phenyl to disinfect it all. It's good exercise, both for the body and the mind, but, I ask myself, how on earth can the womenfolk at home put up with this drudgery day in and day out?

This afternoon the family visit me; Mum, Margaret, Marie, Ted, Else, Bert and Gert. They bring so many good things again, including Streusel Kuchen and beautiful Gladioli. Included in the bunch is a pure white one. After they have left for home, Comelli mixes me a container of red water. I place the white gladi in it and we stand and watch the slender veins of the dainty petals gradually turn red.

It is wonderful to spend time with my family, of course, but I find there is still a hesitancy to ask me what is happening, why, how, when, etc., and, to be quite honest, I doubt whether I can fill in many details for them. However, they are more relaxed about sharing news from home which I am always glad to hear.

At General Inspection and again at Medical Inspection the following day, my Gladiolis are admired. Their names are discussed and again I explain how we have transformed the white specimen into a rose-coloured one.

An incident has just occurred involving two of the A.W.L. lads and there is quite a commotion outside. The lads have scaled the walls and cut the six barbed wires. One of them is Tamke. I had noticed this lad on Fatigue Duty, when we were busy baking our cake on Christmas Day. I later placed him as having played football against Tanunda. When we were exercising in the lane he was sitting near the netting enclosure apparently deep in thought. I got a packet of cigarettes from my cubicle and walked over to him.

'Is your name Tamke?' I asked.

He jumped up from his seat. 'Yes, Mr. Schulz.'

'Do you smoke?'

'I do.'

I pushed the packet through the netting.

'Thank you, Mr. Schulz.'

Tamke disappeared into his cell and I continued my exercising.

So now Tamke has hopped it. Had I been seen handing him something? This thought worries me, so I ask to see Captain Sparks as soon as it is convenient.

'You wanted to see me?' Sparks asks.

'Yes, sir.' And I explain what I have done.

'Ah well, he's hopped it and you didn't know what he was planning to do.'

***

Comelli is permitted to have his gramophone brought into Camp. One of the first records he plays is a 'Laughing Record'. His cubicle soon fills with people and what a noise they all make. The Camp Orderly, Hughie, appears and bellows at them, 'Stop that damned rumpus at once!' There is momentary silence. Hardly has Hughie turned to go back to his cubicle when bedlam breaks loose with greater violence than before. 'The cranky cows don't know any better,' says Hughie with a broad grin on his dial, and lays down on his bunk to rest.

A grey kitten has strayed into the Camp. General jubilation all round with the exception of Hermann Homburg. Comelli immediately appropriates it. It has fleas, of course, and from somewhere he produces Flytox and a spray, and applies the Flytox rather freely. Soon afterwards Puss disappears and Hermann's name is whispered as the reason for this. When we were busy at physical drill during the afternoon Puss reappeared, having apparently just escaped death by drowning at somebody's hands. Drenched to the skin, Puss took up a position in the centre of the squad and immediately behind Comelli. Sitting on her haunches, somewhat dopey and cockeyed, she followed Comelli's movements intently: left; right, left; right; one two, one two, her head swaying from side to side. It proved too much for our instructor, Pastor Stolz. Convulsed with laughter, he ordered the class to stand at ease. Hermann watched Puss with a malicious glint in his eye. He was last to re-enter the Camp and Puss was never seen again.

28 December, 1940

Today is Ernst Pohl's Birthday. We sing: 'Why was he born so beautiful, why was he born at all!' During breakfast Hughie, on extending congratulations to Pohl, referred to the stork's arrival at the Pohl home 39 years ago. I informed the gathering that I remembered being present on that occasion and that one of Pohl's elder brothers, when being asked if he wanted to see the little baby brother brought by the stork, had replied: 'No, I want to see the stork!'

Two weeks into my detention and tempers are becoming frayed. Pengelly threatens to fight Oscar. Hughie tacks a notice on his door proclaiming that only gentlemen are permitted to interview him. During lunch time the notice disappears. Hughie then offers to fight the whole Camp. Eventually it all simmers down to good-natured banter.

That same evening I play chess with Max Hunger. I win the first game easily, but the second is a lot more difficult. I move a unit, just release it for a moment and decide to replace it. Max says, 'A move is a move is a move, Schulz,' and takes my piece. 'I don't play like that!' says I, and upend the board. Max is right, but my nerves are on end. I feel sorry and say so.

While cleaning my cubicle the next morning, I move my bed away from one of the partition walls and find a long hack-saw blade behind the bed. What a find! That was my first thought. With a handle fixed to each end, I could saw little pieces of wood and make toys for Marie. Second thought: What will Captain Sparks say when it is reported to him that I am in possession of a hack-saw? I am sure the blade was not there when I shifted the bed yesterday. So, I decide to report the matter to the Captain.

'You wanted to see me?'

I tell him of my find. He looks at me, then at the blade. 'I'm glad you reported the matter to me,' he said. 'Any idea how the thing got there?'

'No idea at all,' I reply.

'Do you know of anybody trying to plant you?'

I wasn't prepared to say who I thought may have put it there, so just shook my head. Captain Sparks left taking the blade with him.

31 December, 1940

It's the last day of the year and I'm on Mess Duty again. During the day I spend time lining my cubicle with brown paper in an effort to spruce it up a bit. An old blanket I brought into the Camp on my arrest is cut to make a carpet in my cubicle, so now I can walk the floor hours on end and not be heard nor disturb those in the adjoining cubicles.

Sleeplessness seems to be an end result of the situation I'm currently in. I hope that soon I'll hear good news of a release.

My Gladiolas are showing signs of wilting now, so I cut them shorter, cut out the wilted flowers and they still provide a great show.

In spite of the fact that it is New Year's Eve, I'm in bed by 11pm and fall quickly to sleep. An hour later I think there's an air raid happening. Between the top of the door and the roof guttering, where the barbed wires begin, there is an open space of about 18 inches wide. Through this space come four gallon buckets and the tinplate messing gear from our dining room. At the same time Comelli's gramophone begins playing the 'Laughing Song'! All the Camp inmates, of course, are immediately affected, and it's not long before the Camp sounds as if it is full of Australian Jackasses!

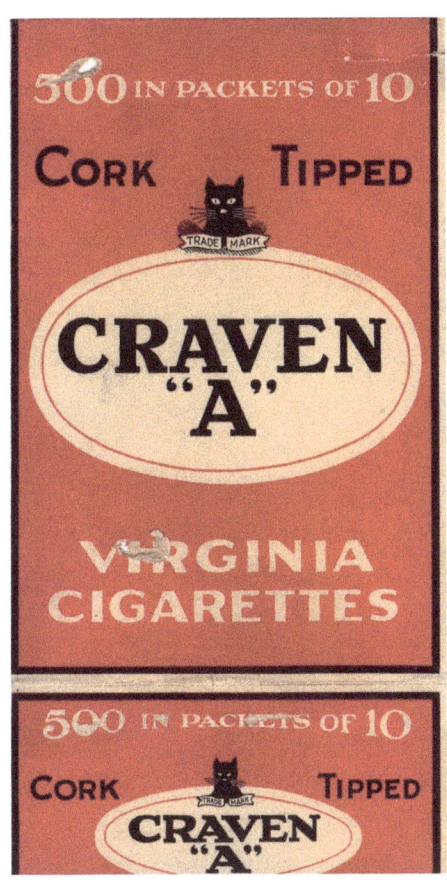

Craven 'A' Packet

Prime Minister's Menzies New Year's Message

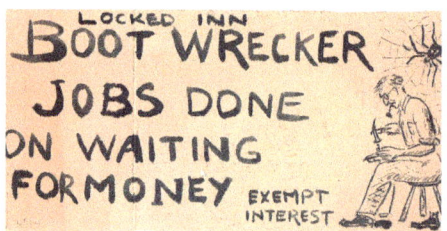

Locked Inn Boot Wrecker

2

1 January, 1941

The New Year has begun.

Prime Minister Menzies, in his New Year Message states:

'We pass into 1941 when the victories shall be ours so long as we to ourselves do rest but true, so long as we look without fear at the truth and are prepared to vow to our country and its cause all that we have and are, without subtraction, without excuse, without folly or selfishness.'

I start the New Year UNDER DETENTION. What will this new year have in store for us here and the world at large? How can I prove that I am prepared to vow to our country and its cause all that I have and are, and that in my past years I have always been loyal and looked without fear at the truth?

Here at Wayville Camp there are two other Australian born men besides myself under detention. We do not know why we are here, although it appears I have committed the unpardonable sin of daring to contest the seat of Angas against a Minister of the Crown.

At tea-time, Kuhri can't find his enamel mug. When it is found at my seat on Table One, he threatens to put me on the mat and to annihilate all and sundry. However, even the biggest bully is unable to counter the banter of an entire Camp. Next morning at breakfast, the mug is found hanging from the electric light cord. The atmosphere is sulphurous, but no storm breaks loose.

Soon after my arrival here I started collecting spent matches. I have 15 bundles of approximately 60 matches. Captain Sparks questions me about them.

'Schulz, what do you intend doing with your bundles of spent matches?'

'I intend putting heads on them again when I find the time to do so,' I reply.

'You're mad, man,' he said walking away.

Eime says, 'Don't take any notice of Schulz, he's a bit cracked in the head.'

I have now been detained for three weeks and still have not heard anything regarding my Appeal. The wheels turn slowly indeed.

Scotty, who is a member of the First A.I.F., with decorations on his coat, doing duty here at Wayville, was brought in yesterday the worse for liquor and promptly put in clink. Scotty measures about 6 feet 6 inches and is of powerful build with a command of language peculiar to Australians. To my mind, Scotty is just the kind of soldier who would be first over the top at Gallipoli. He should not be locked up. He's only just in and is already busy undoing the barbed wire in the far corner!

At breakfast this morning we find he has prised the galvanised iron sheets apart, separating our Messroom from his prison yard. Suddenly he joins us.

'Does anyone have a match to light my cigarette?' he asks, with a huge grin on his face.

Later in the afternoon I learn with delight that he is out again and is asking for his discharge, which of course is refused.

4 January, 1941

Once again, I am awake early. Ruminating, I lean on the bottom half of my door with the top half ajar. The live-stock, for whom these stalls were originally built, I suppose, occasionally hung their heads out in a similar fashion.

My stall has been transformed. On a shelf, built by myself, I have a vase of glorious Gladioli, the second lot brought in by members of my family. Pride of place takes little Marie's photo with beckoning arm outstretched and a winsome smile on her face. In one corner cans containing my films are piled up. Film show paraphernalia rests here and there. Shelving I made by myself out of two petrol cases contains eatables; fruit, nuts, sweets etc. Along on the crosspieces you find knick-knacks made by me from tobacco tins etc., and decorations from patterns on matchboxes, and in front of the little writing table, also made by me, I have nailed the 'Wall Almanac 1941 of the U.E.L.C.A.'.

In a secluded corner there is a large parcel of sole leather generously supplied by J.H.A.Schultz of Tanunda, our local shoe shop proprietor. This little parcel becomes the happy hunting ground of fellow inmates suffering from a torn 'soul'! Upon receipt of the leather, I sent the following note to the donor: You're a brick, Alf, for having helped to save our 'holey souls'!

I set out to say that as I'm leaning over the door, I see Scotty, nicely dressed in his uniform and looking well groomed. Netting and barbed wire separate us. He is busy moving about in the Officer's Mess. Now he emerges from the Mess with a teapot. On his way to the boiling copper he picks up what appears to be an apple or an orange and, in his stride, hurls it with every ounce of strength at his command against the galvanised iron wall of the long building in which his fellow officers are still peacefully slumbering.

While the noise from the throw reverberates through the building, he has already filled his teapot with boiling water. He spies me. 'Will ye have a cup o' tea, cobber?' and without waiting for an answer he proceeds to the kitchen. A few moments later he is at the fence and pouring me a mug of tea through the netting. 'It's a wunderfu' wurrld', he says in his broadest Scottish accent. 'I wuss on yurr side o' the fence yesturrday', and a broad grin flicks across his face from ear to ear. I like Scotty.

Now that I've finished mending my shoes and slippers, the boot last, hammer, nails, and leather are making the rounds in the cubicles. Comelli has nailed a sign over my door:

Locked Inn
Boot Wrecker
Jobs done
On waiting for Money
Exempt Interest.

He has also drawn me sitting on a stool busy putting a sole on a boot, with a large black spider weaving its web in one corner.

Bert brings me all the Electoral Rolls during today's family visit, Sunday, 5th January. A paragraph in the Barossa News reads: '…it is probable that Mr. Schulz will not nominate.' Hell! Won't he?! I intend writing to Bob Richards that I definitely will nominate.

The next morning I'm up early so I decide to awaken the Camp by playing the record: 'My Dark Haired Marie', which the family also brought for me. Of course, my grand-daughter Marie has fair hair, so the Camp now sings: 'Our golden-haired Marie'.

I remember when Marie arrived in Adelaide on her first visit to Grandpa. She had asked her mother, 'Where is Grandpa?' Her mother had replied, 'We'll be there directly.' 'What is Grandpa doing there?' 'He's helping the soldiers.' Upon arrival at Wayville, Marie enters the enclosure with her parents. She has welcomed Grandpa and, after having eyed the men in uniform intently and with pride written over her dear little face, she says, 'Hm, Grandpa, you're helping the soldiers here!'

That of course is not what Grandpa is doing, but conversely the soldiers personified in the Camp Commandant and his staff are helping Grandpa to fit him later again to help the soldiers and the Red Cross. Yes Sir, we must be prepared, we must right now lay hold of the big job ahead of us with both hands.

Never before today did I find physical drill as easy and simple as this afternoon. I can balance on the right leg and do all sorts of exercises with the left; I can balance on the left leg without a tremor and shoot the right leg in any conceivable direction. I am in the rear rank with my back against a galvanised iron wall!

Since my arrival here there have been frequent complaints about postal articles taking so long in transit. Well, the Lutheran Herald No. 1, 1941, dated January 6 reached me here in Camp today, January 6, at 3.45pm.

There's a sulphuric atmosphere at breakfast this morning. Hoeft and Khuri almost come to grips, and Hughie makes it worse because he's not a good mediator. During the first Inspection Hoeft calls Khuri a French ….! Khuri reports to Captain Sparks. During the course of the day new regulations are posted in our Messroom providing for 28 days solitary confinement inter alia, for offenders. I know against whom my vote will go, if a vote were taken as to who should receive the first month.

The prison quarters adjoining, where offending trainees, offending guards, etc. are locked up, is a hive of activity all day. There have been several escapes recently so changes are being made. Besides the overhanging 7 barbed wires, the top of the exercising yards is receiving a closely woven barbed wire roof. That should make a difference. Just recently I heard something which really tickled my funny bone. 'How long has a fellow to wait before the guard finds time to lock him in?' enquires a petulant youthful A.W.L. lad standing outside the locked gate of the detention yard. I have no idea how that occurred but it certainly brightened my day.

Poor Angas has shown signs of restlessness for several days. During yesterday afternoon he looked terrible. After tea he grew violent. Sergeant Link telephoned Captain Sparks, who is kindness personified. The ambulance with the Doctor from Keswick Hospital arrives and Angas is finally induced to put on a dressing gown and enter the ambulance.

Poor fellow! His father and mother are interned at Tatura. His teary-eyed little sister visits him regularly. Angas is only a youngster, what has he done? What has any of us done to be brought here? Angas is just on 5 months under detention and has as yet had no Hearing.

I have been here four weeks today, 10 January. Will another 16 weeks find me in the same frame of mind as Angas Bohlmann was last night?

A few of us volunteer to peel potatoes early this morning for chip potatoes for breakfast. We find a potato resembling a human body and head. It is promptly sent to Comelli, our Camp caricaturist who, by breakfast time has successfully sculpted Eime with a pronounced abdominal appendage. The effigy is then sent into the official kitchen and the cook in turn places it on the breakfast table in front of the Captain's chair. I leave his comment to your imagination.

Comelli is a very talented artist. If he drew you just for love, he would reproduce a fairly correct facsimile of yourself; if you offered to pay him five shillings he would improve you beyond recognition.

***

The Angas Electorate includes 143 electors bearing the name Schulz or Schultz. Am I the scapegoat over whose head the High Priests have confessed all the iniquities of the whole tribe?

Today, 11 January, is not a good day for me. The experience with Angas is extracting its pound of flesh. One moment utter despondency lays hold of me, the next moment I feel happy and must sing.

Before Inspection the Camp Orderly enquires: 'Anybody for the Doctor? There is no reply, so Inspection goes ahead. When the Captain cursorily looks over the cubicle he usually enquires:

'Are you quite alright?' 'Yes Sir', comes the reply. He looks up at me and halts.

'You don't look it!' Then all goes blank. Later, when I wake up, I find medicine bottles in my cubicle and Captain Sparks sitting with me. Our Camp Commandant deserves a medal specially struck for him.

The Medical Officer, who is with Captain Sparks, remarks that my Gladioli seem to have lost most of their charm.

'I will probably receive a fresh supply on Sunday', I say.

'Unfortunately, I will not be on duty on Sunday', is his reply.

That night I lie awake remembering what Herman Homburg has told me about various incidents in connection with his brother Fritz's detention. When Fritz was taken, Herman rang up Sir Walter D and the following dialogue took place over the phone.

'You've got some fairly live committees in your Electorate, haven't you?'

'Oh yes, why?'

'You've got a good chairman of your committee in Tanunda?'

'Yes, why?'

'Do you know a man by the name of Fritz Homburg?'

'Yes, why?'

'Well he has been interned!'

'What?'

The machinery is set in motion. Fritz got a Hearing the following week, despite the fact that there were just on thirty internees in Camp before him. He is released within a few days!

Angas Bohlman had been in the Camp for three months at that time. When they took him away last night he was here just on 20 weeks without a Hearing.

I am now in my fifth week! As God is my judge, I have never uttered or harboured disloyal sentiments. I may have criticised adversely our political, financial, and social institutions, but always with a view to improving conditions. And now I am told that the fee will be 100 hundred pounds to fight myself out of here! To gain my freedom! To go on the stand and convey a message that I feel I must tell! Ah, now we have it! I have the temerity to oppose a sitting member of Parliament! I pray to God that He give me freedom and health.

***

'Here she comes!' That's for Marie as she appears through the gangway carrying an armful of Gladiolis, while the other members of my family are being checked. Every member of the Camp knows Marie now. She has just gone to Comelli's cubicle and he draws a picture for her and gives her lollies. The Herold brothers give her biscuits. Francis Drake finds she wants something he hasn't got so he scouts around with her until he finds it and appropriates it without permission from anyone. When Hughie and another Camp inmate proceed to the kitchen in the Officer's Quarters to collect supplies, Marie is a member of the party, and when they return carrying the tub between them, her golden locks bob up and down behind the tub.

An A.W.L. lad is in clink. He is a yodeller! A Canadian born of Swedish parents. He can't be more than perhaps 22 years old. Shades of Caruso, what a voice! Unfortunately, environment and questionable associations appear to have clouded and limited his repertoire and prevented his vocal chords from radiating all the beauty and charm they are unquestionably capable of. When we exercise along the path that leads past his enclosure he readily obliges with vocal items. Unconsciously, probably, he sometimes swings over into a song that tells of home and mother and the tragedy of a young life not usefully spent. It is mirrored in his features. Apparently, he overslept his embarkation leave, was later picked up, and is now where he is.

13 January, 1941

Today I had a meeting with my son, Bert, and Mr. Harford. We discussed particulars for when my Hearing comes on. Mr. Harford confirms that the legal costs will be 100 pounds. I feel like chucking in my bundle and tell them so. Bert does his best to cheer me up, of course, but when they leave I am not in a good frame of mind. So, in an effort to do something productive, I begin making the following notes to use for my Hearing:

Shortly after the outbreak of war, the District Council of Tanunda received a letter from the Defence Authorities asking the Council to make arrangements for billeting two thousand children from the city if the necessity arose. I attended as a member of the Council and was elected Chairman of the local Defence Committee. After discussion it was decided to draw up a circular letter for insertion in the local paper. Reprints were made and a copy was sent to every rate-payer in the Council area. Within a fortnight replies came to hand from practically every rate-payer. I personally interviewed several who had failed to reply and after a fortnight I was able to advise Colonel Bice that we had arranged to billet our quota. In a short address to the meeting mentioned above, I remember telling those present that Mr. Chamberlain in his speeches, as they appeared in his book, My Struggle For Peace, having failed to preserve peace, it was now our bounden duty to do everything in our power to secure victory, and for the time being follow Mr. Menzies' advice and carry on as usual.

I had done some filming prior to the war, and after the outbreak of war I concentrated on matter suitable for film shows to raise funds for Red Cross and Trench Comforts. At about this time I interviewed Mr. Chas. Edmunds, a Solicitor in Adelaide, and Chairman of S.A. Red Cross, regarding the merits of Red Cross versus Trench Comforts organisations. I failed to keep a correct record of all my shows, but writing from memory, the following are the film shows I gave.

At Tanunda for Red Cross: takings approximately 6 pounds. No charge.

At Eudunda: 5 pounds. Charged either 30 shillings or 2 pounds. Mr. Michael, MP can give the exact figure.

At Williamstown: 5 pounds. No charge.

At Greenock: 4 pounds. No charge.

At Marananga: 4 pounds. No charge.

At Truro: 5 pounds. No charge.

At Tanunda Lodge Hall, for Vine Vale: 5 pounds. No charge.

At Rowlands Flat, 3 times: 15 pounds. No charge.

At Nuriootpa: 6 pounds. No charge.

At Bethany: 3 pounds. No charge.

At Gomersal: 4 pounds. No charge.

At Tanunda, together with Liedertafel and School Band: 20 pounds.

At South Kilkerran: 6 pounds.

Takings while filming Baby Show at Tanunda: 19 pounds.

Baby Show film evening at Tanunda: 11 pounds.

At Sedan: 8 pounds, 4 shillings. Charge 30 shillings.

At Cambrai: 6 pounds. Charge 30 shillings.

On different occasions I have shown films to the men encamped on the Gawler Oval. Captain Blackburn was in charge on one occasion. It had been my ambition to film our men in training as this would then become a stock film for any show anywhere for Red Cross or Comfort Funds.

About four months ago a Penny Drive was arranged by the Red Cross Circle at Tanunda. I got five pounds worth of pennies from the Bank and distributed these among the collectors along the main street of Tanunda.

When War Savings Certificates were first issued, I, my wife, my daughter Else, and son Bert, took one hundred pounds worth of certificates. I, myself, have an overdraft in the E. S. & A. Bank of over seven hundred pounds.

Some months back Mr. Cilento of the War Savings Campaign Committee spoke on War Savings at a Tanunda meeting. Shortly afterwards, on a Sunday, I asked Pastor Hebart to announce that the congregation remain in their seats after the conclusion of the service. I then addressed the congregation on the necessity and urgency of assisting in the war effort and advised those who had not already done so to buy War Savings Certificates.

'Our men have answered the call to arms magnificently,' I stated, 'and it is now our duty to help feed, drill and equip them for attack and defence.'

A number of the older members of the congregation had already bought certificates through Mr. Fritz Homburg's large group in Tanunda, but a number of the younger people promised to subscribe. I wrote to the address supplied by Mr. Cilento advising that a Langmeil Church group would be formed. Mr. A. Basedow, Manager of the Bank of Adelaide, agreed to act as trustee and I was to take the secretary and treasurer roles. Now, as a result of a decision arrived at by the Young People's Society, consisting of members of the Langmeil Church (Pastor Hebart) and St. John's Church (Pastor Held), it was agreed to form a Young People's War Savings Group. Those young people who had promised to invest in the Langmeil Church Group joined up with the Young People's Group and I had perforce to advise the Adelaide War Savings Committee that, for the time being at any rate, the proposed Church Group would not function.

Besides the larger amount mentioned earlier, my son and I recently joined the Tanunda Show Committee War Savings Group. Mr. R. Guerin is the Secretary and Treasurer.

Just prior to my arrest, at a meeting held in Tanunda to stimulate interest in the 28,000,000 pound War Loan, I pointed out in a short speech that small amounts were especially welcomed. Amounts as small as 10 pounds would be welcomed and even these could be paid in instalments.

On Monday 2nd December, 1940, a meeting was held at Tanunda making arrangements for an Australia Day to be held. I was elected Convener and Chairman of the Procession Committee. The Australia Day Committee decided to run a Queen Competition, and I was asked to work on the Queen of Nurses Committee. A few days later I outlined a scheme to Mrs. Dr. Altmann for the raising of money for the Queens and, more particularly, a scheme for keeping a friendly spirit among the Queens and their committees. The Soldier's Memorial Hall was to be engaged as also the Tanunda Club lawn. In the Hall a Paddy's Market was to be conducted. The different Queens: Army, Navy, Air Force, and Nurses, were then to parade on the Tanunda Club lawn with their committees in a tableau and I would film the whole proceedings. I counted on raising 100 pounds from the efforts in the Hall and the subsequent Film Show.

When telling Mr. Winton, our local Barber, of the different activities the Australia Day Committees intended to engage in, Mr. J.C. Meyer, a local resident who had been listening to our conversation, walked closer and addressing Winton said, 'You needn't worry Skinny, they (meaning those of us working for the Queens) will all be behind barbed wire before Australia Day.

Not long after the outbreak of war, I remember having had a discussion in S.L. Winton's Barber Shop.

'I wish I had charge of this war!' I'd said. 'All the resources of the country would be pooled for its duration including banks and companies. The man who enlists offers his life's blood. He is all-in. He would be paid at least the basic wage. Any attempt at profiteering would have to be paid for dearly. Everybody would be called upon to share equally in sacrifices and benefits.'

Until a few years ago I was a staunch supporter of the Liberal and Country Party in South Australia. But, since the outbreak of war, I feel that economically and socially things are going to be different after the conclusion of hostilities.

Having been an organiser for the Liberal Party, I claim to have a knowledge of the Party's aims and objectives. I was prone to condemn everything that ran counter to the Liberal Party's policy. I had never bothered much about the Labor Party's aims and objectives. I did and still hate and condemn strikes. The masses need educating. The youth must learn to love its country, learn to respect it, and then, when the necessity arises, you would have the right driving force to fight for our country to the last ounce. And we would all readily and willingly give our last shilling for the cause. I now honestly believe the best hope for this to work is with the Labor Party.

15 January, 1941

There's huge excitement next door. During the night a trainee was put in Solitary Confinement. In the short minutes while the other A.W.L. lads were taken to the kitchen to collect their midday meal, the newcomer broke through the cell door and somehow wriggled through the barbed wire roof and the barbed fence of the Exercise Yard. A little later when the guard came along with his food, the bird had flown. All patrol vans are on active service and the neighbourhood is being combed with the usual negative result.

Next day there's even more excitement but in a different vein. Somebody's pinched Comelli's gramophone handle. 'I'll wind the bugger with my fingers and play Waltzing Matilda like hell,' he says with murder in his eye. Shortly after that a notice on his door reads: 'Keep out if you want to live a little longer!' Returning from a visit to the lavatory he finds the handle restored but the record gone.

During Medical Inspection Comelli complains to the doctor that he has a pain under his ribs. The doctor tells him that he is suffering from so and so. Comelli remembers some sort of a name and consults his Medical Dictionary. Suddenly he emerges from his cubicle: 'Hell, I'm falling to pieces!' He rushes back to read more: 'Holy Moses, I'm going to go mad the day after tomorrow. Give me a rope to hang myself!'

3

17 January, 1941

I am now detained five weeks. The days are beginning to drag. Angas Bohlmann, Pengelly, Camporeale, and Khuri are notified that they will be Heard next week. This announcement by Captain Sparks, of course, causes much excitement and speculation. When will it be my turn?

This morning the first cook, Cassidy, arrives on the job early and noticeably somewhat under the influence of spiritual sustenance. Strongly worded arguments commence and Cassidy is escorted to clink.

19 January, 1941

I am up early. I always set my little spirit stove ready for the morning and then make my cup of tea just when it suits. It's lovely to have it with the Honig Kuchen (honey cake) my family brought for me during their last visit.

Well, I've had my 'early breakfast' and lean on the lower half of my door. It's just after 5 am. Members of the Provost Staff quartered opposite us are beginning to move about. First one and then another arrives at the coppers with their enamel mugs to prepare a cup of tea before going on guard. But nobody has kept the fire going. The flow of ruddy language almost fans the dying coals into flame. A heap of cut wood, ready to be shoved under the copper is nearby, but nobody would dream of tossing a few pieces on the coals.

At about six o'clock the Cook comes on the scene, and when he has finished telling all and sundry what he thinks of them, well, it's difficult to reconstruct a Sunday atmosphere, and I feel sorry that I had not slept right through to the breakfast bell.

Sergeant Link arrives later with two packets of Popcorn for Marie. He had been unable to procure them yesterday. When I offer to pay he says, 'O never mind, they're from me for little Marie.' So, I hand them to Marie later when the family come to see me, and you can just imagine her delight.

20 January, 1941

What a night! At about 2am I am awakened by loud voices outside, very loud voices. The patrol guards have arrived with some delinquents who don't seem to relish being locked up. More guards appear on the scene.

'Are you the boss?' asks one of the obstreperous ones. 'Well ....!'

'Did you go to the last war?' asks one of the guards. 'Well it's no wonder we .... nearly lost that war!'

And so the bantering continues. It had its humorous incidents, but the spectacle was not an edifying one.

Shortly after 4am I suddenly remember that Cunningham's Comet is to make its appearance this morning. The guard obliges with boiling water for a cup of tea and while he pours I enquire after the comet. He hasn't heard of it but he lets me out of the compound and together we look for it. We agree that a light just appearing over the horizon is Cunningham's prediction, but a conversation later tells me that what we saw was the Morning Star. One of the guards then volunteers to adorn a certain part of his mate's anatomy with a burning candle, when Bromley would be advised of Cunningham's Comet!

Pastor Materne arrives in detention today and I introduce him to all the inmates of the Camp. Every new arrival here adds interest to the community, but it's a sad affair. I lend a helping hand by getting my sewing gear out and fix him up with a bed and straw mattress for the first night, also towels etc.

One of the inmates here is late in tidying his cubicle this morning and when finished with dusting his blankets is told all sorts of complimentary things. Unperturbed he continues and wants to know if 'this isn't a damned free country anyhow.'

Freddy wants to retrieve a ball from the roof. The guard allows him out through the gate to enable him to get on the roof without having to cross the seven barbed wires. Instead of crawling along the gutter, Freddy proudly walks along the ridge capping. Perhaps he intends joining the circus on his release from here.

Two of our little colony were told two days ago to hold themselves in readiness at 6.30 am today, 21st of January, to be taken to the railway station, there to be taken to Hay, N.S.W., the Italian Internment Camp. Throughout the day there is a subdued atmosphere and we quite subconsciously converse in undertones while Vin Caputo and Antonio Camporeale pack their bags and baggage. The Hearing of the Italians' Appeals, I am told, lasted only ten minutes. Their names and a few personal particulars are noted, then they are asked, 'Are you a Fascist?' Unhesitatingly they reply, 'Yes.' That settles it! They return to the Detention Camp awaiting the order to pack for Hay and the Internment Camp there.

Allow me to just establish this fact here. The exercising space of our detention area measures 25 yards 2 feet by 6 yards 1 foot and 4 inches. In this confined area, 25 to 30 men move around from anywhere between 12 to 20 weeks. Nationality and political creed soon disappears and you learn to evaluate the man.

Vin is a quiet, likeable sort of fellow, always ready to learn to accompany on his mandolin any song that is being sung. Antonio, less intelligent but no less likeable, is always wearing a smile and continually collecting used matches and handing them into my cubicle.

We shake hands with them when they are ordered to bring their baggage to Captain Spark's office. Again we shake hands with them when the utility finally pulls alongside. 'Good luck, boys,' and they move out. Old Capitano Caputo, Vin's elder brother who owns two fishing schooners at Port Pirie, (one named Mussolini) is sobbing on his bunk. Pastor Materne, who has arrived here but yesterday, goes in to him and talks with him. We go about our business.

22 January, 1941

A new day. Early this morning I write out information for Mr. Harford, as follows:

In 1931 I received an enquiry from Melbourne for a quotation for printing a book in the German language. The size of the book, quality of paper, binding etc., were stipulated. After having assured myself that the paper was available in Adelaide and worked out the cost of the book, I made a special trip to Melbourne to finalise details. The cost of producing the book was about 700 pounds. There was no doubt about the publishers being able to finance the publication. When I was shown the copy, I found that I was dealing with Jehovah's Witnesses, and turned the job down. The editor of 'The Lutheran Herald' learned of my action and commented on it in the Editorial section of this paper, dated 29 June, 1931, part of which follows:

> *'A Bargain refused for conscience sake. To be asked to print a German book of over 300 pages in 10,000 copies and refuse it for conscience sake is something that merits laudatory recognition. Auricht's Printing Office, Tanunda, was approached from Melbourne for the printing of a devotional book, 'Bible Talks,' and naturally felt very much inclined to enter into a contract. This would have meant work for months and a very handsome profit, things that matter very much, especially at the present time. Before finalising the matter, the book was seen to be a means of propaganda in the interest of the International Bible Students, also called Russelites.*

How far this sect deviates from true Christianity may be learned from the article published in this issue. The printing of such a book by Auricht's would have been a very great help in the Russelite propaganda, as our members led by the fact that it emanated from a printing office which is entirely composed of Lutherans, would have regarded it as something genuine and would have thus been induced to purchase it freely. To assist in any way in the propagation of such false doctrines could not be entertained by Auricht's and thus a cancellation of all negotiations was decided upon for conscience sake. We congratulate Auricht's on their decision and wish them God's blessing. For, no doubt, the Lord will have other means of prospering them...'

22 January, 1941

Angas, Pengelly, and Rothe have been Heard. Hoeft and Khuri are at the Court today. The list is narrowing down.

It is still hot and sultry after tea, so we settle down in our chairs, on benches, and on the ground near the gate leading to our exercising path outside and decide on singing. I produce my Globe Song Folio and Henke gets his steel guitar and we sing the following songs: 'Old Folks at Home', 'Poor Old Joe', 'My Old Kentucky Home', 'Massa's in the Cold Ground', 'Juanita', 'Clementine', etc.

The A.W.L. lads in the Compound across the way are apparently listening and per the guard we are informed that the Canadian yodeller will oblige with a few numbers. We applaud. And did he sing and yodel! We can't see him and he can't see us, but with our ears to the netting we sit in absolute silence, except for a subdued accompaniment by Henke on the steel guitar and listen in the stillness of the night.

If you are brave enough to close your eyes in meditation – well, you remember, of course, how you have felt sometimes leaving the picture theatre when the curtain has just fallen at the end of a dramatic scene, and you are quickly trying to brush an emotional tear from your eye. That is our reaction now.

The next day is still hot and sultry as Hoeft and Khuri leave for Court. Hoeft finishes late in the day so Khuri has just a few minutes and is to continue on Tuesday. They tell us that Hearings are to last only to 5th February and then there will be an interval. It appears that I am to come on after the interval, and a cheque for 100 pounds has already been paid to my Solicitor!

Hoeft's cross-examination makes some remarkable disclosures. It seems we have traitors in the Camp or else the Authorities have very efficient scouts. I am inclined to believe that the latter is the case. I ask Hoeft what induced him to come to Australia. A large poster in New York. Underneath a picture of a large Kangaroo was the inscription: 'Come to Australia, the workman's paradise, the land of freedom.'

Capitano has a meagre command of English. He has a cup of coffee in one hand and a chunk of cake in the other. Much annoyed, in fact, wild as hell, he is holding forth in Italian to his compatriots. Espying me in the lavatory he walks closer, gesticulating, and between mouthfuls protests: '6 o'clock, 8 o'clock, 10 o'clock, 1 o'clock, 4 o'clock, 6 o'clock, 9 o'clock, every time eat, every time, every time! When I home in Port Pirie fishing I just have breakfast, 7 hours fish, half loaf bread and bottle wine, meat and half loaf bread for dinner, more fish and half loaf bread and bottle wine for tea. That's all. Then I go to bed. Here just eat, eat, damn it!'

Anyhow, I am detained and brought into this Compound on 13th December, 1940. The order to detain me is dated 29th November, 1940, and reads:

> *'Whereas by Regulation 26 of the National Security (General) Regulations it is provided, inter alia, that the Minister may if satisfied with respect to any particular person, that with a view to prevent that person acting in any manner prejudicial to the public*

safety or the defence of the Commonwealth it is necessary so to do, make an order directing that person be detained:

And whereas I, Percy Claude Spender, Minister of State for the Army, am satisfied that with a view to prevent the person specified in this Order acting in any manner prejudicial to the public safety or the defence of the Commonwealth it is necessary that that person be detained:

Now therefore I do hereby order that Johann Friedrich Wilhelm Schulz (known as Mons, Monty, and Monsy Schulz) of Tanunda, South Australia, shall be detained.

Dated this 29th day of November, one thousand nine hundred and forty.

(Signed) Percy C. Spender
Minister of State for the Army

An order for my detention to prevent me acting in a manner prejudicial to the public safety or the defence of the Commonwealth was made by the Minister of the Army on November 29, 1940. Is anything I might have said or done by the middle of February 1941, after having been driven to the verge of insanity owing to the manner of my treatment in the course of my detention or the assured feeling of absolute innocence, to be used in evidence against me?

During that first night as I lay on my straw bunk in a stall on the Wayville Showgrounds, originally built to house show stock, the top half of my door was open and silhouetted against the moonlit sky, I could count 7 barbed wires. What purpose were these wires serving? I had been brought into the Compound at about 8.30pm and had not noticed the wires before. I jumped from my bunk and leaning over the lower door (like the prize stock, I suppose) I looked out. About 7 yards separated the two rows of stalls stretching some 20 yards east and west. Strong cyclone fences some 20 feet high supplied the east and west enclosure.

Barbed wires surmounted and surrounded the whole area. Means of egress and ingress was a strongly bolted and padlocked gate. And all this to hold me in safe confinement!

Some little time later the Ambulance took young Angas Bohlmann away. Some said he was being taken to Hospital, others that his destination was the 'Rat House'. His father and mother are at Tatura. He has been waiting for a Hearing since August last.

Soon after Hirsch and Pohl are interned, Hirsch is released on the company's bond of one thousand pounds. A. E. Young, a Chairman of Directors of Millicent Cellulose Works, where Hirsch is employed, is a member of the Tribunal which hears internees Appeals!

Early one morning I called Hermann Homburg into my cubicle. I had hardly slept during the night.

'How many people are there in South Australia?' I asked.

Hermann couldn't say exactly.

I replied, 'There must be some 600,000, and of this number you and I and two or three more Australian born subjects are locked up in here, because we would endanger the public safety etc. At the first opportunity I'll walk out of this damned place!'

'Don't do that,' said my fellow detentionist, 'Don't do that! Stay in here. Outside there is just one big lunatic asylum!'

Would I not have been forgiven had I at that moment exclaimed, at the top of my voice and within hearing of the guards, 'To hell with this kind of democracy!' Then I would be asked at my Hearing: 'Did you say, while under detention, to hell with democracy?'

We've had two days of continuous rain so during that time I've stayed in my cubicle and corrected the brief left by Mr. Harford concerning details for my defence. Next day the family come to see me. Mum, Bert, Margaret, Marie, and Ted bring good things as always. Wednesdays and Sundays are always days of sunshine.

27 January, 1941

Another week enters and it's a Public Holiday today.

I'm usually the first one up in the morning. Hermann joins me early one morning. We want to chat but are afraid of disturbing the others. 'Kannst du Kacken?' Asks Hermann? 'Wenn ich mich in Bischen austrenge.' I reply. We retire to the lavatory. There are two seats, no doors, just a partition so we sit leaning forward and talk to one another round the partition.

The subject under discussion for this morning is farting, and I proceed to inform Hermann of my observations since my arrival at Wayville.

'You can easily tell who is awake in the morning,' I say, 'by the farting that reverberates along the entire length of the row of cubicles. Some sound like the siren of a fire brigade, others like the honk, honk of a motor horn on a flat battery. The first morning attack rattles the walls and dislodges your penny juicy fruits from the crossbeams in your stall. Oscar's fartings are cut short as with a razor blade; Khuri's have frills on them like a piece of old bag hanging on a fence after a heavy gale. Capitano's just peter out until they close their eyes in death. Expressed in concrete punctuation terms, our Wayville fartings represent the full stop, the comma, and the sign of exclamation!

One of my false teeth has been loose for some time thereby making eating a bit of a trial. In attempting a late cut at cricket practice today, I smash the wicket, dislodge the tooth and almost swallow it. This, of course, brings general merriment all round. Later on, Comelli gives me a painting he has produced in recognition of my heroic attempt at cricket that day!

28 January, 1941

Compulsory hot baths are the order of the day. When we have finished, and at the order of 'Quick March', we move off. After having gone about 3 chains we hear, 'Hey, wait a minute!' Emerging from the bathing house we see Comelli and Hunger gesticulating like mad, apparently incensed at having been left behind! Behind in freedom while we are being marched back behind the barred and padlocked gate. The situation is too grotesquely humorous. We assure them that if they promise to be good, they may come along too.

Khuri and Eime leave for their Hearing. We speculate on Khuri taking all day, but both return while we are having lunch, both having been heard.

Schober is asked to appear at the Court during the afternoon, so he leaves at 2.15pm and is back by 3pm. His Solicitor was at the Court, but was unable to produce the witness at such short notice. Schober has been told he is to appear again on Tuesday.

Captain Sparks advises us to hold ourselves in readiness in the following order: Lebeck, Drake, Henke, Pohl, Schulz, and Hunger. Thank God for this news! At 3.30pm Mr. Harford calls to say that he is right on the job. He has already seen Bob Richards and Makin. Makin has spoken to Spender. A letter will be written to Spender tonight. Captain Sparks says I should be heard by Wednesday next week!

29 January, 1941

War is in the air. Just at the conclusion of breakfast, Pohl annoys Drake. There is a little wordy warfare, fists begin to fly and kitchen furniture rocks about. It takes more than one of the Camp inmates to separate the combatants. What a pity! In order to get away from it all, I lend the Italians a hand at 'Messing Duty' outside of the Compound.

One consoling feature here, reassuring and comforting alike, is this. When it comes to the final showdown, when the long looked for hour of Hearing arrives, something or somebody prompts the individual to look for help and guidance elsewhere than to man. I noticed it when two Italians were moved from Wayville to Tatura, and again when one or other here is about to appear before the Commission. He is seen with the Book of Books in his hand.

This morning I am trying to find the passage in the Scripture which Mr. Richards, Leader of the Opposition, used as his theme in a lecture on social injustice at Nuriootpa some time ago. 'The earth is the Lord's and the fullness thereof.' When Bill Herold, who with his brother Max is going up for his Hearing this morning, walks up, he notices I have a Bible in my hand and enthusiastically says, 'Read Psalm 70.'

Max and Bill's Hearing lasts all day and Max has to appear again in the morning.

On a happier note, the Dentist on the Wayville showgrounds, cements my tooth back in. While I'm there, in the Advertiser room, I meet George Steicke and we catch up on news from my home town.

After tea, Sergeant Link advises that the following people are to be ready for Court in the morning. Max Herold, Eime, Johannsen, and Lebek. Eime's inclusion on the list is a stunner. He had been heard yesterday and is now called up again.

30 January, 1941

Max Herold, Eime, Johannsen, and Lebek were heard today. Eime says he was further questioned on a previous statement by him to the Commission that one of the detained men in the Camp is taking information to the Intelligence Department. Eime states that Internee No. 272 (Khuri) was actually named in the Court by Cleland. Life here is becoming unbearable. On top of all this, Captain Sparks announces that Hearings have been suspended for two weeks at least!

There is an ever growing feeling of resentment in Camp over the discrimination in the order of Hearings. Angas had been called up several times. He was about to be heard when Fritz Homberg came in between. The latter was heard and released. His detention was just a mistake! Angas was due for the 'Rat House' a few weeks ago and is on the verge of collapse again. Who is ready to say that his detention wasn't 'just an unfortunate mistake'! I say my incarceration is not only a mistake, it is criminal; a criminal, political perpetration.

Things are going from bad to worse and the Camp is like a morgue. Hughie is preparing a document for presentation to the Intelligence Department on the matter of news carried to that Department. We are all concerned, and Freddy, cutting a cardboard sole for his rubber shoes, very much worn says,' Something has to be done, whatever it is!'

My cubicle is a mass of flowers again; Roses, Dahlias, and Daisies. Bert and Else bring these when they visit me today, 2 February. After much discussion on the subject of Hearings, they leave early to see if they can contact Makin or Harford with a view to expediting my Hearing. It can't happen soon enough. I'm not feeling at all well. I think the strain is beginning to take its toll.

Hughie presents his letter to Major Martin of the Intelligence Department the next day. We shall see what transpires. Interestingly, Khuri is called to the Intelligence Department the day after that. We hope as much for his release as his transference elsewhere.

I show pictures tonight, 4 February, and the show is a big success. Included in the programme is a film from Lenrocks titled, 'Ridem Cowboy'. I had to repeat this film at the end of the show because they all liked it so much. Comelli artistically executes a masterpiece souvenir programme.

5 February, 1941

Visiting Day again and Marie sails around the corner and into Camp before the others have collected the good things they are bringing me from the car. Else assures me that my Hearing is being expedited. What a welcome break to talk of ordinary news with them and general gossip of my good old home town.

6 February, 1941

Angas and Pengelly are taken to hospital by Ambulance. Pengelly has to have his leg bandaged against varicose veins. Angas will be under observation for stomach ailments.

It's hot and sultry; conditions which generally make you feel utterly miserable. A couple of people at the breakfast table are discussing ways of combatting the humid weather and the effect it has on their health. Max Herold says,' I take my Solvol regularly every morning.' He means Sal Vital of course!

Oscar and Freddy have another wordy warfare, but again no fight eventuates. The two are our champion eaters. It would be difficult to say who of the two would throw in the towel first in an eating contest. Freddy ate until he got a cramp in the stomach. One night we found him in agony on the floor with the bed upended. He has just returned from the Adelaide Hospital. Oskar ate until he was unable to eat anything for two days. He is again on the road to recovery. On a previous occasion, when Oskar returned from hospital, he was asked: 'How did you like it at the hospital, Oskar?' 'First they come with the milk, then with the powder, and then with the plurry castor oil!' was his reply.

Tonight, long after lights in the cubicles are out, we have a late session at the cyclone fence. The area is brightened by two powerful searchlights that light up our boulevard bright as day. Wines and wine making is the topic and Hughie holds the floor throughout.

Angas returns from hospital today with an appointment for X-rays tomorrow, 7 February. He returns early following the X-rays to prepare for lengthy observation at the Royal Adelaide Hospital.

I have now been here for TWO MONTHS!

Mess Duty again today, 8 February. There is now only a respite of three days between each duty.

Captain Sparks has found a larger space for us to use for our exercise sessions. He is always on the lookout to relieve our monotonous existence. And while we parade to and fro, officers and trainees gather in groups here and there and, no doubt, discuss the monsters let loose for a breather.

Fifth Columnists! Nazis! Perhaps Huns! And I am now here 8 weeks waiting to be told why I have been detained! My gall rises and a lump gathers in my throat.

A rumour from the Provost Staff has filtered through to our Camp. Japan has declared war on Britain! There is a man-sized job for every one of us outside to lend a hand in the defence of our country, yet some crooked brain has successfully contrived to put us behind barbed wire.

We also hear that Captain Sparks has been hauled over the coals for giving us too much freedom. Didn't he know that a few days ago 3 internees escaped from the Internment Camp in Victoria?

Well, how about this for an interesting Press release?

'The dragnet is tightening around the escaped internee No.273, also known as Mons, Monsy, or Monty. With the aid of tracker Johnny Jones of Kangaroo Reach, the fugitive has been tracked along the Gorge Road, across the reservoirs, since the escapee at times travelled under water to avoid detection. Monty's apprehension seems only a matter of time. It has been ascertained that his favourite beverage is Abbots Lager. All the hotels in the district have been picketed!'

We are all sorely in need of a good laugh these days.

I am up very early this morning, 9 February, and enjoying my cup of tea and eating the last Belgium Bun. I am hoping my family will bring me more good things when they visit later today. Yes, they did and also a beautiful bunch of Phlox, but there is no further news of an early Hearing.

Two days later, Corporal Ardell, returning from his bath, finds Comelli carrying Father Bede's bag and calling the Corporal of the gate. Ardell stops at the gate. 'Well I'm damned, the bl____ fools have locked the Padre in!' Father Bede had provided Mass for the Italians and Khuri.

Pohl sees his lawyer today, 14 February, and learns that our cases are coming on for Hearing for certain next Tuesday. What a sigh of relief!

Pohl's lawyer also reports that one who has come in after him (Pohl), is to be heard before him. Maybe that refers to me.

Next morning, soon after breakfast, we learn that Max and Bill Herold have been released. They can pack up and walk out right now and report to the Intelligence Department on Monday. There are tears in their eyes. We lend a hand to get their things straight. They are going to the city for the day and their wives are coming to collect them tonight after 17 weeks of detention. We wish them well.

Even before the Herolds depart, happiness changes to sadness and tragedy. Angas Bohlmann had had his Hearing before the Herolds. Now he hears they are to be released. Of his own Hearing there is no news as yet. Something seems to snap inside him. He comes out of his cubicle in a hurry and excitedly calling Captain Sparks, asks for a rope. In good faith he is handed a length of rope. Shortly afterwards, Sergeant Major Inwood is sent to Angas' cubicle to enquire what he wants the rope for. 'What the hell's that got to do with you?' Angas rejoins. Inwood retrieves the rope and within a very short time the necessary formalities are completed, the ambulance arrives with a guard and No.250 (Angas) is taken to a mental asylum.

It's been a very trying day with the Mercury just touching 100 degrees Fahrenheit. We sit outside until well after the midnight hour.

Mess Duty again on 16 February. Bert and Else come to see me but have nothing to report about an early Hearing. Bert says he will endeavour to contact Harford re fresh developments.

The list for Hearings comes out early the next day: Oskar, Drake, Henke, Pohl, Schulz, Hunger, and Schober. My name is on the list at last! I ask to see Harford and he arrives early in the day. He has already contacted Bert and will travel to Tanunda today to speak with him.

18 February, 1941

The Hearings begin again. Oskar and Drake are finished by noon and Pohl is called for the afternoon session. He returns after a short while with the news that one member of the Tribunal (Andy Young) refused to sit because, 'he is a personal friend of mine.'

Captain Sparks announces the list of names for Hearings on Wednesday: Materne, Chris Camporeale, and Schober.

I've hung out, got the creases out of my new suit, and shined my boots these days in vain. They win! Camporeale was heard this morning, 19 February. Schober almost finished this morning. Materne and Henke are on the list for tomorrow. The latter probably unfinished. Will I miss the bus next week?

Materne and Henke's witnesses were heard today, 20 February, but their Hearings will continue on Tuesday of next week. There's no further news re my appeal.

A bad day for the game chief at a test match a fast spinner bowled him right out, his bat missing the ball savagely crashed the stumps out, smashed his pipe out, blew his golden tooth out, and frightened Freddy out his feet.'

4

21 February, 1941

I am now here 10 weeks. The temperature is well-nigh unbearable, so I take my bottle of soft drink wrapped in a piece of my underpants and stand in a tin of water wherever there is a little shade. I sit in the lavatory where there are two showers, turn on the two showers and allow the water to splash on my clothes. After a while, however, the surroundings become humid and the symptoms become akin to impending malaria. The best relief is obtained by continually replenishing my thermos flask with hot tea made from boiling water off my little spirit stove.

The loose boxes in which we are housed have galvanised iron walls with a galvanised iron roof that you can almost touch with your hand. It is 106.7 degrees Fahrenheit in the shade. Add to it the depressing environment and Marble Bar is not in it. However, we are promised a cool change and next day we notice the heat really is beginning to subside at last.

There's excitement in the Camp. Angas, who was returned to us from the Receiving Home two days ago, is informed by Captain Sparks that he must pack and hold himself ready to entrain for Tatura on Wednesday or Thursday of next week. To our surprise, Angas takes the news philosophically and whistling, gets on with his packing.

I'm in my cubicle. Captain Sparks comes to Kuhri's cubicle alongside mine. 'Kuhri, get ready to be at the Intelligence Office by 11.45am today.' The Office is at Keswick, which is about a ten minute walk from here. Kuhri is naturally all excitement. Schober, in the cubicle on the other side, congratulates him. 'You're sure to be told that you are to be released,' he says.

Kuhri returns in about a half hour. Hardly in his cubicle, he is called into Captain Sparks' office. Upon his return a few minutes later, his face tells a pitiful tale. It is only when you know Kuhri that you are able to evaluate the tragic position. He says not a word. We know what news he has received and not a man here is sorry.

***

The family comes to visit me on 23 February and, as well as bringing food and flowers, they tell me my Appeal is to come up for hearing on Tuesday. This is the best news so far. The wheels are turning at last.

Dr. Tanko prescribes something for my sore swollen throat next day. Oskar says to the Captain, 'I'd like a drop of Brandy.' 'All right Oskar,' says the Captain. 'And what about a bottle of Champagne for you Mr. Schulz?'

'Be ready for the Court at 10.15am, Mr. Schulz,' is the order on 25 February. I am in high spirits. Materne and I, with a guard, mount the open utility and off we go to Adelaide. About a dozen of my witnesses are there. My Solicitor has arrived only to be told that the case will be heard tomorrow! I feel like crying. I have to stay in Court until one o'clock to wait until Materne's case is finished. On leaving the Court I find my witnesses all waiting. 'We'll see you tomorrow, Mons!' With my guard I hurry back to Camp.

'Be ready to go to Court at 10 o'clock', is the order again next day. Upon my arrival at the Court, I find my witnesses are already there. Soon the case starts. Villeneuve Smith and Harford appear for me, and Eric Millhouse for the Intelligence Department. I am sworn in and Villeneuve Smith examines me.

Then the following of my witnesses are heard: Bert Teusner, R. Guerin, R.Shakes, M. Bell, Arthur Wilson, B. Hall, J.H.A. Schultz, M. Heuzenroeder, Frank Garrett, and Artley Nettelbeck.

At the conclusion of the Hearing at 1.25pm my Solicitors say that I should get a clear discharge. Margaret, Marie, Bert and Else see me after my Appeal and all convey the same hopes.

When I finally get back to Camp I hear that Helmuth Rothe has been notified to get ready for Tatura.

Hunger has his Appeal heard the following day and Angas, Kuhri and Rothe are busy preparing for their journey on the 'Katoomba' to Tatura.

28 February, 1941

I am now here eleven weeks.

Owing to a burst water main we now have water in the Compound. All water for use in the lavatory and for washing has to be carried in buckets from the Provost area.

We transfer a large Polony, about 10 pounds in weight, from our Messroom to the remnant bins. The Polony has been lying in our Kitchen for several days, so we tell the cook what we have done and he passes the message on to Lieutenant Virgo who roars like a bull at the good news. He suggests we keep the Polony out for the Commandant's inspection, so the Cook carefully deposits the prize in an empty pan and the stage is set.

But soon afterwards the scavenger lorry arrives on its daily round of clean-up. Innocently the men clean the pans as per usual and when the Inspection Staff arrive, also on their daily round, well, Exhibit No.1, the aforesaid Polony, is now probably miles away.

The Camp is astir early this morning, 1 March, because Angas, Rothe, and Kuhri must be ready by 9am to go aboard the 'Katoomba'. Angas is as happy as a kid with a new toy, Rothe is late as usual, and Kuhri has dropped his bundle completely. Soon they are off and we wish good luck to the two former mentioned.

My family visit me today, 2 March, and give a glowing report of a very successful Tanunda Show which was held on Saturday. Soon after their arrival, rain sets in and at 4.30pm it simply pours down. My visitors leave in heavy rain but my cubicle is filled with flowers and fruit from the Show.

The next morning, I am astir early. Comelli draws some Show tickets for me, such as, 'Never Seen Worse' Prize, 'Shut the Gate' Prize, 'Consolation' Prize, as well as a larger sign: '1941 Tanunda Show Exhibition Scraps'. Soon I have a miniature fruit, flowers etc. exhibition staged in my cubicle. The various entries are voluntarily supplied by the inmates of the Camp. Both the Field Inspectors and the Medical Inspectors are interested and amused.

Over the next few days, the weather is delightfully cooler. My Show exhibits, especially those in the fruit section, are decreasing alarmingly as their 'owners' eat them.

Hausler arrives to make our total 17. Else comes to visit me. She has driven down in Materne's car and brought Dulcie Materne with her.

It's one week since the Hearing of my Appeal. My nomination as the A.L.P. Candidate appears in the news.

A change of cooks and kitchen staff improves our food by 100 percent, and if you include the milder weather conditions, our overall living conditions are all that can be desired. If only we were not cramped so much for space. Our usual Bath Parade is a Godsend. I help Hausler out by giving him soap and a towel to use until his wife can provide the basics for him.

Toni says, 'Oskar! Mr. Schulz say you and me gotta pay 10 pounds a week taxa when we getta out of here.'

Oskar replies, 'I'm not going to pay 10 pounds for a bloomin taxi when they let me out!'

9 March – 13 March, 1941

When getting water for an early cup of tea, I find that the cook is right out of wood, so I cut a barrow load for him. At around 11.30am a homing pigeon settles on the roof of our shed. We hail it as the dove of peace.

Schrober and Hoeft regain their freedom and Dr. Seith enters our Camp. I wash and disinfect Dr. Seith's cubicle for him and assist him to move into what used to be Kuhri's cubicle.

Upon a phone request on 10 March, the Hon. R.S. Richards comes to see me and informs me that the answer to my appeal would NOT be favourable!!! To all intents and purposes my political chapter is closed. My stocks for release slump badly so, based on that information, I mend holes burnt in my shirt with an eye to future eventualities.

A sergeant gives us 45 minutes of physical exercises which doesn't do much to lift the state of mind I'm in. I guess the Authorities are trying to do their best for us.

Else comes to visit me and she brings a parcel for Oskar 'from the Swedish Consul'. Next day the mains from the bathroom and lavatory are blocked. Captain Sparks blames Oskar, who ate the whole mettwurst sent to him yesterday.

Harford comes to see me on 13 March to let me know that he is going to Canberra to see Spender re my case. I give him the three sheets of notes I have had typed up with a view to obtaining an early release. We discuss these issues, he makes notes in pencil on the reverse side of one sheet which he will use in his discussion with Spender. We also go through the transcript of my Appeal and I underline in red pencil all of the inaccuracies. Whether they are merely typing mistakes or something more sinister, I do not know. Harford makes notes in pencil and will follow this up with the Authorities. One major question I have is, 'Can I demand to see the Warrant under which I was detained and the Evidence brought against me?' It is a question which I hope will soon be answered.

My response to questions asked at my Hearing on 26 February, 1941:

> *I will be 58 next month. I am a married man. I was born at Point Pass. I have three children – two daughters and a son. The eldest*

is a married daughter. Her name is Mrs. Knispel. My other two children are Elsie and Berthold. They live at home with me and my wife. I was in business as a printer carrying on at Tanunda for 15 years. I am now a member of the District Council of Tanunda, Chairman of the Tanunda Civil Defence Committee, President of the Bowling Club there, and Vice President of the Tanunda Show, and Trustee of the Tanunda Children's Orphan Home. I am the delegated nominee of the A.L.P. for the next elections in the Angas district. Nominations are due on the 5th March, a week today. I have no financial, family, or other interests outside of Australia. I have no interest at all in the enemy territory. I am a loyal subject of the Crown and of Australia. I have nothing to justify any belief or suspicion that I have been other than a loyal British subject. I have employed my energy and time in support of the war effort in and about Tanunda. During the last war I actively assisted the Empire. I afterwards went to Rabaul. The Mission formerly conducted by the German New Guinea Mission had been taken over by an Australian-American body, and I was sent there to take inventory of such goods and chattels and prospects for future mission work there might be there. During the last war I assisted on the Recruiting Committee at Tanunda, the Belgian Relief Fund, and the S.A. Soldiers' Fund. Mr. C.A. Pollitt was Chairman of most of those bodies. When I left to go to Rabaul in 1921, Mr. Pollitt gave me this testimonial. (Testimonial put in by Mr. Smith).

During this war I have taken an active part in the effort to stimulate subscriptions to war loans, Comfort Funds, and Red Cross work. I have a hobby, Film Photography. I have employed that hobby to advance the Red Cross Funds, and the Comfort Funds, in and about Tanunda and beyond. I have gone as far south as South Kilkerran on the Peninsula for the Red Cross. I have assisted in entertaining troops in camp at Gawler. I actively supported a movement to have the English language used in Lutheran churches. These handbills shortly describe entertainments at which

I have exhibited films for the benefit of patriotic purposes. These are only some of many shows at which I have exhibited films in various parts of the countryside. I have no precise record of the amount I have assisted to raise. At some of the functions the Chairman of the Red Cross or Comforts Fund would say, 'We have taken some eight pounds, or nine pounds, or ten pounds.' Then there are deductions for rent, and I have no precise record of the actual amount that went to the various funds. My effort has been distributed over the period commencing with the date of the outbreak of the war up to the date of my internment. The films that I exhibited were films of general interest – local Shows, the last Royal Show at Adelaide, the last Tanunda Show when His Excellency the Governor was present – things of general interest. I did film Von Luckner, the German Captain. His visit here aroused general interest, and he was entertained by English and German alike. He was photographed by photographers of the press. The News and the Advertiser men were in front of me, and I had some difficulty to get my photographs. I have no personal interest in Von Luckner, or in his visit here. He was a very public figure at that time in South Australia, and much was made of him. Captain Chapman, a member of the Returned Soldiers, brought him to Tanunda, and he was entertained there. (Bundle of handbills put in by Mr. Smith).

I do not know who Captain Chapman was. I just know his name. He was in uniform. He was introduced to us as a Returned Soldier by Mr. Brown, of the St. Vincent Hotel at Glenelg. That is the only association I can point to between Von Luckner and any Returned Soldiers, other than when Von Luckner pictures were sold at Tanunda. After his entertainment we were told by them that the proceeds of the sale of these pictures would go to the Returned Soldiers' Fund. They were half a crown a piece, and autographed five shillings, and I think Capt. Chapman netted about twenty pounds altogether. I got that from some Tanunda folk who had met Capt. Chapman and Von Luckner earlier. I came down from

Tanunda to go to Parafield. I did not meet Von Luckner there. I did not arrange for him to go to Tanunda, but I met him there, and took further pictures of him there, and attended every entertainment that was tendered to him there. I cannot say just what functions there may have been. I was a member of the party who went to Seppeltsfield, and I attended his concert in the evening. I did not make arrangements for that concert. I had nothing to do with it whatsoever. From conversation, I understand that the Tanunda Liedertafel was approached through Captain Chapman or Mr. Brown of Glenelg, should Von Luckner come to Tanunda. The Liedertafel said they would sing for a figure, which they did. I did not meet him at Tanunda and conduct him to the hall. My daughter and I were not in his company when he went to the hall for the entertainment in the evening. I remember the Cruiser 'Koln' which was here. A special train took a number of the sailors off that cruiser to Tanunda. A spread was given them at the Oval. I was not one of the chief movers in that, other than that I was asked to say something on the arrival of the party at Tanunda. That was at Chateau Tanunda. I was at Chateau Tanunda when they arrived. I was with them at the Oval. I was there when they were there, and I sat with them at a meal, but I was not a member of any committee. I cannot say who brought them to Tanunda, I have no idea.

I know Dr. Becker. I have known him ever since his arrival at Tanunda. I knew him fairly well and thought a good deal of him. I never attended any of his meetings, none at all. I attended a meeting at a Café known as the Vienna Café in Grenfell Street, Adelaide. Only one. Dr. Becker was at that meeting. That was a meeting of the Nazi party. I did not attend two meetings there. The meeting was in about 1934. Dr. Becker was not then installed as Leader of the Nazi party, not from what I saw of the happenings there. In the following year, 1935, I did not attend another meeting at the Vienna Café, I attended only the one. Going home from work one afternoon, Dr. Becker met me in the street, and he said, 'I am going to Adelaide tonight with Mr. Schubert, of Schrapel's, will you come with us?' I said, 'Yes, I have nothing on, I will come with you.' We arrived there, and the room was decked out with flags and pictures, and they were all seated round the table. Most of the evening I wandered around in some of the cubicles at the back where there were pictures and flags and such things, and there was some function on, and Mr. Schubert was installed at some function there. When I met Dr. Becker, he did not say what they were going to Adelaide for. He just said he was going down there that night with Mr. Schubert, and would I come. That is all he said at that time, until we were on our way. He did not say how long we would be away. He said on the way down where we were going, but not at the first conversation. I say that seriously. I was not present at the Vienna Café on the occasion of the celebration of Hitler's birthday. Mr. Schubert, from Schrapel's, was installed in some office. I do not know what office, I have no idea. I could see that was the real reason for coming to town. I could see that when I was there. Possibly when I went home I enquired what office it was. It was associated definitely with Hitler and the N.S.D.A.P., but what office it was I do not know. Dr. Becker was not installed as anything that night. He installed Schubert. I could not say whether Schubert was the only man who took any office. The Nazi salute was given. I am not so sure of 'Heil Hitler'. Either the one or the other greeting that they have. We left there about ten or eleven o'clock. When I made arrangements in the first place to go, Dr. Becker did not say how long we were going to stay, or how long we were going for, or what we were going for. I took no part in the saluting, or 'Heil Hitler'. I remained a friend of Dr. Becker after that. He was always my medical man. In politics I differed with him seriously. I was friendly with him as a medical man, and I was friendly with him in other ways, but I had serious differences regarding politics with him. For quite a long time I was friendly with him in every walk of life, until politics began to take a more serious aspect over yonder.

With regard to Southern Air Lines & Freighters Ltd., I helped to subscribe one thousand pounds to get the prospectus issued. Dr. Becker told us he was a Director, and when I searched the Company's office in Melbourne, the Registrar of Companies told me the other members had just been pulling his leg and taken up his one hundred pounds to qualify as a Director, but he was never on the books. He did tell us he was a Director.

During 1940 I was in Tanunda most of the time, and I had various conversations with different people about the war. I am a friend of Mr. Fritz Homburg. During those conversations, I have never said, 'The British are going to get it fair in the neck,' or anything to that effect. I have not said, 'Hitler knows everything that is going on.' I have never said, 'The Barossa district and Wimmera district will be the only two safe places in Australia,' definitely not. I have never said, 'They are all Nazis living in those two districts.' I knew there was a branch of the Nazi party at Tanunda. You would learn in conversation that Dr. Becker and German Nationals met, not naturalised British subjects, people who came from Germany. They were the only ones I knew of belonging to that party. Nobody else of my acquaintanceship or association at Tanunda were members. I do not know definitely of anybody who was a member. During last year I never said to anybody, 'You are only born of German grandparents, but you should stick up for Germany the same as we do', never.

I am sometimes called 'Mons'. Nobody said to me, 'If that is your version, stick to it, Mons'.

I sometimes go to Seppeltsfield. I have taken quite a number of pictures of different Shows, including pictures of Von Luckner. I had some films of Germany. I have four or five rolls of film at home which I have never shown, and I have only seen two rolls of it myself. I did not get them, or any other films from Dr. Becker. I got *those films from the Consul, in a letter from the General Consul, Von Asmis, in Sydney. He sent them to me. They arrived about a fortnight before the outbreak of war. I have never shown any films of Germany or German life. I have never had any from Dr. Becker. Referring to the pictures generally, nobody has ever asked me what I show the pictures for, and what I do with the money, not that I remember. I have never said that 'this money goes to Dr. Becker, because the bloody British deprived him of his living, and we and the Nazi party have to keep him.' Since I intimated that I intended to go into politics, somebody has possibly asked me what for. I have never said, 'To put some Nazi spirit into this bloody Government of ours.' I do use the word 'bloody', especially since I have been at Wayville. And before that at Tanunda.*

I was educated at Robertstown Primary School, and the Point Pass College, now Immanuel College at North Adelaide. I became a school teacher at Light's Pass. That was the Lutheran school, known as the Light's Pass Lutheran School. I taught at the Lutheran Church School from 1911 until the schools were closed.

I have always taken a rather prominent interest in Lutheran Missions, particularly the Hermannsberg Mission.

I have taken an interest in the German Historical Society. Mr. Krawinkel was the Secretary or Chairman of it, and he wrote letters to the various towns asking different folk to attend. I got quite a number of letters, and I attended one meeting at his home in Rose Park. I was present at the unveiling of the monument at Klemzig, subsequently.

I was a member of the District Council for twelve months. That was the first time I have been in the District Council.

I have never known buttons to be sold in Tanunda in aid of the German Winter Relief Fund. I have never contributed to such fund. Souvenirs of some occasion were handed out at a hotel in Tanunda, and I think I bought a few for the Winter Relief work in Germany. That was four or five years ago. That was the Victoria

Hotel. I used to go there a good deal. I go in there for a drink. In the bar of that hotel maybe I expressed admiration for Hitler. Possibly I did four or five years ago. And the Nazi regime. I might have said he was doing a good job where he was at that time.

I am certain that I have never shown any films that I got from Dr. Becker. I would say I have never had any from him. For the last four or five years I have had nothing else but my own films, or films loaned by Lenrocs or Kodaks.

I remember Hans Bertram, the flyer. Tanunda entertained him, and I was present.

My son Bert went to Germany a few years ago. He was over there in 1935 and 1936 for about fifteen months. That was for the purpose of extending his education in connection with printing. He went from one printing house to another, to pick up some information. He has never expressed any pro-Nazi views to me. He had an admiration for a lot of things, but he said this country was always his. He is working with me now. I have two daughters. I have never stated with regard to either of my daughters that she would not marry a Britisher, or anything like that.

I have never attended any meeting of the Nazi party in Tanunda, never. I cannot give you any reason why Dr. Becker should have invited me to attend the meeting at the Vienna Café, except that he casually met me when I was coming home from work. If he had not met me, I probably would not have been there.

I remember at the last election that Returned Soldiers were used at the electoral booths at Tanunda. I never said to anyone, 'Why cannot we have the same men as last time?' Nobody ever said to me, 'Don't you like the battery of returned men at the booths?' I never said, 'Every Returned Soldier can go to hell, so far as I am concerned'.

I know a man named Forti. I have never been in his place. I have never been in any room attached to his place. He was down in a lane, and now he is in different lodgings, but I have never been in either of the places where he resided at Tanunda, or any room that he rented.

I know the paper De Brueke. That was published in Sydney until the outbreak of war. I was not a local correspondent for that. I was communicated with by the publisher, asking me to be the local correspondent. Having never sent in anything, my answer must have been in the negative. They wrote to me and asked me to become the correspondent, but I have never done anything about it. I was a subscriber to that right up to the time of the war. I had been a subscriber for about eighteen months.

The Victoria Hotel was Hensch's hotel. Someone else is there now, but Hensch used to keep it.

I know Theo Geyer. I know Elmo Rothe, not Hugo Rothe. I have a linotype operator at my place by the name of Pfeiffer. I know a man named Hugo Ahrens. There are three or four brothers named Niejulke who live with their widowed mother. I know Kevin John and Peter Niejulke. I am friendly with all of them.

I believe that Becker was a Director of Southern Air Lines & Freighters Ltd. for some time. Those who subscribed the first one thousand pounds received an intimation from the Director to that effect. Mr. J.H.A. Schultz is a bootmaker at Tanunda.

I was interested in a bookmaking shop about 1938, after the registration of bookmakers. I was not the registered bookmaker, but I was a registered clerk there.

To my knowledge there was not a Club known as the Hitler Club in Tanunda. I have never heard of such a Club. I know Heinrich's store, an old shop which used to be Heinrich's store. There is a little soft drinks and home-made cake shop in a lane, and Mr. Rudie Heinrich and his sister are there. I have never attended any meetings in the back of that shop. I never knew there were any meetings held there.

Dr. Asmis did not write me about reporting for De Brueke. It was the Editor, Von Skurtz. I cannot remember that I replied to him, but in the ordinary business procedure I am sure I did, because I replied to all correspondence that came in.

My son was away for fifteen months. He went over to the Olympics. The Olympics were in 1935 or 1936, and he came back in 1937.

When I went to New Guinea after the last war, I went to make an inventory of the goods and chattels that were transferred from the territory formerly worked by the mission in Germany. According to the ordinances and regulations, the German missionaries had to leave by 1926, and the American-Australian Board had to take over, and I travelled from this country to see what there was in the way of buildings etc. Dr. Thiele paid me. He was the Director of the Lutheran Board of Missions. I studied with him at Point Pass. I have corresponded with him. It may be nine or twelve months since I heard anything from him.

I have never said, since the war started, 'Everything that is printed in the British papers is all bloody lies.' I never said, 'Things don't look too good over there in England, I hope the English get it hot and strong.' I may have said the first part of that, when we were receiving serious news.

I do the printing for the Lutheran Church in S.A., only for one section, for the United Evangelical Lutheran Church of Australia. Hunkin, Ellis & King do the printing for the other German church.

I do not remember the elections in Victoria some time ago when Col. Cohen was a candidate. Mr. Isaacson, Manager of the Bank of Adelaide, saw me in connection with the Federal Election, and at his request I put out a pamphlet in the German Australian language, and probably those booklets or pamphlets reached Victoria, but they were put out for South Australia. I never did anything at all for the elections in Victoria. I never printed anti-Jewish literature when Col. Cohen was a candidate over there.

My printing works are known as Auricht's, and they are not the only printing works in Tanunda. Two years ago the Bank of Adelaide came to us when German refugees were coming from abroad, and gave us some manuscript to print in German to hand out to these refugees. We did that. It is a little folder six inches by three inches, printed on four sides. It was for the Bank of Adelaide. There were thousands of them, and where they went I do not know.

About four years ago I never printed any literature at my works in Tanunda for Col. Cohen. Any information the Police might have in that direction would be wrong. Nothing could be done in that way without my knowing something about it.

I have read 'Mein Kampf', the German edition. I own a copy of it. I underlined some of it.

I have never said anything disloyal. If declarations to that effect are made, they are all untrue. The people who have made those declarations have made a tragic mistake and misunderstood something I have said, but I have definitely not uttered anything disloyal, or acted disloyally. Possibly there have been things I have said which were capable of being misconstrued. I cannot recollect anything of that nature which was said in the bar of the Victoria Hotel at Tanunda.

I have also read Chamberlain's 'Struggle for Peace', and I have underlined parts of that. 'Mein Kampf' is obtainable at any bookseller's in Adelaide. It is in the Penguin Series now.

I had an open quarrel with Dr. Becker in reference to Southern Air Lines and Freighters Ltd. That was about 1937 or 1938. I told him that the whole show was a crook, and he demanded an apology from me. He did not get it. After that my relations with him were cool, other than that if I needed him as a medical man I would consult him. He had made some very remarkable cure of my son early in his career at Tanunda, and I had great faith in his capacity as a Doctor. Part of the funds which I had subscribed for this Southern Air Lines & Freighters Ltd. went to pay for a

Director's wife's confinement, Mrs. Gilroy. She was confined by Becker. I considered that dishonest. That may have been in 1937 or 1938. I said I differed from Becker politically. That was on matters of world politics mostly. At one time I entertained admiration for what Hitler had done. That was early when he came into the limelight, and it appeared that he was cleaning up what was an unholy mess in Germany. He came to power in 1933. I did not entertain admiration for Hitler ever since then. I have publicly stated my disapproval of Hitler's actions when the overseas position did not eventuate as I hoped it would. I hoped that the friendship between England and Germany was going to grow, and be cemented, and finalised, and consummated. When they began to drift apart, and when Hitler started the crucifixion of the independents, as his policy was exposed, my disapproval developed. I bought those buttons for the Winter Relief six or seven years ago.

The Consul General in Sydney would get the standard films that you could show at the picture show. My films were all small films. Some of the big films came to Tanunda and were shown at Tanunda. In conversation with Dr. Becker we learned that you could get sixteen-millimetre films, and I was always anxious to get films of general interest. There was nothing in those films likely to incite disaffection in the empire. They were passed by the censor in Sydney, and a letter reached me that films from the Consul-General had arrived here, and I had to give a receipt for them, and return them. They had been passed by the censor in Australia. They did not contain any political propaganda, or anything likely to incite disaffection, not from their titles. I only put two of those through my machine.

Those letters are letters I received from Col. Bice, Department of Civil Defence, and this one from the Comptroller of Quartering. With regard to quartering, a representative came to Tanunda. We were advised by Col. Bice that their representative would come to Tanunda, and would we make arrangements to meet him. The

Chairman of the District Council invited a number of residents, and we met at the District Council Hall, and a man by the name of Watson from Elder Smiths came up and outlined the scheme. We elected a committee. I was elected a Chairman that evening, and Mr. Harmann, a returned soldier, was elected Secretary. We drew up a leaflet which we sent out to all the ratepayers in the Tanunda District Council, asking them to fill in a form which was also attached, saying how many children they could take, whether they were on the telephone, whether they had cars. This is the tabulated result of the effort. Mr. Fritz Homburg was a member of the Committee. His staff drew up the plans, and they were sent out from my office, and Mr. Teusner's and Mr. Homburg's. We were able to make provision for some two thousand evacuees within a fortnight. The quota was two thousand. This is the leaflet that I had sent out. We supplemented that by personal interviews. When all these circulars went out, and nearly a fortnight had gone by, there were some fifty people who had not replied. I looked most of them up in my car personally. I went around and saw them.

I subscribed to the War Savings Certificates to the limit of my financial power. I arranged with Pastor Hebart to give me an opportunity to address the congregation, and I addressed those present, and explained the War Savings scheme, after I had attended a meeting convened by Mr. Spender in Adelaide, and after Mr. Cilento of the Bank of Adelaide had called on us. In November I made a public address to stimulate investment in the war loan, at a meeting in the Tanunda supper room, stressing the fact that we could take out small amounts of ten pounds. I advocated contributions to the war loan.

My son returned from Germany early in 1937. After he returned from Germany, I never described to anyone the way in which the paymaster would line up the printing staff, and ask them if they were happy, in Germany. Nothing like that. I am sure of that. I never said to anyone that all questions asked by the paymaster of the printing staff were finished by the question, 'And who have you got to thank for all this?' the reply being, 'Hitler, Heil Hitler.' I am quite certain of that. Before the war I never at any time got carried away with my enthusiasm for the Nazi cause.

Inaccuracies in the recorded evidence of my Hearing in Adelaide on 26 February, 1941:

From Sheet 2: 'I do not know who Captain Chapman was. I just know his name. He was in uniform.' I may have been mistaken in saying 'he was in uniform'. It must be remembered we were at war. Every man with a soldier's title is held to be in uniform. Von Luckner's visit was in peace time, and Captain Chapmen may have been in civil dress.

Sheet 3: 'My daughter and I were in his (Luckner's) company when he went to the hall for the entertainment in the evening.' This should read:' My daughter and I were not in his company.......' Neither my daughter nor I were in his company on that occasion. My daughter was on a holiday trip to Melbourne and Sydney in the company of Mrs. Drennan and Miss Barbara Drennen of Tanunda at the time of Luckner's visit to Tanunda. I entered the hall with others who went to hear Luckner.

Sheet 3: 'I knew him (Becker) fairly well and thought a lot of him.' This should read: 'and thought a lot of him as a medical man.'

Sheet 3: 'I attended meetings at a Café known as the Vienna Café.' This should read: 'I attended a meeting.'

Sheet 5: 'I have said, Hitler knows everything that is going on'. This should read: 'I have not said...'

Sheet 6: 'I do use the word 'bloody', especially since I have been at Wayville.' This should read: 'I use the word 'bloody' and have often heard it used especially since I have been at Wayville.'

Sheet 7: 'I would not say I have never had any from him.' This should read: 'I would say I have never had any from him.'

Sheet 7: '*I was not a local subscriber for that.*' *(The paper, Die Bruecke.) This should read: 'I was not a correspondent for that.'*

Sheet 8: 'I know Kevin John Niejalke.' This is quite wrong. There is no person living in Tanunda by that name. Two persons were named. One, Kevin John (John is the surname), and Peter Niejalke. (Incidentally, Kevin John is now in the R.A.A.F. and Peter Niejalke lost his life at Tobruk.)

Sheet 9: 'My printing works are known as Aurichts and they are the only printing works in Tanunda.' This should read: 'they are not the only printing works in Tanunda.' I was taxed with having printed anti-Jewish literature when Col. Cohen was a candidate at some elections in Victoria. I denied this. Asked if there was another printing office in Tanunda, I replied: 'Yes, the Barossa News.' My printing office prints only the church publications and does job printing. The recorded evidence runs on glibly: 'and it is the only printing works in Tanunda.'

Sheet 11: 'Some of those came to Tanunda and we showed them at Tanunda.' This should read: 'Some of the big films came to Tanunda and were shown at Tanunda.'

I must have the above inaccuracies explained!

The following information is in the three sheets of notes given to Harford to share with Spender:

Two days ago the leader of the Opposition in the State Parliament saw me here at the Detention Barracks and informed me that my appeal against my detention had been unfavourably decided upon by the Authorities. Under the circumstances the Labor Party could not further support my candidature at the elections already in progress. We agreed that Mr. Richards call at the Electoral Office and withdraw my nomination. Soon after the Camp Commandant informed me that Mr. Richards had phoned him to the effect that the nomination could not be withdrawn.

With a view to obtaining an early release from detention I beg respectfully that the Minister hear me:

I was born in South Australia 58 years ago and have no interests beyond the boundary of the State. I worked diligently during the last war in raising funds for patriotic purposes, addressing meetings in private schools and Lutheran Church buildings showing my audiences what everyone's duty was, no matter if our forefathers came from the country with which we were at war. During the present war I have raised close on 200 pounds for the Red Cross or Soldiers Comforts Funds, mostly per medium of moving picture shows, the films having been taken by myself. I trust that the film taken by me of Count Luckner's visit to South Australia will not be held a charge against me. As a showman I look for subjects of general interest. I had some difficulty in getting near Luckner on occasions because of cameramen who photographed the Count for our daily papers. Since the outbreak of War I have not shown the Luckner film.

My associations with Dr. Becker in the light of present events were unfortunate. Soon after his arrival in Tanunda he cured my son who had received serious injury to his spine diving into shallow water, and until Becker was disbarred from practising, he was the family's medical adviser. I met him almost daily either at the post office or when the train arrived with the evening paper. We had many arguments on political matters. Early in Hitler's career I subscribed to many of his views and actions. I read 'Mein Kampf' and this book more than anything helped me evaluate its author as the unscrupulous schemer he is. No people received a more scathing pen-slashing than did the Russians. Yet when he deemed it expedient he signed a non-aggression pact with that country and later handed over to it half of defeated Poland. Germany under Hitler is a people without a belief in God, in Christianity, but with a belief only in force. We must fight an ideology that resolves itself into a pagan worship of force. We must fight the dictator to whom all actions are means to an end who crucifies innocent women and children on the altar of expediency.

On subjects similar to the above I had repeated conversation and arguments with Dr. Becker.

A chance meeting with Becker about six years ago when I was returning home from work one day led to my going to Adelaide with him one evening. Started on our car trip to Adelaide, Becker told me that Mr. Schubert who was a fellow passenger was that evening to be inducted in some Hitler Office at the Vienna Café. Arrived at the Café, Becker introduced me to a number of people present who in turn introduced me to refreshments that the manager was ready to sell. I didn't feel disposed to do the honours more than could reasonably be expected. I strolled up and down Grenfell Street for about half an hour until I heard that the actual proceedings were in progress. Schubert was duly installed in some office and standing at the Nazi Salute either the Deutschland song or the Horst Wessel lied was sung. I neither saluted nor sang. Sandwiches were handed round – you had to buy your own drinks. This is the only time that I have attended a Hitler function.

I love my country. I owe it all that I am and have. I have worked and given for it.

I entered politics to contest a seat in the Labor interest, because I believe that after the war Labor problems will be our major problems. The infiltration of communist elements has done incalculable harm to all concerned and particularly to the Labor party. By clever propaganda these elements have exploited the loyalty of unionists – nobody likes being called a scab. My detention has, of course, settled my chance of election. The party cannot champion the cause of a candidate who is held as I am. But I trust still to save my deposit of 25 pounds which I would rather donate to patriotic funds than lose.

I want to be released to carry on work for my country that I love and against which I have knowingly done nothing by word or deed. When my little grandchild Marie came to see me for the first time she enquired of her mother during the car trip 'Where is Grandpa? What is he doing?' To the latter question her mother replied 'Grandpa is helping the soldiers.' When Marie arrived at Wayville seeing so many uniformed men in attendance she said full of pride 'Oh Grandpa, you are helping the soldiers.'

I want to help the soldiers again as in the past. At public meetings I have spoken in support of War Saving and War Loans. I and the members of my family have invested in War Savings Certificates. I am a subscriber to two groups. My associations with Dr. Becker took place at a time when it could be reasonably hoped that his and my country were reaching an understanding. I have been chided or taunted even here in this camp that I was placing too much reliance on British Justice. I am asking no favours, but believe that knowing all the facts the authorities will give me the freedom to which, I respectfully beg to submit, I am entitled to.

Wayville Detention Barracks
13/3/41
J.F.W. Schulz.

***

After Harford leaves I write up other information which I had not spoken to him about but which refers to some other issues in the transcript. I am doing this in an effort to clarify in my own mind that I have not committed any crime against my country. I hope to be able to pass this on to him before he leaves for Canberra.

Firstly, with reference to my attendance at a Nazi social function in Adelaide, I would ask that my attendance at that function be judged in the frame of the social and political atmosphere of that time. I recall to my mind the addresses given in various centres of his electorate by the late H. C. Hawker M.H.R. He spoke at Tanunda expressing satisfaction of what he had seen and heard in Germany. Other men in public life, through the press, related in eulogistic manner their experiences while travelling on the continent, citing Germany in particular.

I have given a Film Show at the German Club in Adelaide.

My printing house has for years done the printing for the Lutheran Church of which Rev. J.J. Stolz is the President. An agreement between the Church and the printery provides that our charge for printing must be at competitive prices. About four years ago, Mr. Methsieder was appointed manager of the Book Depot and he soon began to query my monthly account (70 pounds approx.) for the printing of the Lutheran Herald and the Kirchen Blatt. He had asked for and received a quotation from McAlisters which firm would print the paper for less than we did. I submitted the contract to the legal firm of Homburg, Melrose and Homburg for an interpretation of the words 'competitive price' in the contract. The advice was that a competitive price was not necessarily always the lowest price. The quality of the article produced etc., etc. would enter into consideration. At a meeting of the Book Depot Board, for which I had asked permission to attend, Methsieder said, addressing me: 'You have put money into your pocket which belongs here!' I rose and threatened him. The chairman, Rev. J. Dohler of Murray Bridge, intervened. I asked for an apology. Rev. Dohler supported me saying that the price charged by me for the printing was the price agreed to by the Board. Methsieder apologised and we shook hands. After the meeting, Methsieder said: 'You show films. Will you show the films at the German Club? And what would you charge?' To curry favour, I agreed to show films for the charge of two pounds. I subsequently gave a film show at the German Club, and was paid two pounds. Mr. H. Rothe, who is an internee in this Camp at Wayville, would, I dare say, bear me out as it was he, I believe, who paid me the two pounds.

My visit to Captain Sharland:

My son Bert, who is in charge of my printing business, had intimated by his behaviour that it seemed his duty to enlist also when other lads were joining up. Since his return from abroad, some four years ago, he was given charge of the printery. When it became evident that paper would soon be at a premium in printing houses, he looked up the business firms for whom we do work and enquired what their requirements might be for a period ahead. Two large vignerons had us print in the past: Customs and Excise forms, Account forms, Cartnote Books, etc. For one firm alone we then bought over 100 pounds worth of different kinds of paper.

I am not a printer by trade. Upon the death of Mr. Auricht, owner of Aurichts Printing Office, Tanunda, I helped the family which was in financial difficulties, and am now part owner of the business. The other men on the staff could bring out our weekly paper, the copy for which is supplied by the Editor, Rev. J.J. Stolz, North Adelaide, but apart from that, business could not well carry on if my son were not around. As chairman of the Tanunda Civil Defence Committee, I was in personal touch with Col. Bice at that time and it was my intention when next in Adelaide to mention the matter of my son's possible enlistment to him. When in Adelaide about seven or eight months ago, I called on Mr. Wilson, licensee of the Brittania Hotel, in Gawler Place. I mentioned the matter of my son to him and he said: 'Go to Captain Sharland. I will give you a letter of introduction,' which he did. I had first to transact some business with Mr. Chas. Edmunds, Solicitor, in Currie Street and later casually mentioned the fact of my proposed visit to Captain Sharland and its purpose. Mr. Edmunds said: 'You can mention my name if you like.'

Later in the day I called on Captain Sharland. I mentioned the purpose of my visit, but before I was able to go into any detail, I was under cross-examination on matters not in connection with the object of my visit. From this examination I remember the following. A photograph was placed before me. The centrepiece of the photograph was a large German flag with the Swastika. On each side of the flag stood three or four men. The photo was taken in a vineyard. The background was rising ground planted with vines. The flag was nailed to the trunk of a dry tree. I was asked to say who the men in the photo were. I failed to recognise any of them. Individual ones were pointed out to me. I didn't know any one of them.

Then I was asked which church I attended at Tanunda and who the pastor was. My reply: 'I attend the Lutheran Church and my pastor is the Rev. Hebart.' Question: 'Do you think he is loyal?' Answer: 'Rev. Hebart's relatives live in Germany. He made a trip to Germany about eight years ago. Upon his return, I remember him saying inter alia at a welcome home social tendered him by his parishioners: 'When I came to Australia many years ago I brought a small parcel of German soil with me. I wanted to be buried in German soil. I have now thrown this away. Australia will do.' I have never heard Rev. Hebart make a disloyal statement.' Question: 'Does not Pastor Hebart, when handing Confirmation Certificates to his confirmees, stamp a seal on the certificate depicting the Swastika?' My reply: 'My three children were confirmed by Pastor Hebart and I would be pleased to produce their certificates at once, and would further undertake to produce the certificates handed to confirmees at the confirmation which took place last year.'

I was dismissed without further mention being made of why I had come.

J.F.W. Schulz

Exhibit 5.

Exhibit 5

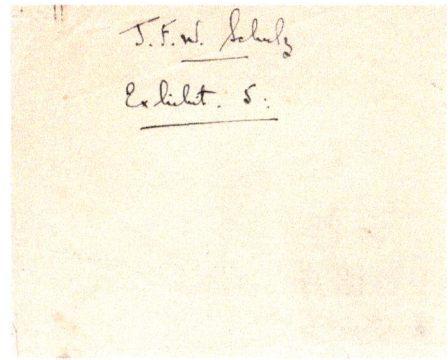

Bank of Adelaide

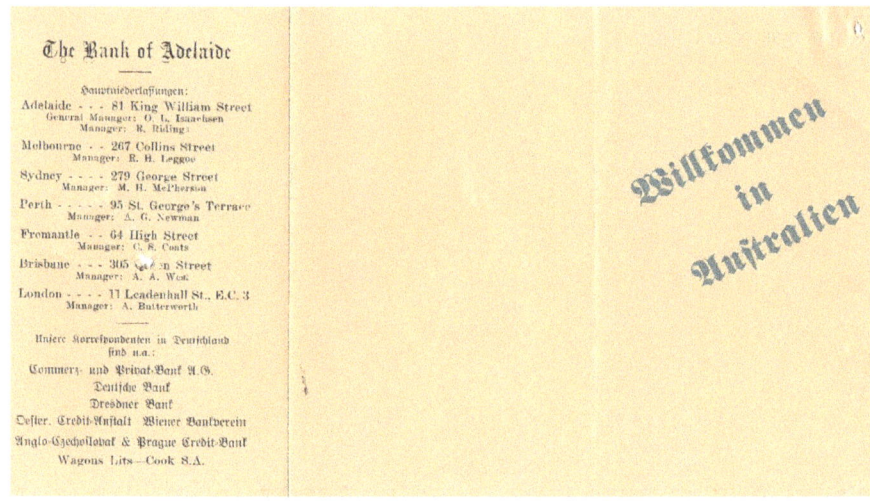

Bank of Adelaide Back

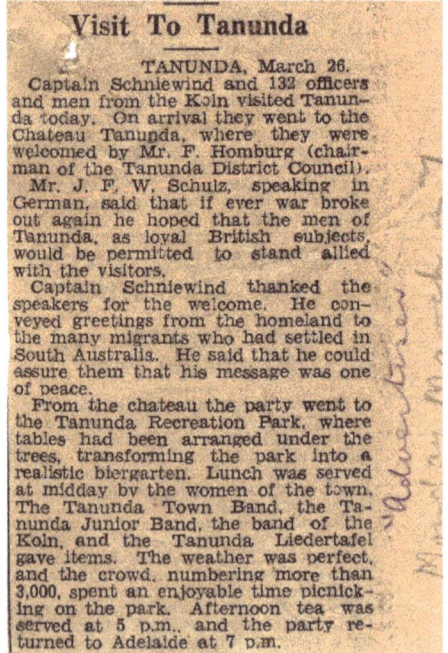

Visit to Tanunda

Jaunuda 26/8/39.

To
The Commissioner for Civil Defence
    Premiers Office, Adelaide.

Dear Sir,
          The Chairman of the District Council of Jaunuda of which I am a ~~Councillor~~ Council member wrote you on July 31st that I ~~was~~ had been nominated as a member for the local committee of the Emergency Civil Defence Council to which letter you replied on the 7th inst.

In view of the present crisis I am looking forward to an early communication from your Mr. Hayward or his representative to enable the local Committee to proceed with the necessary arrangements.

Yours faithfully
J.W. Schulz.

TELEPHONE:
CENTRAL 7136 (TWO LINES).

THE LIBERAL UNION.

PRESIDENT:
MR. O. UPPILL,
BALAKLAVA.

GENERAL SECRETARY:
WM. B. PAGE.

It is requested all correspondence be addressed to
THE GENERAL SECRETARY,
BOX 29, G.P.O., ADELAIDE,
and not to individual officers by name.

No. 16. NORTH TERRACE,
ADELAIDE.

June 20th 1921.

To whom it may concern.

    Mr. J. F. W. Schulz of Tanunda, has been in the employ of this Union as Organiser since June 1920, during which time he has given every satisfaction. He has shown marked ability in organising the Liberal Forces, particularly in Barossa District.

    He is leaving to take up a position under the Commonwealth Government in New Guinea, and takes with him my best wishes for success in his new sphere.

Wm. B. Page
General Secretary.

The Liberal Union

To Whom it may Concern

This is to certify that I have known the bearer Mr. J. F. K. Schultz for many years.

He is a man of considerable ability & bears an excellent character, & is capable of filling a responsible Position.

W. Dague.

Adelaide
June 23/21.

To Whom it May Concern

Vol. 23 No. 9 — April 24, 1948 — Price 11/-, paid in advance 10/-

Behold, the Lamb of God, which taketh away the sin of the world.

O Lord, when condemnation
And guilt oppress my soul,
Then let Thy bitter passion
The rising storm control;
Remind me that Thy blood was spilt
For me, the most unworthy,
To take away my guilt.

O wonder passing measure
To faith's enlightened eye!
For slaves it was the pleasure
Of their own Lord to die!
The mighty God stoops from on high
For me, lost, ruined creature,
And deigns as man to die.

Henceforth my heart shall bless Thee
Whilst here its blood streams move,
With songs of praise address Thee
For all Thy dying love.
Thy sufferings and great agony
Shall be my meditation
Till I am called to Thee.

Lord, let Thy bitter passion
My soul with strength inspire
To flee with indignation
All sinful, base desire.
O let me never, Lord, forget
The greatness of that ransom
Which paid my endless debt.

Christ Jesus is made unto us wisdom, and righteousness, and sanctification, and redemption.

Lutheran Herald

Show Exhibit Signs

1941 Tanunda Show Exhibition Scraps

TANUNDA
Agricultural, Horticultural and Floricultural Society.

FIRST PRIZE

SHOW 194

SECTION _____
ENTRY _____

EXHIBITED BY _____

W. B. SCHULZ, Secretary.

TANUNDA SHOW 1941
EXHIBITION SCRAPS

SECOND PRIZE

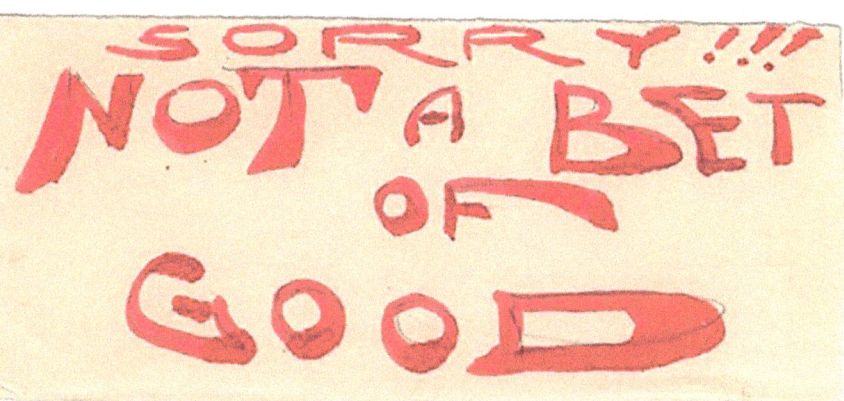

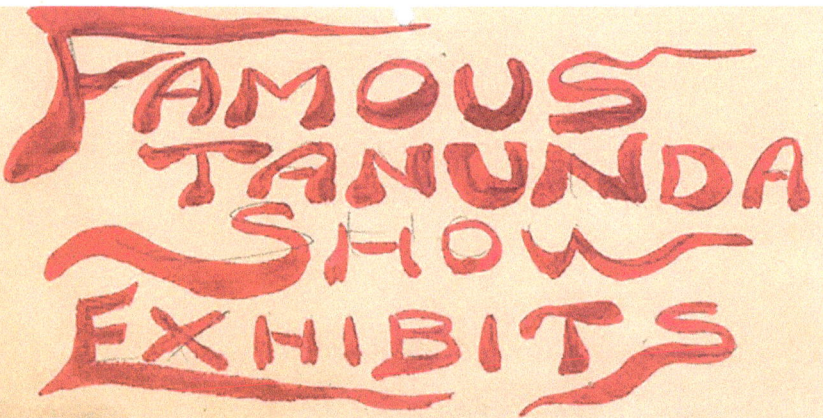

5

15 March – 18 March, 1941

Physical Drill is getting to be a bit tough. Today it was conducted by Sergeant Lee and somehow I injured my thumb. Time will heal it no doubt and I have plenty of that at present.

Oskar gives my neck a shave. When I asked his qualification as a barber, he replied, 'I have helped shaving pigs at home!'

We are experiencing very sultry weather. 'Keep your pecker up, boys,' says Captain Darley after the usual Field Inspection. Fine fellow, Captain Darley. Sorry to hear that he is leaving for Woodside Camp. Quite a lot of rain during the night and today, 18 March. We are going to be miserable if we do not get more protection and northerly winds when rains happen along.

The authorities have notified Eime that we are not allowed to vote at the upcoming elections. I, for one, am very disappointed with that decision but what can I do about it?

19 March, 1941

Today is my Birthday. I am visited by Else, Margaret, Marie, and Miss Auricht, who bring me all the usual good things as well as flowers. Captain Sparks says he must have a piece of the Birthday Cake, so I see to it that he, Sergeant Major Inwood, Sergeant Link, and Captain Ardell each get a piece.

20 March – 23 March, 1941

Eime finds a set of false teeth in the bath shed and takes them into his cubicle. At breakfast he announces his find. Nobody appears to have lost their false molars until Seith is about to commence his meal. Wonderful!

A new sergeant gives us 'feesical jogs' as Toni puts it. I find these exercises very therapeutic since being allowed out for a nice long walk is out of the question.

Comelli is ill again with flu, bad back, and lame leg. At the tea table he says, 'Hell, I wish I was in heaven!

Captain Sparks rings Bert for me. I've had no news from Harford so I've advised Bert to pay no more money to Harford without authority from me.

Two Italians are brought into the Camp on 21 March, then two more, three more, and one more. The next day three more arrive. Also, two Germans, Gehrike and Drucks. What a cosmopolitan Camp we have! Then three more Italians arrive. The last one, who must have said his final farewell in a Hindley Street Hotel 'full of spirit', drops his bundle somewhat limply into the gate of our Compound, picks up his guitar and musically waltzes into the arms of his numerous compatriots. What a babble as one after the other they relate their experiences of 'the last round-up'.

About three weeks ago a party of Italians held some Fascist meeting in a Hindley Street rendezvous. The police watched the proceedings through a window. Sequel: The members of the party appeared in Court. The owner of the premises, where the meeting was held and who supplied liquor, went to gaol. The others paid fines of about 12 pounds each. Then it was intended to apprehend them reasonably quickly for the Detention Barracks here.

None of them, we are told, are naturalised. If report has it correctly, they are destined for Tatura at an early date. Let us hope so. The spitting etc. is unbearable. At about 4pm they are rounded up and marched to the baths for a hot shower!

Mine is the only cubicle with but one inmate. Our colony now totals thirty one.

I wish I had the descriptive pencil of Ion Idriess! As usual I have an early cup of coffee and some cake. At about 6am the two Italians on the left of me start conversing in an undertone. Those on the right soon join in, but a little louder. In the twinkling of an eye the entire nineteen in the whole of the cubicles on both sides of the narrow walk are awake. What a mess! 'Shut up', yells someone, and, as if you had thrown a stone into a flock of roosting cockatoos, an occasional screech in the distance is all that can be heard. How long they will obey the 'shut up' command is problematical.

Mum, Bert, Margaret, Ted, and Marie visit me today, 23 March, but there is still no news of Mr. Harford and his visit to Canberra on my behalf. We shall see what we shall see.

A pall hangs over the Camp. Fritz Henke, Vito Caputo (old Capitano as we call him), Antonio Mezzina (known as the ever-ready and ever-willing Toni), Atura Comelli (the wonderful black and white artist), and Altamurro, have been told to hold themselves in readiness and leave for Tatura by the end of the week.

24 March – 26 March

Another week commences and we are condemned to live in this Italian atmosphere and odour.

Mr. Harford comes to see me, at last, and reports on his trip to Canberra. He tells me he saw Spender in company with Makin and

Curtin and is expecting a reply from Spender during the week. I am not expecting good news.

My turn on Mess Duty again and it's a much bigger job now with thirty one to look after against the sixteen of the past.

Margaret and Else come to visit me during the week. Else has driven Materne's car this time, bringing Hausler's visitors with her.

I am becoming resigned and ready and sometimes almost eager to pack for Tatura. The uncertainty of it all, added to by the sometimes almost indescribable noisy, filthy element of nineteen Italians in a walking space of 22 yards by 6 yards, undermines and weakens my resistance. I feel like chucking in my bundle.

27 March, 1941.

After I had been here for about one month, I told Captain Sparks about a sore on my nose. At Medical Inspection today the Doctor had a look at the sore and prescribed zinc ointment. This I had applied regularly for over a week and the sore seemed to be healing initially but it has appeared again.

About a week ago I again drew the Captain's attention to the sore and Doctor Verco had a look at it. He was in the company of another Doctor. They gave the sore a medical term which I did not understand. Doctor Verco asked me whether the sore had ever received Radium treatment. I replied that it had not. He said he would make arrangements for treatment.

More information on the political front. Following on from a verbal application for a chance to vote for Saturday's Election, we were informed that we could not vote. Eime then made written application. This, we were advised, was sent on to Melbourne with the result that we can vote at the nearest Polling Booth. There is one here on the Wayville grounds. At least three of us are going to exercise our right.

28 March, 1941

At last we have a beautiful spring day and in order to keep my wits about me, I am learning to play Skat. During the day, the Medical Officer tells me that the sore on my nose needs radium treatment. Shortly before tea, Lebeck receives notice that he is to be released. He is to report to the Intelligence Department at 9am tomorrow morning. Good luck, Billy!

29 March, 1941

Election Day. I feel that my immediate future depends upon the result and if I can just save my deposit, well and good. If the unexpected happens and I poll well, there is the instinctive apprehension that definite internment will follow this detention. Another depressing piece of news is that the Camp Commandant has just advised Eime that we will not be permitted to vote today. We have no rights in here.

This evening I show some of my movies, and after the event, Toni lays bare his soul in song. What a beautiful voice!

The Elections are over. At about 9pm I hide away in our Carpenter's cubicle to hear the Election results over the air from the Commandant's Quarter. By lights out time (10pm) it looks as though I might lose my deposit.

30 March, 1941

I am up very early this morning, make a delicious cup of coffee and eat my last pieces of German cake and Berlin bun. It is still very early but soon the Sunday Mail newspaper will come to hand. The paper arrives and I find that I have polled over 700 votes. I have saved the twenty five pound deposit; money the family needs badly, having spent so much in efforts to gain my release, so far without avail.

31 March, 1941

Hughie and I have to go to the Wayville Hospital at 10am this morning. Major Welch just has a look at my nose and, after waiting for an hour, we are told to report again at 4pm when Doctor Messent will examine us. At 4pm we are again at the Hospital. Doctors Welch and Messent are in attendance, but we are not told any results of the examination. It's been a long, hot day.

1 April, 1941

I have written a letter today to the Returning Officer, District of Angas, in Angaston, as follows:

> *Dear Sir,*
>
> *Will you be good enough to read these notes in my behalf at the declaration of the Poll for Angas.*
> *I desire to thank the 700 odd electors who cast their first preference votes for me. I would like the electors of Angas to take to heart the final sentences contained in the message broadcast by His Majesty our King to his subjects at the outbreak of war. '...We can only do the right as we see the right and reverently commend our cause to God. If one and all we keep resolutely faithful to it, ready for whatever service or sacrifice it may demand, then with God's help we shall prevail. May He bless and keep us all.'*
> *To the above message I would like to add an extract from Mr. Menzies' message to our people on January 1, 1941: 'We pass into 1941 when the victories shall be ours so long as we to ourselves do rest but true, so long as we look without fear at the truth and are*

prepared to vow to our country and its cause all that we have and are without subtraction without excuse without folly or selfishness.'

Will you, please, hand my deposit of 25 pounds to my son, W.B. Schulz.

Thanking you in anticipation.

(signed) J.F.W. Schulz.

Bert has made a booklet for me out of sheets of brown paper sewn together, and in this I am pasting newspaper articles cut from the paper I get to read every day, as well as copies of letters I write. My title for this booklet is: Political Pellets.

Today, as well as a copy of the above letter, I've included an article from the paper titled:

STRANGEST ELECTION EVER HELD IN STATE
Labor Candidate Who Has Made No Appearance.

Saturday's State Elections will, in Angas, present the situation of a candidate who has neither appeared before the electors, nor circulated a policy speech. Mr. J.F.W. Schulz, of Tanunda, who had previously been visiting many district centres giving picture shows of films he had taken, and in many instances doing it for patriotic funds, has been absent from the district.

He had been approved in the Labor Party's selection, and his nomination and deposit were duly lodged. His political views were widely known, and many electors have questioned how matters would stand were he to be elected. In reply to questions at one public meeting, the opinion was given that the South Australian Act carried no provision, and that, if elected, so far as the State is concerned, Mr Schulz is entitled to his seat.

It would appear, therefore, that the votes accorded Mr Schulz will be based on the Labor policy, or on personal friendship of those who have heard his views. The Labor Party has given no indication of its wishes. The L.C.L. has given Mr Haese (Independent) its second preference, and Mr Haese has tickets based on a 1, 2, 3, vote from top down. His own name appears against No, 1 and other names are omitted.

Electors, however, must place a figure in each square, in their order of preference, and may vote between 8 a.m. and 7 p.m. Although voting is not compulsory, it is the duty of every elector to exercise the franchise so as to give a real indication of the wishes of the majority, especially at a time when the greatest war in history is being waged on the issue: Democracy or dictatorship.

***

The temperature has almost reached the century today, and just before lunch Captain Sparks tells me that I am to be at the Adelaide Hospital at 1.45 p.m. for radium treatment. So, during the hottest part of the day, I leave the Camp to go to Wayville Hospital from where I am transferred to the Adelaide Hospital. Under guard, of course.

After waiting for some time at Wayville, I prompt the guard to make further enquiries as the time is slipping on. He enquires at the Hospital office. The Officer in charge has no records or papers to take me to the Hospital.

At 1.30 p.m. Major Welch, who apparently is in charge, happens along. 'Oh yes, the internee Schulz is to be at the Adelaide Hospital at 1.45 p.m.' He asks an Orderly to make out the necessary papers. At 1.30 p.m.!

The Ambulance is called into action and in this I and my guard sail forth to the Adelaide Hospital. On arrival there we are told to sit down in the Casualty Waiting Room. We wait for about an hour. At the Enquiry window we are told to hang on for a while. So, after a while a hospital attendant takes us to the Radium Department. The girl at the Office desk can't do anything until I bring a Doctor's Certificate and his direction.

We proceed back from whence we came. The Doctor there is of the opinion too, that I need a Doctor's introduction. I volunteer the information that a Doctor has viewed me daily for 16 weeks, that Dr. Verco last week told me that my nose needed Radium treatment. Another Doctor had confirmed that a day later. Dr. Welch and Dr. Messent at Wayville had apparently been of that opinion also and Dr. Welch had actually signed the document that gained me entrance here.

I was asked to sit down again among the other waiting people while the attendant in charge took the telephone, connected someone, and asked what he should do with the internee Schulz! The latter news item, of course, focused all attention on the rara avis, yours truly.

My guard disgustedly lugged me back to the Radium room. Here particulars were first taken by a charming young lady. Next, a photo of my profile. Why? It was definitely no x-ray. Then Dr. Burnard saw me. It was now about 4.15 p.m.

While taking particulars, he asked me casually:

'How long have they had you in clink?'

'Almost four months,' I replied.

'How long have you been in this country?'

'I was born here,' came my reply.

He looked at me sympathetically. 'That's a bit hard, isn't it?'

I agreed.

He examined the sore on my nose closely and said, 'It's not serious at all, come back next Tuesday and I'll treat you.' Before I left he wrote a card which will gain me direct entrance on Tuesday at 1.45 p.m. I like Doctor Burnard.

My guard and I arrived back at the Camp via Wayville Hospital after 5 p.m. and just in time for tea.

Hughie Eime leaves for the Adelaide Hospital on 2 April in preparation for an operation the next day for his rupture. He will be in the Martin Ward so we are told.

4 April, 1941

Pohl's habeus corpus case comes up for Hearing today. It is listed in today's paper: Cause Lists. Supreme Court. Friday April 4. No. 1 Court (Civil) Before the Chief Justice, at 10.30 a.m. Rex v Clift; ex parte Pohl. I paste the small cutting in my Diary.

We have rather an interesting morning. While we are absent at the Showground baths, the Camp Staff, following complaints made about the sudden appearance of bugs in the Camp, hold a bed inspection. On our return from the Bath Parade we find some of the beds which belong to the Italians, in the middle of the Compound, absolutely infected with bugs. Stretchers and mattresses alike.

The aggravating, noisy, nonchalant manner of the recently arrived Italian coterie has received a sudden check. A display of gold wristlet watches with bugs and lice shying off at a tangent when the girlfriends put in an appearance on visiting days, doesn't rhyme too well. Thank goodness the never ceasing monotone singing has received a check for a time, at any rate.

Some of the bedding and stretchers are burnt and gallons of Kerosine is used to kill and disinfect. Comelli makes a painting for me and writes the following on it: 'The Game Chief wants to keep the fleas off his small goods!' 'The Game Chief' is a reference to my Kangaroo shooting days.

5 April, 1941

What a day! What a mess! We, in No. 1 are on Mess Duty. We have scarcely finished with fatigue work when the order is given: 'All quarters are to be cleaned right out ready for disinfection.'

All day yesterday, Officers from Corporals to Colonels inspected 'Bug Alley'; old Captain Arnold from Wayville Hospital even going over chinks and cracks with a microscope. Hundreds of bugs and lice had come to an untimely and violent end yesterday, but there were apparently still plenty at large, hence the disinfection order.

What a mess! The crusade is of course directed against the Italian quarters, but since unquestionably the vermin is now exploring fresh fields and pastures, it is deemed advisable to attend to the entire Camp. The Commandant and his Staff have received a bit of a shock. They have apparently been somewhat lax in allowing dirty beds and bedding into the Camp. On top of that, we understand bugs were mentioned before Chief Justice Murray in the Pohl case yesterday.

What a mess! All cubicles have had to be cleaned right out. My cubicle, though it is the only one in the Camp with but one inmate, is fairly stocked up, what with films, projectors, screens and a hundred and one other things. I have had quite a bit to shift. I even unearthed my golden tooth again which the Dentist at Wayville had been unable to replace following its forcible dislodgement during strenuous cricket practice some two months ago.

But what about the cubicle adjacent to mine! Its two Italian inmates are here but two weeks. To begin with, their duty beds and bedding emerge into 'Bug Alley' followed by remnants of fruit, olives in oil, watermelons, and poultry apparently cooked in oil from the manner in which it slithers all over the place.

The walls of the cubicle have been papered with pages from Pix Magazine, depicting actresses and females in various degrees of undress. All the papering is ordered down. The occupants of the cubicle turn to their work half-heartedly. The paste used in papering has apparently been well prepared, for when the disinfectors commence their work, they have to apply Phenyl here and there on Hollywood stars who have refused, partially at any rate, to vacate the stage.

We are promised fumigation for Monday! What with the Pohl case, and rumours of Mr. V's enforced retirement, things have assumed quite an interesting angle here.

Visiting Day on 6 April. Mum and Else, as well as my brother Dolf and his wife Irene come to see me. It's my brother's first visit and he was quite surprised to see how homely I have made my cubicle. At least, as homely as I can under the circumstances. Mum and Else are concerned about the sore on my nose but I've told them I have great faith in the doctors at the Adelaide Hospital and am sure all will soon be well again.

Pohl's case is on for Hearing today, 7 April, and I am to report at the Adelaide Hospital tomorrow at 1.45 p.m. Captain Sparks asks if I would care to walk to the Hospital and I readily agree.

Ideal weather conditions which makes life here easier to cope with. During General Inspection the Field Officer, a Lieutenant Colonel we are told, enquired of some of us as to how long we have been here and how long since the Hearing of the Appeal. He shakes his head in my case. Eleven weeks before Appeal was heard and five weeks since the Appeal.

8 April, 1941

A wonderful day! I have dinner early and at 12.45 p.m. leave for the Adelaide Hospital per foot with my guard to get my Radium treatment. Captain Sparks lends me ten shillings as I want to buy something for Mum's Birthday tomorrow. The guard is told that I have permission to buy something wherever I like, also that I may visit Hughie Eime in Martin's Ward.

While waiting for treatment I meet Jim who is down from Tanunda to have sores treated. The guard says, 'Forget me and talk to him if you like.' We have an interesting chat and he brings me up-to-date on a few things which are happening in the Valley. More gossip than interest, really.

The Doctor inspects and examines my sore. He prescribes a pot of ointment and says, 'There's hardly anything there, but I will give you this to apply to the sore and I would like to see you again tomorrow at 2 p.m., and again on Thursday.' That eliminates my people from coming down on Visiting Day tomorrow, the first missed visit since my arrival here.

After I am through at the Hospital and have a short chat with Hughie, my guard and I start on the return journey. I call at Bauer's, Tobacconists, and buy a smoking mixture that I am fond of. We have a rest here and there and arrive back at 'headquarters' at about 4.30 p.m. Altogether a delightful outing.

At the Camp I find that Pohl's case has as yet not come on for Hearing. He is to appear again on Thursday.

Max Hunger and one of the Italians have been taken to Wayville Hospital for treatment of some kind.

9 April, 1941

As usual the Italians fill the kitchen with arguments and noisy procedure at breakfast, and I have a few words to say on their conduct and behaviour. Not that it makes much difference. No sooner have I finished talking than they are back at it again.

'Popeye' is back with an A.W.L. ticket and sings and yodels in his approved old manner. What a tragical, wasted life; ready to enlist in the defence of the country but determined to avoid actual participation in fighting. His singing, as good as ever, is exciting less interest and approbation, and rightly so.

As the 'Provost Company' is unable to provide a walking guard for me to the Hospital, I am driven and the driver acts as guard. Entering by the wrong gate at the Hospital we finish in a cul-de-sac at the rear of the Nurses Quarters. Having no time to lose, we leave the car there and proceed to the Radium Department. We are directed to the Waiting Room and after a while I am asked into one of the treatment apartments.

Seated in an easy chair, a small object is fastened across the bridge of my nose with adhesive tape. With the door ajar the guard can see me. An occasional look assures him I have not bolted. 'What about rescuing our bus and bringing it around here?' I suggest. 'A good idea,' he agrees. Showing some hesitation, however, I assure him that I will be good! He leaves.

Shortly afterwards, the Sister who is attending me, enters to have a look at how the application is sitting, then leaves again, closing the door leading into the Waiting Room. Soon afterwards I hear the guard ranking his utility into position and presently his footsteps sound in the hall. The door to my apartment being closed, I notice him carefully turn the doorknob. The door refuses to yield because of the Yale lock. 'Mr. Schulz, Mr. Schulz,' first silently but presently with more firmness. 'OK,' I answer.

After about half an hour the Sister comes in again and, consulting her watch, informs me, 'You have had half an hour, the application must remain a further three quarters of an hour.'

About half an hour later the guard speaks again. 'Mr. Schulz?' 'OK Chief,' I volunteer. The Sister enters. 'Did you call?' 'No, it's only my guard wanting to allay his apprehension that I might have bolted!' She smiles her sympathy.

By and by I am released from the Hospital. Even though I had phoned home that I would not be at the Camp today, I found Else waiting for me at the Hospital. She had driven Materne's car down again. I gave her two shillings to buy some chocolates for Mum's Birthday.

All too soon I am back in 'Bug Alley'. Altogether, it has been a wonderful day; the green parks and lawns, the beautiful flowers. How little do we appreciate nature's loveliness generally!

Fritz Henke, Oskar Johannsen, Vito Caputo (Capitano), Toni Altamurra, Camporeale, and Comelli are told today that they must be ready to leave for Tatura today week, 16 inst. Later in the day, while walking back to his cubicle, Eime is heard to shout: 'All trains express to Tatura!' Our original small group is getting smaller by the day.

Regularly when the old bespectacled guard is on night duty, he comes to my door punctually at 6 a.m. 'Mr. Schulz, the water is boiling, in fact it is bubbling over.' Out of bed, coffee from home into my billy, through the unlocked entrance gate, and over to the boilers. In less than three minutes I have the loveliest cup of coffee and together with Streusel Kuchen or Berliner Pfannkuchen from home, what a glorious early morning start.

Before the Camp actually bestirs itself, I have washed the floor of my cubicle, made my bed, cleaned up and generally tidied everything up. When the morning paper arrives, I sit back and smoke my pipe of peace.

The third big bug hunt! There is another thorough and I understand, final clean-up ordered. A regular 'Bedouins on the March' outfit. I tie two neckties together and with this tie-rope round my mattress and blankets, together with the other thirty inmates, set out for a vacant allotment at the rear of the Showgrounds carrying our huge swags. It needs only a black billy dangling at the side and a hundred-foot colour film will be worth a little fortune at some future date.

At 1.45 p.m. I leave for my second treatment at the Adelaide Hospital. Pohl, to his Appeal, and I leave in a truck. The guard, Corporal Gill, like practically every one of them here, is considerate towards me. We had to return by tram and reached the Camp again at about 4.30 p.m. I am to report again at the Hospital on Monday, 28th inst. On the way back the Corporal only winks negatively when I suggest that he introduce me at the Gresham Hotel as an Inspector under the Food and Drugs Act!

Good Friday, 11 April, 1941

The radio programme for the day according to the Advertiser gives Richard Crooks, Lawrence Tibbet and the Trinity Choir singing the 'Crucifixion' from 9 to 10 a.m. I move my chair closer to the fence to listen to the Provost wireless, but the continuous, never-ending haranguing conversation carried on by the Italians makes it quite impossible to follow the singing.

I inform Captain Clift that it is now six weeks since my Appeal. When will I hear news of the outcome? The days drag by so slowly and my patience is wearing thin.

Easter Sunday, 13 April, 1941.

Bert and Mum visit me. Bert informs me that the reply received by Mr. Guerin to his letter asking for my release stated that the Authorities could not see their way clear to alter their decision. What does this answer imply?

Comelli brightens my day by presenting me with a small Easter painting and card which he has executed. He has drawn me spread out on my straw bed with chickens hatching from their eggs beneath me and a balloon of wording which reads: 'Hurray! After 4 months of hard seating I got some chicks.' He has a great sense of humour. I remember when he and I were peeling potatoes once on Mess Duty. I'm going like blazes when I notice a broad grin on his face. He has found a suitable murphy and is busy modelling me! I stick my knife through the spud. 'Oh hell!' says he and makes the peels fly.

I am almost through Volume One of Lawrence's 'Seven Pillars of Wisdom.' The writing is solid but very informative.

Warm, sultry weather on 15 April. Captain Sparks and I are going through the documents Bert brought on Sunday: the return of 25 pounds and Declaration papers re Election expenses. The papers will be returned to me tomorrow for my visitors to take back home with them.

The one from the Returning Officer for the District of Angas, dated 9 April 1941, reads as follows:

Dear Sir,

I enclose cheque for 25 pounds, being refund of deposit lodged with your nomination as a candidate for this district. Will you please let me have your personal acquittance for the amount.

Under Section 140 of the Electoral Act, within eight weeks after declaration of the result of the election, to file with the Returning Officer for the State a return (fifth schedule) of your electoral expenses with vouchers for same.
Yours faithfully,
Ernest Feist (signed)
R.O. Angas

16 April 1941

Visiting Day. Margaret and Marie with Mrs. Materne arrive first followed by Else and Miss Auricht. Else brings a parcel for Oskar, who is also to leave for Tatura.

The Camp is a hive of activity today since our friends destined for Tatura are busy packing their things. Fritz, Oskar, Comelli, Toni, Altamurra, Capitano Vito Caputo, Camporeale. We are sad at heart to see them sent for the duration.

The cubicle alongside of me is vacant, until old, dirty Salvatora of the Hindley Street bug infected boarding house moves in. Suffering from a bronchial cough, he only sleeps in fits and starts and his continual expectorating almost makes me vomit.

Next day, on returning from our bath, we all have to do the -------- parade. Since the advent of the Hindley Street Italians, anything and everything is expected, and inspected.

This week brings me up to eighteen weeks since the start of my Detention!

Mum, Bert, Else, Ted and Marie visit me on 20 April. I give Bert the Candidates Deposit form to enable him to receive the 25 pounds return which he does from Sergeant Major Inwood today. The receipt reads:

> Barrack Detention Rooms 20th April 1941
> Received from Captain Sparks O/C Barrack Detention Rooms WAYVILLE
> Cheque from E. Feist. Returning Officer for the sum of 25 pounds also attached Documents in relation thereto.
> W.B. Schulz (signed)
> Witness: C.S.M. Inwood R.R. VC (signed)

Expenses returns are due on Wednesday.

21 April, 1941

For the last few mornings I have begun to sleep in and then have to hurry to be ready for breakfast. This morning the Cook and his assistant are having an argument over milk with our Mess Orderlies. As a reprisal, no doubt, we get scanty rations for dinner. No potatoes, and only carrots for half a dozen men, and a supply of very ordinary meat. So, we complain to the Captain and get a further supply of carrots which are all eaten.

While our Orderlies, Hunger, Seith, and Drake, are washing up, I notice the Cook's assistant tipping carrots into the refuse pan. Soon afterwards the Cook and his assistant go to the pan evidently to establish the fact that we have thrown carrots away. However, our evidence is too strong and upsets the malicious conspiracy. We're going to have some fun with the Cookhouse, it seems.

Little Joe aspires to become an expert tennis ball catcher and catches a fast screw throw fair in the eye. He bolts first into his cubicle and then into the washhouse. Emerging from there with tears trickling down from the injured eye, he looks heavenwards and makes some remark in Italian which evokes roars of laughter from his compatriots. He is evidently much pleased to learn that he can still see.

Salvatora goes into hospital today, 22 April, and I am not praying for his speedy recovery. Next day Margaret, Marie, and Else come to see me just as rain commences to fall steadily.

23 April, 1941

Today a letter is sent from Villenneuve Smith & Harford to The Hon. P.C. Spender K.C. Minister for the Army, in Canberra, a copy of which is given to me. It reads as follows:

>Sir,
>
>RE J.F.W. SCHULZ
>
>*On the occasion of the writer's visit to Canberra for the express purpose of placing before you the facts contained in and arising out of the evidence relative to this man's detention, and appealing to you for his conditional release, you were good enough to place at Mr. Harford's disposal after the formal conference with you at which the Hon. Norman Makin was present the means of submitting to you in writing the most significant and favourable, together with unfavourable features detailed in the evidence of this case before the Advisory Committee here for the purpose of re-consideration by you of his, our client's detention.*
>
>*At the conclusion of the interview you will recall that it was agreed that you would read not only the written submissions, but also the evidence, and let us have your decision one way or the other on the following Monday. The writer appreciated your promise to do this, having regard for the special circumstances of the case, and particularly realising that it is impossible for you to review*

the evidence in the multifarious cases coming to your notice. Consequently the fact that we have heard nothing further from you embarrasses us in our relationships with our client and his family. No doubt the exigencies, the extreme pressure of vitally responsible and heavy work devolving upon you, rendered that impossible. We do, however, respectfully request that you will at the earliest opportunity give further consideration to the written matter submitted, and particularly to the fact that no evidence of any kind in contradiction of the evidence submitted on Schulz's behalf was placed before the tribunal, and we submit a substantial case on the evidence stood absolutely unanswered.

The material available from the cross-examination and as detailed in the submissions placed before you when carefully considered is in our respectful submission hopelessly insufficient to detain any person.

Suggestions were certainly put to Schulz. They were answered by him and they were unsupported after denial by any evidence contrary to his. We respectfully, but none the less emphatically, repeat on behalf of our client that the evidence supports the indisputable fact that Schulz is a loyal Australian. It is conceivable that the British subjects and men with whom he lived his life and was so well known in Tanunda would have testified as they did in his favour – schoolmaster, stationmaster, and every available Justice of the Peace and well- known citizen. These men would have refused their very attendance if the slightest suspicion in their long line of knowledge of him had manifested itself.

The long detention already suffered by Schulz is surely a sufficient punishment for any slight indiscretion, and we do not admit of any, except perhaps the most aggravated and worst construction put upon his son going to Germany at the time of the Olympic Games, or the filming of Von Luckner, or the one visit only without any suggestion of membership to the Nazi Club Meeting in Grenfell Street, Adelaide. It was not suggested and there is no evidence that Schulz was ever a member of the Club, or that he ever went other than on that one occasion. Surely these things, whether separately or cumulatively, cannot be taken as a case warranting his further detention, but that upon the whole of the evidence you would be justified, Sir, in favourably considering his release upon such conditions as you see fit to impose.

Although comparisons and indeed contrasts of cases are invidious, it is known that there have been instances of release upon conditions of German Nationals. Schulz is an Australian born citizen, his wife, family and the whole of his interests are here, and along with the citizens who testified in his favour, he again asks for your clemency in granting to him a conditional release.

We have the honour to be,
Your obedient servants.

***

Hughie returns to us on 24 April after his operation for a rupture. He was at the Adelaide Hospital initially, then at St. Margaret's Convalescent Home in Semaphore. He considers it was a wonderful holiday from here.

Anzac Day, 25 April, 1941

We do remember them. The weather is certainly cooling down now, but the days are not unpleasant.

I have just finished writing a letter to the Intelligence Department, as follows:

Dear Sir,

Today, Anzac Day, I take the liberty of writing these lines. The very serious position in which we find ourselves and the part played by the Australian Forces in Greece during the days just passed brings to my mind the suspense and anxiety the parents of the boys who are personally known to me and who are now at the front, must be suffering just now. I cannot share the feelings expressed or implied by some of the men in whose company I am now when news from the war came to hand. Permit me to say that any utterances or actions of mine which I may have, in less troublesome times, expressed in connection with the war have been incorrectly interpreted. I sincerely desire to help. Cannot I perhaps fill the position of a hospital Orderly somewhere? I am prepared to go anywhere. If not, I plead to be allowed to return to my own work and lend a hand at Red Cross or Comforts efforts.
  Yours respectfully,
  J.F.W. Schulz (signed)

27 April 1941.

Bert and Else visit me and they bring reports of an excellent finish to the Tanunda Queen Competitions. The effort realised over 800 pounds.

Shortly after dinner, Drucks and Pengelly have a real dinkum fight. Freddy got the worst of it and when floored on one occasion, I noticed him sending appealing gestures to heaven, invoking the aid of the angel Gabriel to carry him high and dry. After the fight, Freddy walks up to Drucks' cubicle with blood on his nose and mouth and says, 'Shake hands Wally, I don't mind a fight as long as it is a fair one!'

I get ready early on 28 April as I must be at the Adelaide Hospital at 9 a.m. to report for an inspection of my nose treatment, which I underwent a fortnight ago. The guard and I walk back in ideal sunshine.

Ernst Pohl's big day in Court today, 29 April. He says he feels he has no hope of a reprieve.

30 April, 1941

The last day of the month. Some of us were hoping for a decision on our Appeal by today. The seriousness of the war, no doubt, overshadows everything else. We have been forgotten.

May, 1941

I have an altercation with Don Salvator. His coughing and vomiting at night becomes unbearable, and then he has the nerve to complain about my snoring!

It is now 20 weeks since I arrived here. 5 months, and a whisper is around that a batch of 'Germans' is due for Tatura at an early date.

Bert receives a letter from Villeneuve Smith & Harford dated today, 2 May, which he brings me when he visits today. It reads as follows:

> *Dear Sir,*
>
> *RE YOUR FATHER.*
>
> *The writer has to report that he did attend before the Hon. The Minister for the Army and put submissions which were reduced to writing and promised the consideration of the Minister. We enclose a copy of our letter and the reply which we have this day received from the Minister and which unfortunately speaks for itself.*
> *Yours faithfully,*
> *(signed) Villeneuve Smith & Harford*

The attached reply from Percy Spender, Minister for the Army, dated 29 April 1941, reads as follows:

Dear Sir,

RE J.F.W. SCHULZ

I acknowledge your letter of the 23rd instant relative to the above-named internee. I regret that you have not been acquainted with my decision, viz. that Schulz was to remain in internment. After perusing the file, I gave this direction and was under the impression that it had been conveyed to you. This decision cannot be varied, even in the light of your letter under reply.

Sincerely yours,
Percy Spender
(P.C. Spender)
Minister for the Army.

Happy Birthday

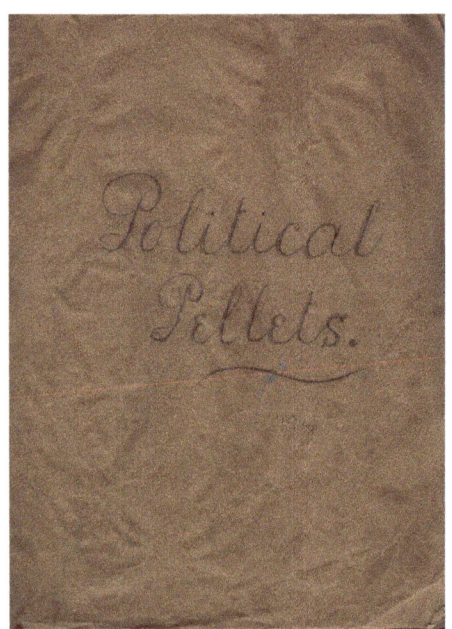

Political Pellets

The Game Chief wants to keep the fleas off his small goods.

Here is the Game Chief back from hunting big day.

Hurray! After four months of hard seating, I got some chicks.

Happy Easter

6

On 4 May Mum, Bert, Margaret and Marie visit me and Sergeant Major Inwood tells me the news: Tatura this week. Not a happy day for my family. They will not be able to visit me twice a week as they have been. Our lives have taken a turn for the worse.

I receive a signed, handwritten note from Sharland on 6 May certifying 'that a film of the visit of Von Luckner to South Australia, the property of J.F.W. Schulz, is in the possession of this Sector. G.S.O. 111 (M.I.) 4 Military District.

Today is the last day I cover the date in pencil on my Wall Almanac 1941 of the United Evangelical Lutheran Church in Australia. From the beginning of this year I have been crossing out each day in the hope of release and return to my family. My hopes for that were dashed on Sunday 4 May when I was given the worst news imaginable.

On 13 May I write to The Hon. R.S. Richards, Leader of the Opposition.

> *Dear Sir,*
>
> *I have been informed by the Camp Commandant that within a few days I am to be transferred from here to the Internment Camp at Tatura, Victoria. This means in effect that the Committee that heard my Appeal did not believe the evidence given by me on oath. I desire to assure you, Sir, that I did not commit perjury when giving my evidence before the Committee. Here at Wayville my name is entered as a German, I believe. I will never change my name, but*

I am not a German. I was born here 58 years ago and this is my country. I may differ with the powers that are as to the methods to be adopted as to our country's future welfare, but even my further internment is not going to shift me from doing whatever is in my power to prevent this country ever having to suffer a similar crucifixion to that of the innocents of small European nations.

We have here at Wayville just now an internee who has already been at Tatura for a term. From him I learn that so far as he knows there are no more than half a dozen Australian born internees at that Camp. Am I to stay there for the duration? I have offered my services to the Authorities as a Hospital Orderly wherever I might be sent. Surely, I cannot be considered dangerous serving in that capacity?

Respectfully yours
(signed) J.F.W. Schulz.

I receive a reply to the above letter on 15 May which reads as follows:

Dear Sir,

I beg to acknowledge receipt of your letter of 13th inst. I have no knowledge of the intentions of the authorities, but I will forward your letter to the responsible Minister asking if any information can be given on the points raised by you.

Yours sincerely,
(signed) R.S. Richards

On 20 May, P.C. Spender, Minister for the Army, replies to the Hon. R.S. Richards:

Dear Mr. Richards,

I am in receipt of your letter of 15th instant, with which you enclosed a letter from Mr. J.F.W. Schulz, who is at present interned at the Wayville Detention Camp.

I shall furnish you with a considered reply within the course of a few days.
Sincerely yours,
(signed) P.C. Spender

2

TATURA INTERNMENT CAMP

2 JUNE 1941 – 19 APRIL 1942

7

8 June, 1941

These notes follow a long break dating from the Sunday five weeks ago when I was informed that my destination was NOT HOME but TATURA.

Were it possible, I would like to wipe this spell from my memory. But impossible. Satisfied that I had done nothing to deserve detention, much less internment for the duration, I had lived surrounded by the atmosphere of early homecoming. To see those near and dear to me in familiar surroundings, to play and converse with little Marie when she would show me and speak to me of many things and happenings while I was absent 'helping the soldiers.' And now she came for four long weeks to enquire again and again, 'Grandpa, when are you going on your long holiday?' Then she would hug and kiss me and tell me to, 'Keep smiling, Grandpa,' in which she had apparently been carefully drilled by her parents.

Information filtered through to us that one detentionist had been approached to act as stool pigeon in the Camp at Wayville and that another inmate had been asked to supply information which would lead to the apprehension of more citizens. This prompted me to seek an interview with the Camp Commandant. I placed the above reprehensible facts and tactics before him and demanded early transference to Tatura. However, he could do nothing.

Eventually, on Monday evening, 2 June, nineteen of us boarded the second division of the Melbourne Express at Mitcham and, via Geelong, reached Melbourne by midday on Tuesday, 3 June. There was some confusion at the station and while the officials were straightening matters out, we were marched into one of the luggage rooms or left parcels office with iron grills on two sides. Passers-by no doubt wondered at the strange collection of 'left-luggage goods' awaiting delivery.

After some time a lorry arrived which took us to Broadmeadows, about twelve miles distant from Melbourne. There were no seats on the lorry, which was closed in and did not permit standing up. The nineteen of us squatted, knelt, or lay about as best we could. We had not eaten since breakfast at Ballarat.

The midday meal was over when we arrived at Broadmeadows. We were marched to the Messroom by guards with fixed bayonets. An Orderly placed a Dixie filled with cold chops on the table indicating that that was our dinner. The table being devoid of eating utensils of any kind, we enquired how we were to eat these chops. 'With your bl.... fingers if you bl.... well like,' was the reply. Pointing to a pile of tin plates piled on a ledge along the wall some distance away, he continued, 'You can use those bl.... plates if you like, but see that you bl.... well wash them when you are finished.' We declined to partake of the questionable looking chops and, discovering a tin of Blackberry Jam, we dined on jam and bread which we washed down with a cup of lukewarm tea.

The twelve Italians who were members of our party were put on board a train at about four o'clock in the afternoon en route for Hay, we believed. Actually, they were returned direct to Loveday. From Adelaide to Loveday via Melbourne, having of course passed Tailem Bend, the nearest stop to Loveday, en route to Melbourne!

At about five o'clock a number of Tatura internees, who had been before the Tribunal in Melbourne, appeared at Broadmeadows and together we spent an enjoyable night. There were amusing incidents marching from our quarters to exercise, to the latrines, etc. Guards with fixed bayonets were posted at the door inside the hut throughout the night. I listened with amusement to von Sk. pleading to be allowed to go to the closet without delay, and while the guard was busy securing the necessary escorts, von Sk. was having a battle royal with nature's imperative call.

At 8 a.m. on Wednesday we boarded a train for Murchison East and after a further lorry ride of some twenty odd miles, reached Tatura at midday. Together with Francis Drake, I was directed by the Camp Supervisor, Dr. Haslinger, to take quarters in Hut 28.

And now I return to today: Sunday 8 June. This morning I attended Church Service in B Compound conducted by Missionary Zimmermann. I will forever remember this service opened by a choir of men all dressed in burgundy coloured greatcoats. During this afternoon I was the guest of Rev. W. Flierl in Hut 138. Wacke, Pilhofer, Doehler, Metzner, and others were present.

For the next few days I am busy getting things straight in my quarters and making my new home comfortable. With some acquired wood I make a table and shelving. Iron shutters on hinges take the place of windows, so Drake and I make improvised window panes by soaking drawing paper in boiling dripping, procured from the Kitchen, rendering the paper transparent and durable. It is strenuous work getting the framework ready, lifting the heavy galvanised iron shutter from its hinges, fixing the improvised panes and replacing the window, but the result justifies the effort.

The nights are very cold and showers of rain fill the days. On a visit to the Library I find August von der Flatt listed, a booklet I wrote some years ago. What a surprise!

There is a scarcity of matches at present which is making life here somewhat difficult. The 'ewige Lampe' (everlasting lamp) tides us over but the question is how to secure the necessary kero? Looking down the alley-ways of the huts just prior to bedtime, where lanterns and pots are regularly placed, affords an amusing spectacle.

Today, 11 June, I receive a letter from Mr. Richards which he received from Mr. Spender's office, dated 20 May, in connection with the letter I wrote to Mr. Richards last month. It reads:

> *'I am in receipt of your letter of 15th inst, with which you enclosed a letter from Mr. J.F.W. Schulz, who is at present interned at the Wayville Detention Camp. I shall furnish you with a considered reply within the course of a few days.'*

This letter was forwarded to Wayville on 26 May and has obviously been chasing me all over the countryside ever since.

This evening I attend the Kameradshaftsabend (fellowship evening). This is the only one I will ever attend because I CANNOT Heil Hitler.

'Schnapps' the Camp dog does not like khaki uniforms, but he does like to participate when ball games are in progress.

I've lost my cigarette holder and before tea, on 12 June, when the Camp Supervisor, Dr. Haslinger, reads out the day's notices etc., he announces that a cigarette holder has been found in the Camp. I've now got my holder back.

An hour after dinner this evening, Francis Drake is lying on his bed with a magazine in his hand, snoring! Life in Tatura Camp is obviously much too tiring for him.

13 June, 1941

After an exceedingly cold night we have a cloudless sky and a wonderful sunshine filled day.

The Provost Paymaster returns me the seventeen shillings and six pence taken from me upon my arrival here. The envelope contains seventeen one shilling chits and six coppers. When you buy a penny bun you receive eleven pence change in coppers. These you pile up in an allotted place and see how long they last. A cup of coffee and piece of cake in Café Well-Blech costs four pence, if you find it inconvenient to make your own tea in the Kitchen and eat penny cakes from the Bakery. The latter is by far the cheapest. I begin to learn the value of money!

I have just finished writing a letter to Marie letting her know how much Grandpa is enjoying his holiday here as well as being of so much help to the soldiers. I have also written to Bert asking him to include my large screen when sending the previously requested films over to me.

14 June, 1941

What a wonderful day! At last I am having some repairs done to myself. Dentist Fent, on Dr. Becker's recommendation, gets busy to replace the tooth I dislodged at cricket at Wayville Camp.

I get to play my first game of Skat here at Tatura and am slowly getting the hang of it.

'Pygmalion' is the star attraction at the Kino this week and is running for the third night.

The Church service in B Compound next day is provided by Pastor Wache, and later on Missionary Horrolt turns me a long cigar of New Guinea leaf.

This afternoon I watch an exciting game of Handball on the Sports Platz, with bearded young men participating in the game, and later I get the chance to watch the feeding and handling of white mice. I wonder what Marie would say if she saw them?

Carl Hoffmann and Methsieder receive notice to leave for Wayville, Adelaide, tomorrow morning. Methsieder's order is later countermanded and he stays here.

I am half way through the book, Pastor von W. Raabe, by Dr. Hunger.

We experienced a bitterly cold night last night and my knitted fox hunting cap is a godsend to me, keeping the chill air off my ears and head. This morning ice covers all exposed water in the Compound.

17 June, 1941

A fine day at last. Watching bearded young men participating in football matches amuses me. As far as I am concerned, bearded men are always old men. At the first Soccer match that I witnessed, I marvelled at the agility of the 'old men' participating, only to learn later that these 'old men' whose beards, when running against the wind, blew over their shoulders, were but thirty years old.

Next day there is a Soccer match among the veterans here. One rather corpulent player playing all out without result is upbraided by a fellow player: 'Mensch, was machst du den da für 'nen Mist!' (Man, what kind of crap are you doing?) All spent and doubled up he replies in despair: 'Verflücht, ich hau' ab!' (Damn, I've had it!)

19 June, 1941

Thirty-four internees from Queensland arrive today, after having been interned there on an average of six months. It is an interesting, humorous, yet pathetic sight to see these men march through the large gates into the barbed wire enclosures for an indefinite stay. They are a weather-beaten tired party and apparently glad to find rest, though enforced, at last. Three of the new arrivals are quartered in our Hut 28.

Every new arrival is weighed and measured. My weight: Fourteen stone four pounds. My height: Five foot eight and a half inches.

The cold, wet weather continues but my day is brightened up with the opportunity to listen to the final rehearsal for the first Choir Concert. Tonight, the Queensland arrival, sleeping on the floor on my left, talks throughout the night. He has brought little clothing with him so I give him a guernsey.

Arrangements are afoot for lining the huts and fixing windows. What a godsend these additions will be! Huts 8, 9, and 10 are cleared for ceilings, lining of the walls and windows. Only ceilings are put in and the disappointment is great.

Last night Captain Kohler gave us an hour's worth of reminiscences of his time on the raider 'Moewe' during the last war. The 'Moewe' sank some 300,000 tons during her adventurous two trips 'auf weiter Flur' (over a wide expanse). Captain Kohler spoke in a most humorous strain: 'Ich denk' es laust mir 'en Affe!' (You must think I'm a monkey.)

I attend the first Chor Konzert des Deutschen Mannergesang vereins Tatura (German male choir). I wish Fritz Homburg and the members of his Liedertafel could hear and see Dr. Gruber conducting the Choir and Orchestra. What a genius! Dr. Brose is at the piano and Dr. Steinberg, who was schoolmaster to the Viennese boys, is first violinist. A musical treat second to none I have ever heard.

On Sunday, 22 June, I attend Church service in B Compound led by Preacher Meier. Today's theme is Volkstum und Christentum (nationality and Christianity). After the service, as he did last Sunday, Missionary Horrolt took me to his hut and made a six- inch cigar of New Guinea leaf for me. Some cigars!

This evening I listen to stories of how wood was obtained for shelves etc. in the early days. They were told by a contractor that they could have a heap of 'offal' (wood) outside the gates. A party lined up at the big gate to carry the timber inside. They left the 'offal' and carried a heap of good timber into the Camp. When the contractor arrived next day and a search was made in the Camp, there was not a piece to be found anywhere. It had all been cut up that night and fitted anywhere and everywhere!

23 June, 1941

Küchendienst (kitchen duty): Hut 28 has to serve coffee and tea in the three Mess Canteens, wash the cooking utensils, and peel today's supply of potatoes, which is one bagful. And did those peels fly! The sooner they are done, the sooner we are out of there.

I hear that Muller of Angaston has been released, so I give him a message for my people to send me some of my old spectacles. I have broken the frame of mine and temporary repairs have been affected with Johnson's adhesive plaster.

24 June, 1941

Muller of Angaston, Popkin of Renmark, and Heinke of Port Augusta are released today. Our good wishes go with them.

Dentist Fent finally fixes my tooth and fills a second one to the cost of fifteen shillings. My spectacles also need overhauling again and I see to this with another layer of Johnson's plaster.

Today I received a letter from Richards which he had received from Spender, dated 3 June, and which had originally been sent to Wayville after I had left for Tatura. It reads:

'I desire to refer again to your letter of May 15th, enclosing letter from Mr. J.F.W. Schulz, who is interned.

In view of the general terms of his letter, it is difficult to reply to questions raised therein, as you request, otherwise to inform you that if Mr. Schulz is transferred to Tatura he should expect to remain there for the duration of the war.

As regards Mr. Schulz's offer of his services as a hospital orderly, I have no doubt that the Camp authorities will give it due consideration.'

So that says it all.

25 June, 1941

Ceilings are being built in our huts. It's an education to sit, apparently reading, in front of our hut and watch how the contractor's wood disappears from under the nose of the guard. All the furniture from inside the hut is placed outside while the ceilings are put in.

Letters from Mum and Else arrive today; the first from home to reach me here at Tatura.

> *Tanunda, 17 June 1941*
>
> *Dear Dad,*
>
> *We received your welcome letter on the 15th of June, and were very pleased to hear from you and also that you had a good journey and feeling well. It has been bitterly cold here the last few weeks and we also had plenty of rain and it looks like some more. We gave your address to Marg and Ted so that they can write to you too. Our Lemon tree was so loaded with lemons we could not make use of them all so we offered them to Mr. Doering, who gave us nine shillings a case. We were quite pleased. We are all well, and I hope you keep the same.*
>   *Love from all*
>   *Mum*
>
>
> *Dear Dad,*
>
> *Just a few lines from me too. I suppose by now you have settled down in your new quarters, and have got into the general routine of things. We missed going down to see you, it seemed so strange not to be going down.*

The town is very quiet just now, nothing important has happened, very few people go to golf now, petrol rationing and so on. Your friends always enquire about you and wish to be remembered.

The mushroom season is very slow, the weather has been too cold, although we have had a few nice meals, I believe we told you we found quite a number just outside our gate, where the candle pines were planted.

Have you everything you require? Mum says just write and ask for whatever you want and we shall send it. I go up to Margaret's place per cycle once a week and then Steve comes for tea and we usually play Bridge after tea. Marie likes visitors and usually puts on a 'turn' for us. Mrs. and Miss. Auricht send regards to you, the old lady needs a lot of attention, the cold weather does not agree with her.

Our poor old puss is not too happy today, she is limping badly, most probably was in a fight. She is great company for us, and we should hate to lose her now. Mrs. Slatter has offered us a cocker spaniel dog, she is having two given to her, we don't know if we shall start with dogs again, but I know Mum would like a 'pom' again. Do you have good meals? Perhaps you would like some honey biscuits or anything else?

At the pictures each Saturday night they have a quiz Show. Steve runs it for Dick Hawkes. They ask all different questions and have cash prizes and free picture tickets, and it has become quite an attraction. In the daily paper last week, the death was given of Mr. Edmunds, the big Red Cross worker in Adelaide, you would know him. Mr. Alf Zander has been notified that Bob is missing with the A.I.F., it is a great shock to their family. That is all the news for this time.

Love from all,
Your daughter Else

Today, 26 June, is an especially good day because I receive a letter from Margaret with a few lines enclosed from Marie.

> *Nuriootpa, 19/6/41*
>
> *Dear Father,*
>
> *We were very pleased when Bert came up here on Monday to show us your letter which we were anxiously waiting for. By now I expect you have settled down to your new life and feeling somewhat 'happier'. We are always thinking of you and wondering what you are doing from day to day.*
>   *Today it is very cold and wintry and I have made a nice big fire in the dining room and Marie and I are well up in front of it, but of course you can imagine what Marie is like, she wants to write too so I said she can write a few kisses to Grandpa presently but she just can't wait. Granny Knispel is here with us again she arrived on Saturday morning and at present is with Ern's then coming here with us. Yesterday afternoon Marie and I went for a little walk and called in to see Mrs. Summerton, she had the misfortune to break a little toe just through a simple knock against a chair and the result is foot in plaster of Paris. Poor old soul she still hasn't got over her grief yet although it will be twelve months the end of this month. At the present moment Marie is having a lovely time with the curtains having quite a swing with them. A fortnight ago we had another tragedy in the town. Harry Krause the baker committed suicide terribly sad left a wife and two children and with not a penny, financial difficulties I believe and his business had gone to wreck and ruin. Now Marie wants to write a few words.*
>   *Keep smiling Grandpa till we see you again lots of kisses from Marie.*
>   *Hoping these few lines find you well and happy. I'll close with all our love.*
>   *From Marg, Ted and little Marie.*

Later today I reply to Mum's letter, dated 17th June, and let them know I have received all the letters sent me from home. I also tell her that today I had my first Italian lesson in a class of thirty pupils. This class is conducted by Dr. Bartolini and I am looking forward to mastering another language.

27 June, 1941

A wonderful sunshine filled day! It makes one feel glad to be alive. In the Orderly Room I am told that approval is given to my films gaining entrance into the Camp. Now we can have film shows again as we did in Wayville.

Next day I volunteer to help scrub the floor of Messroom 3. Twelve of us do the work and Dr. Haslinger provides coffee and Berlin buns for us as our reward.

Missionary Horrolt is our preacher at Church this morning, 29 June. I attend the service even though I can feel the beginnings of a cold coming on.

30 June

My cold has grown much worse during today and I certainly don't feel like doing anything but resting. But, our hut has a busy day with the carpenters arriving to put our ceiling in. We are fortunate to be able to move back in just before tea.

Good news again! I receive letters from Bert and Else. Bert's first letter is also included. I think he must have missed the postal deadline that week.

Tanunda, 16 June 1941

Dear Dad,

We were glad to hear that you had arrived O.K. I had been watching the mails keenly every day for your letter – of course we had no idea just how long it might take in transit.

The main purpose of this letter is to advise you that I am herewith forwarding five pounds to you in the form of a money order. You will have been wondering why there were no funds to your credit on arrival at Tatura. Well, during last week, the money which had been paid in at Wayville was returned to me, and I was advised to forward it to you per Money Order to Tatura. This I have now done. The Order is made payable to you, and you will have to sign your full christian names when cashing it. It is made payable to Johann Friedrich Wilhelm Schulz at Tatura, Vic. I trust you will have no difficulty in securing the cash. Another thing. You will note I have punched the sheets on which our letters are written. This has a special reason. As soon as I can, I intend making a cover for you so that you may file all letters received from us. I thought you might like that.

Work at the office is going along quite nicely, and the staff send their kind regards. Mr. Obst was at a relative's wedding in the south-east over the holiday weekend. The trip will be something new to him.

I will close this letter now, or the clock will beat me and I'll miss yet another mail. You'd better let me know in your next letter when you wish your next lot of 'baccy to arrive, so I can make arrangements.

Your son
Bert

Box 83, Tanunda, June 23rd 1941

Dear Dad,

Another week has gone by and it is again letter writing time.

The first news I have this time is I am working at the Office now, my first day today. I do Folding etc. and Bert says there are lots of odd jobs for me to do. We have had lovely sunshine the last few days after all the wind and rain and all the gardens are looking nice and fresh and green.

The Adelaide Electric Supply men have been busy in the streets the last few weeks, they have been erecting large iron and concrete posts all along the main street. They usually attract quite a large crowd in the street, with all their apparatus and gear.

We hope that you have received the 'Barossa News' and 'Leader', we have had them sent on to you.

Marie and family were down to see Grandma yesterday, she always enjoys having a game with puss.

Goers' have moved from their place in the main street, up to Miss Riedel's house near the Police Station, which they have bought. The place needed a terrible lot of repairing, it had been neglected very badly. I daresay they will be starting to demolish the old place in the street soon, and start on the new Bank building which should look well situated there.

We had word from Aunty Irene, I will send them your address, so they can drop you a line sometime.

I daresay you are more settled down now Dad, and have you everything you need?

It is Annie's Mother's birthday this Wednesday, 25th, I believe she is going to be 73.

That is all the news from me this time.

Love from your daughter Else

Tanunda, 23 June 1941

Dear Dad,

Next time I think I'll have to write before El, for she seems to beat me with all the news. She has mentioned the Adelaide Electric people – they sure are fast movers. It has been interesting to watch the progress made day by day. The biggest eye-opener to everybody seems to have been their method of making the holes for the posts. You must imagine an oversize in auger bits at work, for the diameter of the hole they drill in the soil must be at least two feet. And the whole plant is driven by a petrol motor mounted on the back of one of their hefty lorries. This monster drill, or bit I suppose it is, they send down six feet for the average pole weighing eleven hundredweights, to nine feet for the whoppers at the corners, weighing up to thirty hundredweights.

You may or may not remember me telling you that we were cutting down the sugar gums at the back of the printing office. Well, we've sure made a mess of them! The back yard looks as though it has been struck by a tornado – trees lying all over the place. We've lopped the limbs off them, too, and all that remains is some hefty work with the cross-cut saw. There are quite a few tons of wood in the five trees we cut down. Mum says it's not much good on its own, but makes a good fire mixed with other wood. Wood at the present time is almost worth its weight in gold. You will still remember the time when there would always be somebody knocking on the back door to sell you wood. Now it's just the other way around. Twenty-seven shillings a ton is an average price for both cut wood and stumps. Terrible, isn't it?

Now that you have settled down after the change-over, how do you find things? It seems from your first letter to us that gardening is possible. That should suit you for part of your time. What about trying mushrooms? We had four meals from the little patch by the carob hedge we told you about. They must have established themselves there when Helling carted the soil there to fill up the hole alongside the road.

Don't forget to tell me exactly how I must forward tobacco or any other parcels. I am waiting until I hear from you before I forward any parcels. Just check up on the postage question again, will you? You told us we must put stamps on all letters, yet I believe that others are sending letters to their relatives minus any stamps!

I still haven't made up your cover for our letters, but don't despair. I intend using a fitting similar to one Short's use in their price lists, but so far I haven't been able to obtain it.

Believe me, we're looking forward to your second letter. You wrote the first on the 5th June, and it reached us on the 15th, so we realise there is probably some unavoidable delay in transit.

As I write this I hear strange noises from outside. It's that cranky cat of ours, just landed home. (11p.m.) And she seldom comes home without bringing some trophy along. Judging by the noise, it must be a frog this time. Frogs and bats are her specialty.

At the office things are going along satisfactorily. With but one paper, and that fortnightly, you will realise that there is generally a fair bit of spare time hanging around during the off week. I am trying to concentrate on more and more jobbing work. As you get amongst the business folk, however, it's always the same old story – they think only the city can do things. The answer usually is: 'We didn't know you went in for those jobs!' You know, gummed receipt books, and so on.

El is going to be a big help at the office now. Poor old Mrs. Auricht is really a problem for Miss Auricht now, and she hasn't much time for the office work which she used to attend to.

When you left, I made arrangements for the 'Barossa News' and the 'Leader' to be posted to you, and the 'Lutheran Herald' is also going forward. Is there any other paper you would like to receive?

> *Mum whispered in my ear before she went to bed that I should include her kind regards with mine before posting away this letter.*
> *Your son,*
> *Bert.*
> *P.S. Note the flash envelopes!'*

1 July, 1941

I have just written letters to Bert and Margaret and my cold is now much better, thanks to the Becks Powder given to me by Hans Scheiner.

Our hut takes its turn at wood-sawing next day, although the rainy weather presents some difficulties.

Kurt Hoerisch, and Strauss of Murray Bridge have been notified of their release. I send messages of good cheer to my people with them.

Today, 3 July, I have my third Italian lesson. The weather is awful; wet, dirty and cold, but I receive a very interesting letter from Else dated 28 June, and this brightens me up considerably.

> *Dear Dad,*
>
> *Well, there has been quite a lot of excitement in the town this week. On Wednesday last a telegram was received by five men at the Chateau saying they had won ten thousand pounds in Tattersalls. The men are, Reg Kleemann, Wally Kleemann (his brother), Pat Keil, Cox Heinemann, and Edgar Kassebaum.*
>
> *Reg K. had paid in a double share and he gets over three thousand pounds, the others about one thousand six hundred each. There was great excitement at the Chateau and Mr. Ian Seppelt turned on the Champagne and I believe the Hotels are doing quite well too.*

Today there is a scratch football match on; a team is coming up from Adelaide (Commercial Travellers) and a collection is being taken up for Patriotic Funds.

Alf Zander's have heard no more news of Bob, they are hoping still to get news saying that he is a prisoner of war.

I am getting into the work nicely at the office now. I go the half day from 1 p.m. till 5.50 p.m. and Bert is giving me one pound. There is plenty of work in again now. Last week I took stock of the Book Depot books and cleaned out shelves etc. We also did a job for the Club; printed little booklets of Rules and Regulations. These I folded and stitched, and then there is the sewing of the Catechisms.

Alfred has gone to Eudunda this weekend, his last time, as petrol allowance will not enable him to go very far now.

Little Marie came down with her letter last week, she was bright and happy.

Mrs. Bartsch (cake baker) has been very seriously ill in the Hospital, lung trouble and pleurisy, but seems to be getting over it again now.

Werner, Bert, and Gert hiked up to Margaret's last night (Sat.) and have not yet returned; it is now Sunday afternoon, so, evidently they are being well entertained up there.

It was a year last week that Ronald Schulz died, how the time does fly. Winnie is still in the Office at the Mill, we received a small order from them too this week.

Martin John is short-handed now too, as Walter Fietz has gone into Camp. Walter was telling me they had word from Howard who is in the front lines fighting in the Middle East.

You remember the Jack Scherer's? They went into a Butcher shop at Renmark from here, well I believe she turned out rather a 'bad egg' and now they have a separation.

You also remember Miss Alice Lange my School teacher? She died suddenly last week in Adelaide. She was keeping house for Mr. Keats who had recently returned.

> *We have been cleaning up the back garden. Steve, Bert and I got to work and it won't be long before we shall have it looking nice and clean.*
>
> *On Wednesday is Dulcie's (Cookie) fiftieth Birthday. She still gets around like a two- year- old. She certainly does not look it.*
>
> *Well, that seems to be all the news for now, we received your letter asking to have your films etc. sent so Bert will no doubt drop you a line tomorrow.*
>
> *Love from all at Home and keep smiling.*
> *Your daughter,*
> *Else*

4 July, 1941

We are advised that three more S.A. internees are to arrive tomorrow. My tip is that Vincents, Seith and Hunger will be the three.

During the day I give my final signature to enable me to draw money against my five-pound account. Part of it is already mortgaged.

Later on I visit 'Das Veruchte Cabaret' (The Crazy Cabaret). Very humorous!

Next day there is some sunshine amid the cold weather and we find that the new arrivals from S.A. are: Max Hunger, Dr. Seith, H. Hausler, C. Vincents and Carl Hoffmann (returned). Only Hughie is left at Wayville!

Sunday, 6 July, 1941

Our preacher for Church today is Pastor Wittmann and I hope to always remember something of this sermon. Church going and church service is different here to the 'orthodox formula'. It is somewhat more down to earth.

Good news! We receive windows in our huts next day and altogether things are looking up, but because of this work I miss my Italian lesson.

Three more internees arrive on 8 July and they are quite a cosmopolitan trio: A Belgian, a Frenchman, and a naturalised German.

9 July, 1941

Today all the huts are supplied with timber for a locker, table, and chair. We will soon be living in luxury! The weather is still very cold but a hot shower helps to warm me.

I've just seen a very amusing sight: a party of internees are out looking for mushrooms and they are followed by three guards with fixed bayonets. Maybe the bayonets will come in handy for cutting the mushrooms out of the ground!

A letter from Else arrives today dated 3 July.

> Dear Dad,
>
> Another month gone, how the time does fly, but of course when one is busy you notice it more.
>
> In my last letter I told you Bert had received your letter re the films and would attend to them, but he says he is waiting for word from the authorities first, before he sends them on. Your last letter arrived last night. Bert and Mum will answer to that over the weekend. Mrs. Auricht was delighted to receive a remembrance from you and she sends back every good wish and hopes you keep well and happy.
>
> Today I learned to do the wrappers etc., it was quite a big job but the first time is always the longest, but I like the work very much.
>
> Prenzler's and Kilmiers have additions to their family; Prenzler's another boy and Kilmiers a little girl, so Gert is an Auntie again.

Fancy you learning Italian? We will have to learn it too so we can converse with you when you come back home. We were pleased to hear you enjoy the food and also have plenty of blankets, we often wish we could just hop down to Wayville and bring you a few things from home, but maybe we shall be able to come over one day soon to see you.

Gert had her Birthday on Tuesday, it is a year since she and Bert were engaged. Bert has to sing a solo in the Choir in church, he usually practises in the bathroom in the mornings!!!

Well that is all the news for now, hope the short note will interest you.

Love from all at Home,
Your daughter
Else xxxx'

10 July, 1941

Today I report to the Authorities here that I am due to appear at the Adelaide Hospital on 21 July for treatment to my nose. I await their reply with interest.

I receive a letter from Bert dated 6 July. With his letter I also receive a supply of pipe and cigarette tobacco. I unwrap my parcel of tobacco and smoke my pipe of Bauer's mixture!

Dear Dad,

There's a good fire going as I write this letter, so you can guess you're not the only people having cold weather. Today has been a real snorter, with a steady drizzling rain almost all day, and certainly not the kind of weather one likes on a Sunday.

I received your letter written on the first of July on Friday evening last, the fourteenth, so delivery of letters has sure been expedited! And today (Sunday) I received an official receipt from the

Paymaster of the Camp at Tatura for the five pounds forwarded to you per Money Order.

I have made arrangements for four ounces of Pipe Mixture and four ounces Capstan Fine but to go forward to you per post. By the way, you might let me know whether we have to add postage when sending you parcels. Until I hear from you I shall add postage to parcels. I can't locate the 'self-made merchant' books at home, and will endeavour to get them in the city, as also the books by Valentine, if available.

Regarding the sending of your films and the large projector – On 13 June you wrote us: 'Last week I wrote you to send me my films. Possibly this letter would first go to the responsible department for authorization to send the films. If the films are being sent on I would like you also to send the large screen carefully packed...' According to this I have been waiting for this other letter of authorization. So far nothing has arrived.

Now, in your letter of 1 July you say: 'The letter written by me asking for films and large screen only left after the authorities had given permission. I don't need the projector.' If permission to send the films etc. depends upon me receiving the letter mentioned by you in your letter of 13th June, and which, you thought, would first go to the responsible department for authorization, well, I haven't got that permission, for I haven't received that letter.

It may be, however, that I have misunderstood, and everything is O.K. However, you know that the films are worth a lot to you and it wouldn't be very nice if they went astray, so before I send anything, either films or screen, I will wait for your reply to this letter. If all my caution proves unfounded, you will probably feel like kicking me in the pants for wasting time, but you'll have to save that for a later date.

Some more news on the subject of mushrooms. For tea tonight we had another meal off the patch by the Carob hedge. That makes it the fifth meal we've had off that one spot, which you could cover *with a wheat bag. It seems remarkable that such a small patch of soil could bear such a crop.*

We've been doing a bit of hiking lately. Several Saturday nights we've walked up to Nuri to Ted and Marge's. Gert has come up with me and last Saturday night we stayed there. They enjoy it and so does young Marie. She prattles away on any subject under the sun, and is always making us laugh with some funny remark.

While I think of it; you say you receive the 'Leader' and the 'Barossa News' but do not mention the 'Lutheran Herald.' The 'Lutheran Herald' has been posted on to you regularly since you left Wayville. Business at the office is going along satisfactorily and there's always plenty to keep me busy.

Cheers,
Bert and Gert

Letters and parcels from home make me forget all else around me. What matters it whether the Russians flee before the German avalanche or cities go up in flames! With news from home I am content.

12 July, 1941

A glorious day! At breakfast Dr. Haslinger calls for volunteers to go mushrooming. I make one of a party of sixteen. We leave in two parties of eight with four guards for each party. Mushrooms are plentiful and my bagful is enough for our whole family at home! I get enough ready for a big feed for myself. At about 4 p.m. I have the meal ready, toast and all, with the result that I ate little at tea-time and was ready early for pictures commencing at 6.15 p.m.

Missionary Walter leads the Church service the next day.

14 July, 1941

It's been raining all day, and I'm very glad the mushroom hunt wasn't postponed until today. We have to form in queues to receive our ten shilling allowance.

I receive a letter from Margaret, Ted, and scribbles from Marie.

Nuriootpa, 8/7/41

Dear Father,

Ted wanted to write to you this time but at present doesn't seem to find the time for anything. They have Mr. McMurry the Stocktaker at the shop again so Ted has been helping him a bit at nights and then Ted is also short-handed in the Salon. His man is in Camp, so I said I would write and he will next time. My word it must be very cold for you over there judging by all the woollies you have to wear, but believe me it's pretty cold here too at present, today especially it is bitterly cold. Marie doesn't seem to feel it though. Today she has gone out with Granny Knispel, she is with us again now. They have gone around to Bert Knispel's. I didn't want her to go because it is so cold but she cried bitterly so I had to let her go. Now for a bit of news about our little 'Mops'. Yesterday afternoon I went out for a little while and left Marie home with Granny, anyway Granny had been outside for a while when she missed Marie so she went inside to look for her and there she stood in front of the bedroom mirror cutting away at her hair to her hearts content. The left side is practically all cut away except for a few strands and she has quite a fringe in front. I didn't know what to say I was cross but at the same time had to laugh, and when Daddy came home to tea she ran up to him and said 'Daddy what do you think of my hair?' She looks too bad now I don't know what to do with it. Now the scissors is hanging up on the wall. Last week Marie and I went to Adelaide with Uncle Bert and when I told her we are going to

Adelaide she said, 'Are we going to see Grandpa again, Mummy?' There has been an outbreak of diphtheria in the town. Two cases have been reported up-to-date. I hope it doesn't become serious. I am pleased Marie is over with her injections then if she should get it Dr. said she would only get it in a mild form. Dr. gave her two pennies for being such a good girl when she had her injections, now she thinks he's not such a bad Dr. at all.

Marie has just arrived home and I asked her what shall I tell Grandpa and she said, 'Tell Grandpa I made a mess of my hair.'

Lots of love from
Ted, Margaret and Marie.
Keep smiling Grandpa.'

15 – 17 July, 1941

We finally have sunshine after an awful lot of rain. I receive medicine for my throat and cold at the Hospital. They have asked me to call there after every meal. On the morning of the 17^{th,} I wake with the worst sore throat I have ever had, but by taking more medicine during the day I find my throat begins to respond. Another party goes mushrooming again but I stay behind and nurse my cold. While they are out I get in touch with little Dr. Singer, who is an expert on economics and currency problems.

More letters arrive, this time from Mum and Else, dated 11 July.

Dear Dad,

I'm very pleased to hear that you feel quite comfortable now. Yesterday afternoon, we had Ted's Mother, Marg and little Marie here. On Sunday I am going to their place for dinner and tea. El and Steve are going to Vic Lindner's for dinner and tea and Bert to Gert's place, now we are all out for a change.

We have terrible cold weather again and not too much rain.

Our Minister called here the other day and he wishes to be remembered to you.

I hope your cold is better again.
With love to you
From Mum

Dear Dad,

It has been bitterly cold here this week, I don't know when we have experienced such cold weather before.

In a previous letter I mentioned to you about the Jack Scherer's having a separation, since then we have heard the case was dismissed as she (Mrs.) had no grounds for a case against him. The case went on for quite a while. I believe there was quite a lot of scandal etc. and also a few Tanunda people's names were brought up too.

So far we have heard that Edgar Kassebaum, one of the Tatts winners, has bought a house. The one belonging to Jack Traeger's next to Hele's in Bridge Street.

This week at the office I have been doing the alterations (here some words have been cut out of the letter by Security) of 'Lutheran Herald' and 'Children's Friend'. It is quite a lengthy job and Bert wants it done very thoroughly as there has always been a lot of trouble.

All the small bits of paper Bert has been cutting up and I have been stapling them and they make nice little pads, he had an order from Benno.

Marie certainly looks a trick, now that she has cut her hair, and she is so proud too she thinks she did a great job too. 'Cookie' and Ed Heuppauff and Steve and I played Bridge last night. We have been playing a series, and take the score each time, but Ed goes into Camp next week so that will end.

There are not many flowers in the garden now, it has been too cold and the plants are very backward. It is time to put Gladiolis in again now. I want to put in a big lot.

Frank Hale is over from Melbourne on leave for a week, he usually comes over with a car load, they say they come off cheaper and have a little more time.

The usual crowd still go to golf week-ends, they must still have good supplies of petrol.

I hope the warm weather comes soon we want to start tennis soon, but now it is too cold.

The footballers have an occasional match when they can arrange it.

The Electric light men are still on the job, it will still be a long job.

That seems to be all the news for now. I am pleased to hear the thick cardigan is suitable, if you want anything knitted just say the word.

Love from all.
Your daughter
Else

18 July, 1941

My throat is improving, especially with the wonderful sunshine we are experiencing today. When the mushroomers went on their outing today, they had very little luck. I guess the weather hasn't been conducive for more growth.

I enjoy my Schwartzbrot (ryebread) and Wurst (sausage) as a change from the ever-recurring soup, sometimes Eintopfgericht (stew), and decide not to go to dinner today.

19 July, 1941

It is a bitterly cold day today. Mr. Bitzer leaves on parole for Toowoomba to visit his wife who is seriously ill. I'm currently watching haircutting in process on the steps leading to the door. Both of the men stand; the operator moving a step up or down as suits his convenience. Necessity is definitely the mother of invention in this place.

20 July, 1941

Missionary Wagner conducts today's Church service. Later, at Café Wellblech, I buy four Saiten Wurstel (Vienna sausage) for six pence and these I have for my dinner in the hut.

21 July, 1941

It is raining again so I decide to have dinner in the hut eating the boiled ham I saved at tea last night. Hearty tea at night adds to the discomfort of my room-mates during what are termed their reposeful hours. I am told I snore. My namesake in our hut complains of the hammer and sickle monograms drawn with pencil on the inside of our doors.

22 July, 1941

A dreadful cold and wintry day so I stay inside and spend practically all day reading. Owing to our Italian teacher's illness and his going to Melbourne for treatment, the Italian lessons receive a break.

    A parcel from home arrives today. In it are two Valentine books and a paper file which Bert has made as he thought I might like to keep all of the letters together that my family send me. I also receive letters dated 17 July from Else and Bert.

Dear Dad,

Another week has slipped by, and it is letter writing time again. Today was the first sunny day we have had for ages after all the rain and wind. The rain has done wonders to the crop and farmers are very pleased.

Little Marie spent the afternoon with Grandma today, whilst Margaret and Mrs. Hasting went to visit a friend around in the Hospital. She is so good and plays by herself and also has a grand time with the pussycat, which usually takes up her time.

Gerald Tuohy has been digging the garden at Auricht's and next week he is coming here to do a few jobs for us. He is a very good worker too.

Mr. Herbert Heuzenroeder has been spending a few days in Tanunda. We saw him (through the office window) leaving Moritz's place this afternoon carrying a white bag. Bert said, 'most probably complete with snakes.'

Last night the Blind Institute ran a Ball here, there was a very poor crowd, it was very interesting to see one of the men making a speech of thanks, in Braille.

'Bubbles' McGee (Schulz) and her husband and little boy are over from Sydney holidaying with Mr. and Mrs. Jack Schulz.

Mr. Obst 'Shouted' at the Office yesterday, he was so pleased that Bert had located a 'squeak' in one of the machines.

The most outstanding news this time is that I am having my bottom teeth out next Wednesday. Mr. Harris is drawing them and I am just having injections. There are ten to come out. I thought I might as well have them all out as the two gold crowns at the back were causing trouble and would have to come out, so a few more won't matter. I am not getting the plate right away, (most people do now) as there is an extra charge of two pounds two shillings to have them remodelled later on after the gums have finished shrinking. I would much rather wait too, I don't like the idea much of a plate right away. Audrey had her top teeth out recently. She had them drawn at three o'clock was home at four, complete with new plate and had steak for tea. I asked her how she got on, she said, 'Good oh, only the gums were a bit sore the next day!!!'

Hope you enjoy the books by Valentine. I wanted to read them first, but Bert wanted to get everything away together, they sounded a bit 'lovey', hope they are by the right Valentine.

That is all the news for this time. We are all well and happy and hope you are the same.

Love from all at Home.
Your Daughter
Else

Dear Dad,

I got your letter of the 11th July yesterday evening, so I set to work right away this morning to pack away your films and screen. I felt a lot easier when I knew definitely that it would be O.K. to send them. They left per this afternoon's goods rail. You asked me to advise the cost of railage on the parcels – this amounted to nine shillings and ten pence.

I also wrote a covering letter to the Commandant, as follows: 'Sir: Upon instructions I received from my father, Mr. J.F.W. Schulz, P.O.W. 3077, Camp A.1., I have dispatched to you per today's Goods rail the following: 1 package containing 18 reels of 16mm Cine Films and 1 package containing Film Screen and Tripod.'

So, the packages should get to you safe and sound. I have also sent you, per parcel post 2 books by Valentine: 'The Rising Mists' and 'Youth in Revolt.' I got hold of these in the city and am told that others may be obtainable interstate. They are trying to get whatever titles they can for me. El thinks the two I have sent you are love yarns. With these two books I have forwarded the loose-leaf binder which I said I would make for you to file your letters as received from us.

I trust your quarter pound of pipe mixture and the two packs of Capstan Fine Cut reached you O.K.

We are still picking mushrooms from our patch – it seems just too easy doesn't it?

People are always asking after you – although you might be far away, you are certainly not forgotten in the district.

Your son,

Bert.

(To use the Binder:

Pull the top metal slide down and over to right. Bend up the two tongues, when sheets may be filed. Bend down tongues and slide top into position.)

23 July, 1941

The weather is improving. There is a rumpus during Inspection when a Sergeant endeavours to remove a Hoheitszeichen Kreuz (Swastika) from the wall in Hut 21. The inmates refuse its removal. The Commandant also orders that all blankets used for partitions must be removed and returned.

Next day finds closure regarding the H. Kreuz incident. The emblem is to remain and our blankets are allowed to remain as partitions.

Perfect weather for the next two days. I'm on Tischdienst (table duty) on the 25th and the next day I have my first washing day. I tackle everything but the good shirts. Everything is on the line and I am anxious to see how it will turn out.

27 July, 1941

Missionary Baer is our preacher today. Later we give Dr. Gruber a surprise party on the occasion of his Birthday. He is ill in bed with the 'flu so the orchestra visit him in hospital. He is most impressed.

28 July, 1941

There is a most beautiful sunrise this morning with an opposite rainbow. I had never thought this phenomenon possible: sunrise – rainbow. At the same time as this, a serious altercation has arisen between Dr. Haslinger and Fritz Weber. At present I'm not quite sure what it is all about.

I spend time today filing all my letters in the file I have received from Bert, and later on, I receive a letter from Margaret, Ted, and Marie dated 23 July, as well as one from Elsie and Ernie Bruhn of Mount Gambier.

Nuriootpa, 23-7-41

'Dear Dad,

your letter today, and I can assure you we were delighted, as we are always looking forward to your letters, and a toss-up as to who reads firstly, which is not very hard to guess. Ha ha. To date we are all enjoying fairly good health, especially Marie she is a real 'wag', she has a weakness of going out visiting, in other words, 'running away' to the neighbours. Keeps one busy, believe me, but I guess it is better for her to be that way, than the other. We also had her immunised against Diphtheria, which has been completed about four weeks ago thank heavens. As there are two cases here now, also a number of Measles and colds. Well Dad we have just completed Stocktaking, a trying job, but very interesting in some respects, regarding Stocks etc. We had Mr. McMurry with us this year, he used to do it for the late Chief, unfortunately we were unable to get him last year, but probably will have him again in the future, as he is a grand fellow to work with and that helps a lot. I see by your letter you have been out mushrooming too, that is more than we have done this season, although we have had a meal, as Mother was kind enough to send us some, but as for around here, there seem to be very few about, I think the conditions have not been favourable at all this season, too cold. We have had very useful rain this month, approximately three inches so far, which the farmers and orchardists can make good use of. Our garden is looking quite nice at present, quite a number of our shrubs are flowering and making a nice show. Vegetables not many, but our lemon tree is loaded, we also had several oranges off our trees and quite nice too.

My Mother has been over here for a holiday, and is staying with us at present, she is quite well, with the exception of Rheumatism, of course. This time of the year is bad for that type of thing. Business is still very good, marvellous the way it keeps up, of course stock is hard to get, however we are doing quite satisfactory to date. Smokes are very hard to get, we just seem to get a few to keep us going. Yesterday Marie spent the day with Grandma, Auntie, and Uncle Bert, and did she have a grand time. She went to Gramps with Uncle and then to the Office, so you can imagine what a time she had. Well Dad I will now conclude hoping you will soon get rid of the cold you've got.

Your loving children
Marg and Marie and Ted

Browne's Road, Mt Gambier, 23-7-41

Dear Uncle Willie,

We had a letter last week from Dolf and Irene and they sent us your address, so Granny Bruhn has asked me to drop you a few lines, we often think of you and now we know your address can often write to you as I guess you look forward to your mail.

Grandfather Bruhn had a very bad turn yesterday, the Dr. came and said he had a growth in the stomach and it has burst and he was vomiting blood, the Dr. said it was very serious, but he is a little brighter today. The girls are all here and Lucy sat up all night with him.

Auntie Bertha has just arrived, she is very well. She often hears from Freddie from overseas.

The weather is so cold and wet down here, real miserable.

Well Uncle news is scarce, I will try and write more next time. Uncle Paul is here looking for work.

Cheerio for now, we would like to hear from you soon,
Fondest Regards from
Elsie and Ernie Bruhn

29 July, 1941

I'm on kitchen duty again and after days of leisure this is rather an exacting duty, but you do feel all the better for it afterwards. I've also ordered books on Economics through the Canteen Agency from Melbourne. These books have been recommended to me by Dr. Singer, a lecturer in Economics.

I receive a letter from Else, dated 25 July.

Dear Dad,

You remember me writing to you in my last letter that I was going to have my bottom teeth out, well they are out, so you can imagine that at the present time I am nursing a very sore jaw. Still it is not too bad, only one caused a bit of trouble and he (Mr. Harris) nearly had to give me a 'whiff', but I told him to go ahead. I would rather stand the pain than have an anaesthetic.

Bert is also having a few fillings done by him at present. I am having a few days off from work, Werner is helping in my place so long. There is plenty of work in again, Gramps have several nice big jobs for us again. The last few days have been lovely and warm so I can sit out in the sun and recuperate.

Mr. Tuohy has just finished digging and cleaning up our back garden and pruning the vines and roses. He is an excellent worker, you would hardly know the place now.

I have put in a few more roses in the front garden, they are so lovely and do not need much attention.

What a feed of mushrooms you must have had, I daresay it reminded you of the times at home when you used to go out looking for them.

Marie came to spend the day on Tuesday, and we did have some fun, she is a real trick now, talks like a young lady, and certainly listens to everything you say and then goes home and tells her family.

Bert had to go to Gramps, so she went with him in the 'Singer' and had a great time too. She then stayed the rest of the afternoon at the office, I took all her toys down, and she enjoyed herself very much. Miss Auricht brought over afternoon tea and she was all there too. It is amazing the appetite she has but of course we can see where it goes, she is growing bigger every day, and getting fatter too. She just looks a picture of health now.

Mrs. Hebart had a nasty accident, she burnt all her face, from blowing on to the fire in the kitchen where she had some rubbish which would not burn. She spent a few very anxious days, but last reports are that she is progressing satisfactorily.

In a few weeks' time the Tarac Co. at Nuriootpa are going to produce Power Alcohol from wheat, so Steve will have more than enough work to do, he says, 'no holidays this year.' He sends along his kindest regards to you.

We were sorry to hear you have only received only one copy of the local papers. I purposely had not written you all the news in the letters, as I thought you could read them all in the papers.

Hope you have received the films etc., I think I could just about guess whose picture will be first on the screen.

I have to change my nib here, the other one is not doing too well as you can see.

Bert was in Adelaide yesterday on business again and he also enquired about several more 'Valentine' books for you.

Miss Auricht has just called in on her way to Basedow's to play Bridge and to see me and when she saw me writing to you she said, 'Remember me to your Father.'

Mum has managed very well through the cold weather, and has managed to keep off her old Bronchial trouble so far.

That is all the news for now, hope you are well and keep smiling. Love from all at Home,
From your Daughter Else. Xxxx

30 July, 1941

Kuchel from Hut 17 lends me his book on Economics: Wealth, written by Edwin Cannon, and I commence studying in earnest.

A pig is killed in the Camp today. The pig was bought privately by an interned butcher, and tomorrow we are promised (for sale) every known sausage yet manufactured. My mouth is watering already!

31 July, 1941

There is intense activity on the Kegel Bahn (bowling alley) today with work in progress for Tennis Courts and a Bowling Green. How wonderful the anticipation to be able to take part in tennis and bowls at long last! All the work is done by internees working six hours per day at one shilling per day!

Achtung! Zum Zahnarzt antreten! (Attention! I have to go to the dentist!)

During the morning I buy a Bratwurst (sausage) from our butcher, fry it and have it for dinner. It reminds me of meals enjoyed at home with the family.

8

Camp Life at Tatura. Impressions after two months. It is the end of July.

When the first bugle sounds at 7 a.m. day is just breaking, mostly cold and dreary, and just at that hour bed seems the last thing you wish to leave. But there is no alternative. Within a quarter of an hour the second bugle sounds and the die-hards or wake-slowlies have to dress and wash hurriedly indeed to escape being detailed for fatigue work meted out to late comers. The washhouse and bathroom after the first bugle, resemble a rudely disturbed ant's nest. The men who have Tischdienst (table duty) for the day are usually found racing for their wash or bath, followed presently in an endless stream to and fro, of the seven hundred inmates of A and B Compound.

In the large Messrooms, each capable of seating two hundred diners there is soon a hum of voices and a rattling of kitchen table utensils. One of the men on duty serving the meals, in a loud voice, calls the tables to come forward in the order named by him. The order, of course, varies ensuring a longer or shorter wait for every table in turn. After the meal each table attends to its own washing up and in turn each hut, numbering on average twenty inmates, washes the paraphernalia used in preparing the meal and sweeps the Messrooms.

Returning to their huts after breakfast the men are soon busy tidying up: beds have to be made up, the floor swept, and possibly the face needs a shave. From 9.30 to 10 o'clock is Inspection time by the Camp Commandant or his representative Officer. On his appearance at the door of each hut in turn the 'Hütten Altester' (hut leader) calls the Roll which is checked by a Sergeant accompanying the Officer. A bugle call announces the completion of the Inspection whereupon everybody may go about his business.

What a cosmopolitan community. Practically every nationality is represented, every political, religious and social creed. Contrary to expectation the dyed in the wool National Socialist is by no means in the majority. You happen across huts inhabited solely by Jews and Jewish refugees; then there is a fair sprinkling of naturalised British subjects. The element, now in part naturalised who may be called 'Flichtlinge,' those who absconded from ships at Australian ports of call and those who left Germany surreptitiously, is of course represented. A small percentage, including myself, are Australian born British subjects, and there is a sprinkling of Italians. In addition, you find those professing no political creed: Jehovah's Witnesses, Seventh Day Adventists, and representatives of the Christian Science sect.

When war broke out between Germany and Russia and I expressed surprise at this turn of events, I was taken aback somewhat at the statement of a fellow internee: 'What else can you expect! Hitler breaks every pledge or pact when it suits him.' The permeating atmosphere nevertheless is one of unbounded faith in the Fuhrer, of whom just now close at hand an elderly internee lays it down vehemently to a group of sceptics or critics: 'Make no mistake, Hitler has a direct telephone line to heaven! How else could he do what he is doing without making a semblance of a mistake?'

The Jehovah's Witness man is quite sedate and altruistic. On a recent Sunday he carried around a picture drawn and painted by himself depicting David and Goliath. Goliath's sword being held by David stood higher than that lad. It was dripping red with blood. Goliath's head, almost half the size of David, was being held by the hair by David. Blood was all around. Just how Rutherford's disciple was proving the inevitable and early approach of Armageddon with the aid of his picture, very crudely executed, I was not able to, nor did I care, to learn.

1 August, 1941

Work is going on apace on the Sports Ground. While on an exercise walk today, I pick up an idle pick, doff my coat and pullover, and lend a hand. When I sign off, bathed in sweat, Schuster tells me that 'King George is now indebted to me to the tune of Two Pence!'

I attend the Cabaret tonight. Head of the show is Elimar (Bushmann), juggler and magician of the Berlin Wintergarten, and Wirth's and Sonnley's in Australia. It's a very good show. The best act is Hampel selling tin plates that fall off a shelf when a lie is told.

2 August, 1941

Today I bought a length of Jagdwurst (sausage) from the butcher, Helmuth Bartels, and I am looking forward to quite a few meals of this.

There was a bit of bad luck at the Soccer match today. Kissling broke his leg and was taken in the Military Ambulance to Maroobna Hospital, twenty-two miles from here.

3 August, 1941

at today's Church service. The Text for today is Romans 8:18.

4 August, 1941

I am involved in Tischdienst (table duty) and wood-sawing all in one day. There is currently extreme activity on the Sports ground and I've been told that the tennis courts will be ready first.

After today I am free from Tischdienst (table duty) for eight days, from Messedienst for a further fourteen days and from wood-sawing for about three weeks.

Even better news is the fact that today I have received letters from home, dated 30 July from Else and 1 August from Bert and Mum.

Dear Dad,

Since last I wrote to you I have had quite a lively time with my teeth or rather, with my gums. My gums usually bleed quite a lot, but this time only about a day, and then I started getting terrible pains and by Sunday I was just about ready to 'throw my towel in.' Well, Sunday night about nine o'clock the gums burst and three days of congealed blood had to come out. They stopped about six thirty Monday morning. Bert and Steve took it in relays to stay with me and on Monday I paid another visit to Mr. Harris and he said why it had clogged was on account of those gold crowns I had in the back, he said they had dry sockets, which were poisoned and collected all the clean blood that was trying to get through. I have to see Mr. Harris again today, but I must say I am feeling ever so much better now and I hope to be at work again tomorrow. So much for that.

The wattle tree behind the flower house is in full bloom now, it has grown taller than the house and it looks really lovely now.

The Adelaide Electric Supply men are working in front of our place today, they are still hard at their job. I think the change-over is in September.

Jean Homburg and Maurice Kleemann are being married in the middle of August in the Church of England. They have asked Lorna, Claire, and myself to decorate the church for the occasion. Brian Anderson is still up at Darwin. I think he and Lorna intend to be married this year too. Claire and Mel Goers have broken off their romance. Claire is keeping company with a boy, an old pen-friend of hers from the West, who is in the A.I.F. I believe Mel is joining the Air Force.

The Wally Kleemann's (the Tatt's winners) have bought a car like ours, only black. I also hear Mrs. Reg Kleemann is buying one, May Goers is trying to sell them hers.

Mum asks if your cold is quite better now, she sends her love and will write later. She is just plucking a 'chooky' for Margaret. They are coming down this afternoon again.

Bert sung his solo in church on Sunday with great success, he is receiving congratulations on all side. Some people are still wondering who it was, someone said, 'Mr. Obst.' Bert was terribly insulted.

Arthur Woollacott has been sent to Mt. Pleasant to relieve for a few weeks and Mr. White is here on his own.

That's all the news for now.
Keep smiling.
Love from all at Home.
Your Daughter
Else xxxxx

Dear Dad,

We had some very nice days this week, yesterday the sun was quite warm and it was lovely, so El, myself and Marg and little Marie visited Auntie Anna. She is very weak, her hands are quite crippled from Rheumatism and she can hardly do the cooking for herself. She wants to be remembered to you. El went to work this afternoon, she wrote you all about her troubles. We told Mr. Laycock about Marie's Kangaroo rug, he was not quite sure if he promised you that, anyhow everything was alright he wants to do one up for her. A week later he changed his mind and told Bert that he is making one for you and not for Marie he said you can give her something else. He made one for Dr. Becker. I suppose he thought it is not quite right you not getting one, so we can't do anything just let him do what he wants.

Hope these few lines find you in the best of Health as it leaves us. Love from all to you.
Mum

Dear Dad,

Once again you hear from me. I feel that I haven't written you quite as often as you have probably expected, but I hope you will forgive me. I know that El writes you all the news there is, so it isn't as though you don't hear from us at all. I find my time pretty well cut out keeping up with things at the office, at home, and generally.

The time as I write this is 4 p.m. and you'll wonder why I'm home and not at the office. Well, I've been shifting wood at the wood-heap to make room for a load of stumps coming in tomorrow. I've got hold of a very big load at a good price and what we can't use will go up to the office. Well, I've just finished shifting the wood, and am writing this while I cool down before going back to the office.

I don't go out so very much nowadays, but last night Gert and I went to see a Film Show by Mr. Lou Borgelt, on Central Australia. It was a really good show. He went up with Mr. A.G. Bond of Bond's Tours, by plane, and quite a number of shots (in colour) showed the various towns en route. You'd have loved seeing the show, I'm sure: Glen Helen Gorge, Palm Valley, Jay Creek, Mt. Sonder, etc. And he did quite a long trip with Missionary Gross of Hermannsburg. And right through the show we saw the Chev. buckboard which you took up. I quite expected Borgelt to mention your trip up with the buckboard, but nothing was said. Perhaps he didn't know you took it up. Surely, he must have known of your trip?

As Mum mentioned in her letter, we told Cliff about the 'roo rug for Marie. Now, El told him of your wishes, and I also chatted him and this is what he told me: 'I've got the skins all ready for a single bed rug, and I'm sending it to your Dad,' emphasizing it as I have underlined. He reckoned you could give Marie what you cared to, but he was sending you the rug. You may wish to write him, but he seemed set on sending you the rug.

I sent you half a pound of your pipe mixture last week, and trust that by this time you will be enjoying it. Rhodesian perfumed was not procurable, but what has taken its place seems O.K.

By the way, August Geyer and his son Ted are going to Central Australia in a week's time.

Cheerio

Bert

'P.S. *I'm expecting you to acknowledge receipt of anything we send you – tobacco, etc. Have your films arrived? Have you still not received any further local papers – 'Barossa News', 'Leader', 'L. Herald'?*'

5 August, 1941

It's a cold and wintry day. I am indoors and spend most of the day in bed because this is the warmest place to be, and so I proceed diligently with my study of Wealth by Canon.

6 August, 1941

Out of bed at bugle call and over to the washroom when Drucks calls out to me, 'Have you heard that Eime arrived at midnight?' 'What?' I reply. Sure enough, Hughie had arrived at midnight and what a joy did he bring me! News from Bert and parcels of cheer from home, tobacco, cigarettes, cigarette papers, fruit and sweets. I sat down and cried; and I think of those in my hut and those in the whole Camp of seven hundred odd who have no-one with kind thoughts for them.

All of this and a letter from Bert dated 4 August.

Dear Dad,

This letter is in reply to yours of the 28th July, which we received last Friday.

I have enclosed herewith a M.O. for five pounds, and it is made payable to J.F.W. Schulz, at the Military Post Office, Tatura. I trust it reaches you O.K.

Wayville Camp rang me the other day saying that Eime had received notice that he was to be moved to Tatura. He wished them to let me know that he was willing and would be pleased to take along any small parcels for you. So, I got a few smokes, etc. for him and sent two packages along for you, contents as follows: 2 pairs of glasses, half-dozen packets Baffra cigarette papers, 4 small packets of Black and White cigarettes, 2-ounce tin Capstan Fine Cut, 2-ounce Pouchpak Capstan, a package of 'Ranch' Rhodesian cigarette tobacco, some Licorice Allsorts (from Marie), Figs, Crystallized Fruit, Walnuts and chocolate. I trust they will bring you good cheer.

Have you had any picture shows of your films as yet? I am waiting to hear how the films and screen arrived. I spent several hours in packing them, so the long journey should not have damaged them.

We went for a little outing yesterday, and took Mum, Marge, Ted and Marie along with us. Everybody enjoyed it although we ran through a few showers of rain.

Excuse this short note – I am due to leave for the Lone Pine Bureau Annual Meeting in about ten minutes. A party of us is cycling out.

Cheerio!
Bert

7 August, 1941

Today the authorities take stock of all goods handed to internees on their arrival here; blankets, palliases, kitchen utensils etc. Finally, the cold snap we have experienced for the last several days is passing away. Hopefully winter is on its way out. Today Materne, Hunger, Eime and I play enjoyable Skat.

8 August, 1941

It's time for a bit of spring cleaning so I give all bed clothes, blankets etc., a thorough dusting and airing, and finish up with a hot shower.

9 August, 1941

I have an appointment with dentist Fent who fixes my tooth for the second time. It looks like tooth issues are running in the family at present. During the day I get the chance to watch the killing of a pig and a calf. Rumour has it that all 'B' Compound is to move into 'A' Compound! I wonder what that is all about?

Since news of my move to Tatura was first given to me, I have felt somewhat depressed about the whole issue to the extent that my Diary entries, on reflection, are quite meagre and lacking in much detail at all. Also, because of the cold I am suffering from, I have been spending time in bed during the day in an effort to not only keep warm but to allay any further decline of my health. Today I decided it is time to once more write a letter to the Minister for the Army, (Intelligence Department), and state my case for release.

Sir,

After eight months internment I beg respectfully that you give the matter of my release further consideration. In support thereof, I desire to correct some of the evidence as taken down during the hearing of my appeal, to amplify some of the evidence and to state my position in the Camp here at Tatura.

It was shortly before I was transferred from Wayville, S.A. (early in June) to Tatura that a copy of the evidence taken at my appeal was made available to me. It covered some twenty sheets of foolscap type-written. It was not read to me for signature as being a correct record of the evidence taken.

The report has it that I said: 'Hitler knows everything that is going on.' I denied ever having made that statement. The report also states: 'I have given a number of Film Shows for Red Cross and Soldier's Comforts. I do not know how much money was collected at these shows.' Allow me to amplify this. Whenever asked to show for patriotic bodies I readily agreed. The arrangements were left in the hands of the local Committees including the sale of tickets. At the conclusion of a show I was usually told the amount collected, but I kept no record. The amount collected at centres as far away as more than one hundred miles from my home town was near the two-hundred-pound mark. My expenses for car hire totalled less than seven pounds. When I was unable further to carry the expense of buying and taking films I appealed for assistance to M. W. Seppelt of the firm B. Seppelt and Sons. Mr Seppelt gave me a cheque (not from the firm) for ten pounds to film subjects for screening at patriotic functions. (I have received permission to show my films at Tatura. How much would I prefer to continue my work at home!)

The report mentions my participation in War Savings Certificates. Delegated by the Tanunda District Council, I attended at the Adelaide Town Hall when Mr. Spender explained the War

Savings Certificate Scheme. The members of my family and I bought one hundred pounds worth of Certificates, and besides that I contributed a small amount weekly to the Tanunda Show Group and was directly responsible in forming at least one other Tanunda Group. About the time of my detention a Queen Competition was begun in my home town and on the actual day of my detention samples of buttons from Adelaide firms were in transit to my address for Queen buttons. (I believe the headmaster of the local school, Mr. Guerin, took charge of them.)

In the course of my appeal I was asked: 'Do you use the word 'bloody'. I simply replied in the affirmative. I have used the word, but I doubt if the members of my family have heard me use the word and my acquaintances rarely. I am reported to have said that I used the word 'bloody' 'especially since I have been at Wayville.' What I actually said: 'I have often heard it used, especially since I am at Wayville.'

I have only read the report once and the above quotations may not be verbatim.

My visit to a Hitler function in Adelaide some five or six years ago can, of course, be viewed with suspicion. But this happened at a time when signs of rapprochement between England and Germany were in evidence and I desired nothing more fervently than that the two peoples might live in harmony and work in co-operation.

My position at Tatura:

I left Wayville on June 2, and arrived at Tatura on Wednesday afternoon. After obtaining some of my luggage and arranging for a straw palliasse on the ground, the bugle sounded the evening meal. At the meal it was announced that the usual Wednesday evenings 'Kameradschaftsabend' (fellowship evening) would take place. I attended the one held on the day of my arrival only, since I cannot join in the salute that is given at the close of the function.

Just now about one thousand pounds relief money from Germany is being distributed among internees. Even if I so desired

I could not participate being 'only an Australian.' Another two hundred and fifty pounds from a relief centre is due shortly for 'Reichsdeutsche' (German citizens) only.

Sir, Australia is my country, the country in the service of which I desire to give such strength and ability I possess. I respectfully ask you to appreciate my position as an internee at Tatura and review your decision regarding my continued detention.

I would willingly appear to answer any questions that might be asked of me, granting me that right laid down in Magna Charta that every person shall be deemed innocent until proved guilty.

Believe me
Respectfully yours.
J.F.W. Schulz (signed)
P.O.W. 3077

10 August, 1941

Watching the butchering in the cold air has brought on another cold and sore throat; the worst so far. Because of this I miss the first Church service since I arrived here. My warm bed is the best place to be under these circumstances.

11 August, 1941

I have an anxious night because my throat worries and pains me. The doctor's prescription has a wonderful effect and I'm hoping that soon I will be well again.

A pair of wonderfully knitted socks arrive in the post, but I'm left to wonder; where did they come from?

12 August, 1941

I am battling against going to the hospital and the bitterly cold wind blowing as hard as it is does not improve matters. I decide to stay in bed and eventually feel that the temperature is leaving me.

The entire members of 'B' Compound, some two hundred and fourteen odd, are ordered to move into 'A' Compound, to make room for a similar number from Camp No. 2 which is about eight miles from here. The latter are those that were rescued from the 'SS Arandora Star', which was torpedoed while conveying some thousands of German prisoners from England to Canada.

The crossover of the 'B' Compound complement into the 'A' Compound is such a mess. Every one of our huts has to fill up, taking twenty men each. All lecture halls, concert and picture halls are commandeered for quarters and Mess Halls. Dr. Haslinger deserves thanks for the manner in which he has handled the difficult problems which have often occurred.

13 August, 1941

The new men for 'B' Compound arrive. The two Compounds are separated by two barbed wires about five yards apart filled in by barbed entanglements. The gate from 'A' to 'B' is closed. The new arrivals line up on their side of the fence and our men on theirs and greetings and conversations pass across. The guard's attempts to stop this verbal intercourse proves of no avail.

At the Kameradschaftabend (fellowship evening) this evening about forty of the men now in 'B' Compound suddenly put in an appearance. They had managed a hole through the entanglements and later got back safely. There were some amusing incidents to be seen in crossing over, especially when pastors and missionaries break the law.

Today I received my books on Economy from Melbourne at a cost of one pound eleven shillings.

14 August, 1941

There is intense activity between 'A' and the new 'B' Compound. 'B' has no Canteen, Store, or Café. They transfer their money done up in little parcels with a clever throw across separating barbed entanglements. Orders are given and soon a Leberwurst (liver sausage), cigarette tobacco and Schwartbrot (ryebread), go sailing back.

'A' Compound has erected a small stage and with their gramophone equipment and the cinema loud speaker, they send a musical programme of German marches and airs across to the new arrivals.

The hole in the entanglement is growing larger, perceptibly higher, and with shades of night falling, you'll find 'Rothveen' intermingling with the men in 'A' Compound.

Hughie Eime writes a letter today to the Commandant on behalf of the British subjects interned at Tatura, and gives me a copy to file in the folder Bert made for me. The letter reads as follows:

> *Sir,*
>
> *I herewith beg permission for the Internees in the Tatura Camp, who are British subjects either by birth or naturalisation, to be recognised as a body which through its representatives to be elected, may place their several needs or grievances, or whatever affects their status as British subjects, before the appropriate authorities.*
>
> *The recognition of this body is not intended to interfere in any shape or form with the domestic workings or discipline of the Camp, which is already ably represented, but to deal entirely with representations to be made to the Hon. The Minister of Defence and other outside authorities.*
>
> *Thanking you in anticipation.*
> *I am*
> *Yours obediently Eime. (signed)*

Today I receive a nice long newsy letter from Else dated 10 August.

Dear Dad,

We received your last letter on Friday, we always look forward to receiving them. I am O.K. again after my teeth episode, and can eat practically anything again, only not nuts!!

You are certainly going in for sports over there, anyway it keeps you fit as well. We shall attend to the bowls, tennis racquet etc. this week and send them along.

The weather seems to be brightening up here a little now too, I am pleased the cold weather will be over soon and then we start tennis again.

There was a farewell to Ron Schilling on Friday last, he is in the R.A.A.F.

Last week the Band gave a concert to raise funds for themselves (Band) and there was a very good attendance. The takings were over seventeen pounds.

The Angaston Races were on Wednesday last, I believe the attendance was not as good as usual, not as many cars as usual came through, the petrol rationing has certainly made a difference, although there was a special train.

Mr. M.E. Heuzenroeder celebrated his 70th Birthday last Sunday. We called on him and he asked after you and sends regards. He was terribly thrilled about a cable which he received from Phyliss from London. She is very well and Ken Charnaud her husband is a Major in the army now. He showed us some snaps she had sent him, she is still the same and Ken is getting fatter than ever.

Mr. Gus Kleemann, Mr. Ernst Kleemann and another brother from Waikerie have just returned from a trip to Central Australia. They went up by train, and were away about three weeks.

Audrey has been staying up with her people for a week. Little Jimmy is growing up too, he is a lovely little boy and will be two years in November. The family certainly makes a fuss of him. Splinter had been playing in an Orchestra at the Tivoli Theatre for a week every night, so Audrey came up here. Splinter works at the Wheat Board.

Mrs. Hentsch is really very bad now. She wanders around all over the town. They are continually out after her and people are complaining, I think they will have to take her away soon. Poor Mr. H. is feeling it very badly too.

Traut Held has been transferred to Gramps Melbourne office now, she is very pleased but accommodation in Melbourne is very hard now, I believe.

Dulcie and her boarders, five in all, won ten pounds in Tatts last week. She is very excited of course, they were only one ticket off the ten thousand pound draw that time.

Are you receiving the local papers now? They are sent regularly from here each week, I hope you do because all the 'little bits' of news are interesting to you.

Well, news has run out once again, so I will say 'cheerio' for now.
Hope you are well and keep smiling.
Love from all at home.
Your loving daughter
Else xxxxxx

15 August, 1941

Today is the warmest day we have had so far and I am enjoying every moment of that warmth. I really don't enjoy trying to keep warm and free of further bad colds by having to spend time in my bed.

I spend time outside watching two teams of soccer players from across the fence march onto our sports ground accompanied by marching songs and then proceed to play a wonderfully combined game. A proper match between representatives of their players and our players will be interesting. Incidents culminating in two broken legs recently has somewhat dampened the ardour of our players.

I receive a letter from Bert today dated 12 August.

> *Dear Dad,*
>
> *A few lines from the Office to accompany a parcel I am forwarding under separate cover. I have looked through your books but found only 'Old Gorgon Graham' which I have forwarded together with another book which should interest you: 'Dewdrop Danby.' Will see what other Gorgon Graham books I can get.*
>
> *As I write, the Adelaide Electric men are hard at work on the line outside the office. The power is off all day today, but the foreman told me it would be the last time before switching to Adelaide supply. When they will actually switch over, nobody seems to know. The main trouble now seems to be the scarcity of motors. Our motor for the Linotype has been here in the office quite some time, but of course, not in use. We are still waiting, however, for the other two motors.*
>
> *They are always anxious at home to hear that you receive all parcels we send you. It would be a good plan if you were to acknowledge receipts.*
>
> *I have made arrangements for getting hold of some bowls, and will be sending them along, together with a tennis racquet, within a day or two. Will advise when I have railed them.*
>
> *In the last few weeks I have been preparing for the Show Annual Meeting. I hope to have the books audited this week, and the annual meeting will probably be held in the last week of the month.*
>
> *So much for the present then, Dad, and keep smiling.*
>
> *Your son*
> *Bert*

16 August, 1941

The new arrivals in 'B' Compound, at least two teams of eleven each, accompanied by supporters, march onto our sports ground to play Handball today.

The gap in the barbed entanglements, which was closed by the authorities during the day, was again opened at night and men from our side, so I'm told, went across to listen to a lecture on Russia by Dr. Erler, leader of the new arrivals.

17 August, 1941

Today we have our first Church service in 'A' Compound, and our preacher is Wittmann.

Under adverse weather conditions, a vocal and instrumental concert was given 'across the fence' to the inmates of 'B' Compound. A 'Begrüssung' (greeting) to the recent arrivals is to take place tonight to which 'alle die sich zum drei Reich bekennen' (all those who are loyal to the third Reich), are invited.

19 August, 1941

We have had the warmest, most ideal weather during the last two days. 'B' Compound march and sing on their way to the Sports Ground. A humorous interlude then occurs. When the internees are due to return, the guard is found asleep on duty at the back of the Sports Ground and fails to respond to their calls!

20 August, 1941

I'm spending most of my time reading books on Economy now, and playing Skat almost every evening.

21 August, 1941

More studying of Economics, and a letter from Else dated 17 August.

> Dear Dad,
>
> Well, it is raining cats and dogs today, no weather for going out hiking, so letter writing comes next.
> We have plenty of work at the Office, and it looks as if I will be going down a full day now instead of half. We have another order of Cookery Books and Gramps have come in for more jobs, so it is good that the work is there.
> Yesterday there were three weddings celebrated around here. Jean Homburg and Maurice Kleemann were married and another of the Braunnauch girls to a Liebich boy and 'Seedy' Lietschke to Margaret Hoffmann, Mrs. Richard Hoffmann's adopted daughter.
> Last week Mr. Len Winton and a carload were returning from Williamstown and the car hit a tree and somersaulted and came to rest on its wheels again. No-one was injured. Some of the occupants were; Winton, Peter Mayr, 'Seedy' Nietschke, and two others, I am not sure who they were.
> The building where Gun and Teusner's office is, is having a frontage built on, it should look very nice when finished and quite an improvement in the main street.
> Bert had the Show Auditors, Frank Rothe and Mr. Obst in last week, they remarked how well the books were kept and everything orderly and neat.

> *I heard the other day that the Bowling Club was not in a good position and members were asked to pay ten shillings to help the Club along. The Tennis Club seems to be the only financial Club in the town. We have about twelve pounds in hand.*
>
> *I have some lovely daffodils out now. I wish I could bring them to you, they are so lovely, the poppies are in full bloom now too.*
>
> *Mum is well, she said she leaves the letter writing to us, she always says she did not have such good schooling as we did!!!*
>
> *We hope you received the small parcel we sent along with Mr. Eime and enjoyed its contents. Mum asks about your sox, are they still in good order, and do you darn them yourself? Perhaps they are not in such good order then!!!*
>
> *If there is anything you want in clothes just let us know and we will send it to you. How is the weather there now, is it getting warmer?*
>
> *Steve's brother, Phil, is in Tobruk now, and has met some Tanunda boys there. Zander's have not heard any more news of Bob, it is several months now since he was reported missing.*
>
> *That is all the news for now.*
>
> *Love from all at home.*
>
> *Your Daughter*
>
> *Else xxx*
>
> *P.S. Bert says I have to learn to use the Typewriter again. I am his private Secretary now.*
>
> *Else.*

22 August, 1941

We experience a fine morning which, unfortunately, is followed by thunderstorms and rain later in the day. I get a letter from Margaret, Ted and Marie, and included is a photo of Marie. I also receive a letter from Annie Auricht. Both of these letters are dated 18 August.

Dear Father,

This letter will probably be a bit of a scrawl, I am taking advantage of the nice sunshine and writing outside. Marie told me to tell you she has had another 'go' at her hair, despite all my warnings but this time I punished her so I hope it will be a lesson. Last Wednesday afternoon we had a gift afternoon in our new Sunday School Hall. The Hall was opened about three weeks ago on a Sunday afternoon, it is a beautiful big building it has a nice stage and fitted out with chairs in sets of three, of which we gave one set, but to get back to the gift afternoon, Mrs. Held opened the fete and Marie afterwards handed her a posy (as you will read by the cutting) but Marie got quite upset afterwards because Mrs. Held put the posy on a chair behind her and Marie said to me, Mummy she doesn't want it. Marie gets very excited when she sees a snail you know, so the other day she came running in to me very excited and said Mummy there is a snail on my sand pit you know one of those things with pins on. She is really very funny now some of the things she says.

The snap Marie is sending you was taken at a birthday party of Donald Rhind he lives just at the back of our place, but Marie wouldn't be snapped with the others so they managed to get her on her own. Have you received the parcel that Marie sent for you? I hope by now you have recovered from your cold and feeling well again, we are well Marie especially she is as fit as a fiddle. Else and Bert are working hard at the office and you can rest assured that Bert is 'keeping the home fires burning' he is after business where ever he can get it. So you have no need to worry about that. Last Wednesday afternoon, Annie pushed to Freeling on bike. She

called in here but I wasn't home. I hope these few lines cheer you up again we are always thinking of you and awaiting your return.
    Lots of love
    From
    Margaret Ted and Marie'

Tanunda

Dear Mr. Schulz

And how are you?
    It is so dreadfully cold here these days that we hardly know how to get warm, Mother feels this winter more than any other year, but I suppose that is quite natural because she can't work about at all and just has to get warm sitting by the fire. The last few days she has been fairly well but some days I really don't know how to stick it and there is so little I can do for her.
    The Dr. comes to see her every three months now and that is a big weight off my mind and to know who I can call in, if the emergency should arise. Mother is always glad when Dr. Altman comes and quite enjoys his visits.
    Today I dug up our first potatoes and were they a size, potatoes never tasted so good before.
    Both the cats have been ill, first one and then the other, for a fortnight it was just like having a patient in the house but I cured them with Nux Vomica and castor oil, the hot water bag had to be filled every four hours so it was quite a business, every morning I was afraid to look in their box thinking they might be cold and stiff. For five days they just lay in the box and never had anything to eat or drink bar the medicine, however they are well again, when quite a lot of people lost their cats.

Bert and El will be telling you all the office news so I won't go into that only to say that everything is going on very satisfactory and I thought you might be glad to hear that from me. El is certainly a great help but apart from that she cheers me up quite a lot seeing her every day and she has got her father's cheery disposition.

Thanks for the greetings you occasionally send to Mum and me in your home letters.

Well partner take good care of yourself so that you can come back to help us in the best of health.

Mother joins me in sending you the kindest regards and hoping to hear from you someday soon.

Very sincerely yours
Annie H. Auricht

23 August, 1941

A rainy day though not cold.

24 August, 1941

Missionary Munsell takes today's Church Service. The entire sermon practically consists of adulation of Hitler's prowess and there was even a prayer for the success of his arms! It's almost enough to put me off going to these church services ever again!

For the greater part of the week there was no tobacco procurable at the Canteen. It opened its doors today from eleven to twelve o'clock, and report has it that forty- five pounds worth of tobacco was sold in that hour.

25 August, 1941

Rumour has it that today's paper would bring interesting news. Great annoyance when there is NO PAPER DELIVERY. 'Nuff said!
    At long last my films have arrived!

26 August, 1941

I am promised delivery of my films today – but do not yet get them. The Intelligence Officer on duty for some weeks relieving, has handed over to his cobber, who has first to gather up the threads apparently before getting into his stride. I try to wait patiently.
    Fortunately, I receive two letters today dated 22 August, from Bert and Else, and that helps to relieve the frustration felt at not having been given my films.

> *Dear Dad,*
>
> *Yesterday I forwarded to your address, per Goods Rail, the following:*
> *4 Bowls*
> *1 Tennis Racket*
> *For the Bowls, you must thank a friendly neighbour, and for the Tennis Racket you owe thanks to Margaret. I hope they reach you O.K.*
> *El has written to you today also, in reply to your letter to her. But there's one piece of news she hasn't written you. By the midday mail today, we received a letter from Auntie Bertha of Mt. Gambier – she's the one you've got to thank for the pair of socks you received. She tells us she often wonders how you're getting on, and says she would like to hear from you sometime. She also writes that Uncle Paul and Auntie Maggie are staying with her while they look about for a suitable place. So it sounds as though they intend*

settling down at the Mount once again. Uncle Paul has a job in the Railways Department, it seems.

I'm glad you received all the goods sent per Mr. Eime. The Rhodesian tobacco was some I still had on hand. I've been smoking little lately.

Have you received the films now?

The other day I picked the largest lot of mushrooms yet, from our patch by the roadside. FOUR POUNDS. Beat that if you can. I took some round to Gert's people, and we had two meals at home.

I gave Gerald Tuohy your regards. He was pleased to hear from you and said 'Tell him he was sadly missed at Bowls last season, if ever anyone was missed!!' So, you're not forgotten.

Our annual Show meeting is to take place next Thursday, and I'm enclosing the Show balance sheet, it may interest you.

I have noted your advice regarding local papers – henceforth only the 'Leader' and 'Lutheran Herald' will go on to you.

They have been going regularly so far, so I cannot understand why you haven't been receiving them.

So much for the present, and, as Marie says --- keep smiling!

Your son

Bert

Dear Dad,

We received your letter this morning. Today it is raining cats and dogs again, I always seem to choose a rainy day for letter writing. The creek has come down quite high. I think it is the highest it has ever been during the winter months.

I don't know if I told you in a previous letter that Frank Fischer had enlisted, he is at present in camp at Wayville.

Colin Offe has been given a farewell too. He is the youngest of the Offe boys.

Several Tanunda Bandsmen have been playing in the Adelaide Competitions. Jack Traeger (Nuri.) came first in the Trombone Solo, Gal John, second in the Euphonium Solo, Aubrey Kernich second in Champ. Solo (any Instrument) and Aubrey Kernich third in Cornet Solo also. May Goers played the accompaniment to all the pieces.

It was May's Birthday on the 19th and the Band Boys (for whom she had played) gave her a surprise party at John's.

I do not remember writing to you of the death of Mrs. Matchoss wife of the late Pastor. She had been in ill health for quite some time and passed away at the Angaston Hospital.

I have seen the rug from Cliff, it is not quite completed yet, and will be sent on to you later. It's a gorgeous rug and it will be nice for you in the cold weather. (Don't smoke in bed and burn it!!)

Little Marie was down yesterday, she is very clever now, you can't put anything across her though, she tells you off in a few minutes.

Her birthday will soon be here again on Sept 18th. How the years do fly, she will be going into her fourth year. Margaret will be thirty this year on the 29th Aug.

There is no Football here now. Steve tried to get a few matches but now all the lads are in camp and there are not sufficient players.

I still go to the Freytag's to cut their hair, Tussie always enquires after you and sends kind regards. Her brother still has the little shop, although I heard that he had gone insolvent.

Baker Hoffmann is building a house at the back of Harmann's Bakery next to Stoll's place.

Mrs. Hurst is a keen golfer now too. She and Mrs. Rheinold Graue always go out. We have not been out this year so far, I will wait for the warmer weather and tennis.

Tomorrow Dulcie and Vic Lindner are coming in for the evening, they have been very good to us, and we often go out to their place. Dulcie has a new Healing bike it's a beaut too, she puffs a bit after coming up the cutting.

I have tried to make enquiries about the socks, and so far have not been successful, the only other person I can think of is Auntie Irene, I will drop them a line and enquire.

My gums are healing nicely now, and I am O.K. again, but I occasionally get a lovely bout of Indigestion and then I run for the powders etc. It is a month since I had them drawn the time will soon pass and I will be able to get my 'denture'. More refined than 'plate'. (ha ha)

Cheerio from all at home.
Love from
Else xxxx

27 August, 1941

The Garrison Sports are scheduled for today so there is no hope of having my films given to me. I'll just have to hang on and wait patiently.

Hunger and Seith haven't got their beds yet. They left Wayville with the others over two months ago!

28 August, 1941

At last! Today I receive my films and screen and am as happy as a child receiving toys at Christmas.

Owing to overheating of the stove in Messroom 4, the hot stove-pipe ignites the ceiling just when we are retiring for the night. The fire-fighting effort was hilarious! No-one seemed to know what had to be done, but in the end, calm was achieved and the fire was quelled.

I have begun writing the draft of a letter to Mr. Richards, as follows:

Dear Mr. Richards,

Early in June, soon after my arrival here, I received the letters sent me by you which you had received from Sydney. Thank you. I have somewhat settled down to the routine existence here. I have no complaints on the score of food and quarters. As regards social intercourse the position is different. As an Australian it is impossible for me to take part in the regular comradeship evenings, and my experience among the cosmopolitan community here makes me feel then that I do not fit in. Recently over one thousand pounds was distributed among inmates of the camp. I was automatically excluded being 'only an Australian.' Another two hundred and fifty pounds is to be distributed shortly but to 'Reichsdeutsche' (German citizens) only. (The moneys, of course, come from German sources). My family, of course, provides me with whatever I need, I only desire to put the position to you. I desired to improve my knowledge in economics, when I am facetiously told that I need not bother my head on that score, since the economic affairs of the country will in the near future be laid down for me. Thanks to the help of the camp supervisor I have ordered and received four valuable books on economics from Melbourne.

I try not to see the barbed entanglements around me, preferring an existence of temporary stupefaction, and I pray that I may be permitted to walk out from here without bitterness in my heart.' (Remainder of letter missing.)

29 August, 1941

Margaret's Birthday. I am getting together a present for her and one for Marie, whose Birthday is next month. Am sorry I will not be able to film Marie for her fourth Birthday. I rewind and check up on my films.

30 August, 1941

Sunshine has given place to a cold, dull day.

31 August, 1941

The preacher today for Church is Gotzelmann.
 I attend the lawn Concert and collection for P.O.W.'s from overseas; eight hundred have arrived and are quartered in a nearby Camp. The collections in 'A' Compound realised three hundred and twelve pounds, and in 'B' Compound one hundred and twenty- two pounds. A wonderful effort. Dr. Seith contributes six pence!
 Two meetings of Australian born and naturalised internees has been presided over by Burghart. It was decided to send an appeal for help to the Red Cross in Berlin for assistance similar to that received by Reichsdeutsche.

1 September, 1941

I'm up earlier than any previous morning, and on going through my films I find that the Military Censor has cut out the last half of my Hermannsburg film. Why?

2 September, 1941

Sultry today with a little rain in the morning. I give my dungaree suit a wash to remove the blue.
 I receive a welcome letter from Else dated 29 August.

Dear Dad,

This afternoon we journeyed over to Nuri to spend the afternoon with Margaret, it being her birthday. We also took over Mrs. Vic Lindner, and Marie was getting very upset as we were a little later than usual and she thought we were not coming.

Mr. Paul Heinrich died this week, he died of a heart attack quite suddenly.

There has been another shocking tragedy in the district. Mollie Harman the young girl in the Ladies Hairdressing Salon at Summerton's, died four days after receiving severe internal injuries, after a motor accident.

She and Margaret Zerna (Stockwell) were going to Adelaide in Mollie's little Austin 7 tourer car, when near Dayveston the car skidded on the side of the road, after much rain, and turned over three times.

Margaret was pinned under the car only receiving lacerations and severe shock. She had to have fourteen stitches in her thigh. Mollie was thrown out and was picked up unconscious and taken to Angaston Hospital. Dr. Hoopmann and Dr. E. Britten-Jones from Adelaide tried in vain to save her life, she died four days later never regaining consciousness.

She was such a happy-go-lucky type of girl and very popular in the district and also in her work, it has been a great shock to all.

Old Father Jericho from Nuriootpa also died this week, he was 87.

Have you received the Bowls and Racquet yet?

We have the rug here now from Cliff, it is just beautiful and Bert will most probably send it tomorrow. He (Cliff) sends along every good wish to you, he hopes the rug will give you some happy thoughts of olden days out amongst the 'roos'. He had a letter from

Stan and Os, they may be going up north on a 'shoot' in Oct., they also remarked that the party will not be complete without you.

The dark bluey skin in the rug Cliff sent is a beaut. Mr. Juttner the tanner, said he would give pounds for it.

Mr. Noll sent down a lovely bunch of red tulips yesterday, they are a real splash of colour in his garden now.

The Show meeting was held last night, Bert said it was a very quiet meeting, and he has been re-elected Secretary again.

Our pussycat is very spoilt, just at present she will not eat anything but mince-meat, so now pussy has a standing order with the butcher.

Edna Schultz and Frank Fischer are being married tomorrow week. Frank is in the A.I.F. now, and Edna will come home to live with her people again.

Mum sends regards and hopes you are well, as she is at present.
I will close now hoping you are well and keep smiling.
Love from all at Home
Your Daughter
Else. xxxx

3 September, 1941

Sergeant Howard of the Intelligence Department today presented me with forms which I was asked to fill in in duplicate. When finished, the form read:

> *I, Johann Friedrich Wilhelm Schulz, born March 19, 1883, at Point Pass, S.A., desire that my name and personal particulars not be communicated to the German Government direct or through Consular offices.*

When asked by me what the form purported, the Sergeant replied that the form was intended to supply the respective Governments with the names of all who might require assistance or whose relatives were enquiring after them.

Two pigs were killed today. Will we have more sausages?

4 September, 1941

Outbreak of the war two years ago. The Camp celebrates the event with Faustball (fistball, a sport similar to volleyball) in the forenoon and Handball in the afternoon.

5 September, 1941

I procure old timbers and make my first attempt at inlay work.

6 September, 1941

Spend all day laying out a butterfly tray and commence cutting out timber. I also receive a letter from Bert dated 2 September.

> *Dear Dad,*
>
> *Here I am once again with a few lines for you. I hope to have a bit more spare time for a week or so now - a thing that hasn't happened for a long time. Show Annual Meeting is over, Income Tax Returns have been sent in, and everybody's happy.*
>
> *Shall I tell you something of the Show Annual Meeting? Mr. Guerin is president once again, so you will understand that we are*

holding another Show. At present it is too early to say where any profits will be allocated. It has therefore been decided to carry on as in normal times and leave such decisions until the profits are actually in our hands. I was re-elected Secretary. But I pointed out to the Committee that my responsibilities at present were greater than when I had applied for the position 2 years ago. I explained that the Committee might find someone who had more time than I for the job. They reckoned it wouldn't be so hard this year and wanted me to carry on – so there you are.

I think things will be O.K. though, because El is a great help these days, and she can do a lot of the addressing and circularizing work for me.

Regarding the business – I have found it advisable to buy a motor bike for use when hunting up work. I picked up a little two-stroke for twelve pounds. It's just a bike of course, but does the work. Just at present it's a fact that if you want work, you've simply got to go out after it. Plenty of customers have told me that with them it's a matter of 'first come gets it!' I'll send you a snap of the bike some time.

Talking of snaps – We were up at Ted's the other Sunday and I took several shots of Marie and Ern. Knispel's two boys – Robert and Don. Am sending two snaps of the kiddies, and also one of El and our cat, named 'Miss Pattercakes.'

Last night I was out at Lone Pine for the Bureau meeting once again. I had made a proposition at the Annual meeting that one of the older members be asked to give us a talk on the early history of Lone Pine Bureau. I understand they asked Monty Ellis, but he didn't arrive on account of illness – so 'Dick' Hentschke gave a paper on 'The Good old Times'. The style of the paper seemed familiar to me; I was sure Dick hadn't written it. So after the meeting I asked him to show it to me. He did so, and then I knew who the author was. You will probably remember the paper, as well as the author! Dick sends you his heartiest greetings – he is always asking after you. (Who isn't!)

I don't know whether El has written you this or not – but the shops in Tanunda close at 5.30 p.m. now. This applies, of course, only to the stores, not workshops or factories.

I am pleased to hear that you have at last received your films and screen. Perhaps by now you have also received your tennis racket and bowls. May they help to keep you cheerful.

So long, for the present.
Your son
Bert

7 September, 1941

Church service – preacher is Meier. I do a little bit of work on my tray.

8 September, 1941

A number of Australian born and naturalised internees are called into the Orderly Room to give fingerprints. Bohlman, Rothe and I are not included in the list. The others have a hurried meeting and decide to protest against giving fingerprints. In the Orderly Room they ask the Sergeant for the regulation empowering the taking of fingerprints. He is unable to produce the regulation and no fingerprints are given.

9 September, 1941

It's an ideal spring day today. A parcel arrives from Bert containing Cliff's Kangaroo skin rug which is admired by many here in the Camp.

Bert has also included 2 packets of cigarette tobacco and 4 packets of cigarette papers. I am indeed blessed.

10 September, 1941

I work throughout these days on my butterfly tray. If only I had the requisite tools for this work. My knife can do wonders, but it's tedious work.

12 September, 1941

I receive two letters today; one from Mum, dated 8 September, and the other from Margaret, Ted and Marie, dated 9 September.

> *Dear Dad*
>
> *I feel like writing a few lines to you again.*
> *Today we did not wash because El went to work in the morning, it is a very cold and rainy day again, after the lovely nice weather we had, still the rain is very good. Last week I wrote a letter to Mrs. Johnson and thanked her for her kindness, she will be very pleased to hear from you too. Mr. Irrgang took ill last week again, his old complaint Asthma he was very bad, they had shifted out of their old place and are living in that house opposite the Church, it looks quite nice the garden is all done up, they still keep 2 cows. I am very pleased that El can help in the Office she likes it too.*
> *Next week we will be going to Marie's Birthday she is 4 years then, we will miss you, don't worry we always think of you. When Marie saw that nice rug, she said when Grandpa comes home from his long holiday I'll get that rug, she is a very clever little girlie now.*

One of Ed. Hage's children about Marie's age can't talk yet. They seem to have bad luck with all their children.

Hope you keep well
With love
From Mum.

Dear Dad,

We received your very welcome letter some days ago now, and we were glad to know you are so far enjoying fairly good health. Marie was delighted with the letter, telling everybody 'Granpa' had written her a letter and that it was for herself only. So far we are all well, I have been fortunate enough to escape sickness. The weather has been very wintry the past week, and have had 160 points of rain since Saturday, of which everybody is very glad of, excepting the 'washer woman', as you can imagine would gut them about getting things as they should be. Business is going along very well, but gradually getting harder as things are getting more difficult to get every day, however we cannot complain. We have been overtaken with more misfortune our Lady Hairdresser, meeting with an accident at Daveyston on Saturday week. She was on her way home to Glenelg when overturning the car and totally wrecking same, she was thrown out and rendered unconscious and not regaining it again, passed away at Angaston Hospital on Tuesday. We are finding it difficult to replace her as Lady Hairdressers are very scarce too, at present we have one of 'Maeder's' girls, he has been kind enough to help us out, and is also trying to get another for us. Mrs. Summerton is keeping fairly well, and at present is spending a holiday at Glenelg with her daughter, as the children have a weeks' holidays. I had a ring from Mum today, and everybody is well too, and very busy, my word Bert is doing a great job at the Office, and is out for all business he can get. I got a quote from him *for some account forms, the other day, so will put a little his way, too, as no doubt he is as keen as mustard and you need not worry as he is the right man for the job, and always goes about his work in a cheerful manner. Mr. Hosking, A. Rensch, and Bronte Ellis send their regards to you, and often enquire as to how you are keeping.*

On Saturday afternoon I built a bench in the Garage with the assistance of 'Arthur', so one will be able to do a few odd jobs now. Our garden is still quite colourful and when the weather breaks we will be getting it ready for summer flowers etc.; and by your letters you must be quite an expert at gardening too, no doubt it is a great 'hobbie'. I will conclude hoping you are well.

Your Loving Children
Marge, Marie and Ted

13 September, 1941

I give my first picture show to a full house and am booked for repeat shows.

14 September, 1941

Church service – preacher today is Missionary Holzknecht. The weather here is changing again and we are back to windy and cold.

15 September, 1941

It has rained practically all day. I give my second picture show.

16 September, 1941

I spent all day working on my wood inlay work. Received a letter from Else dated 12 September.

> *Dear Dad*
> *We received your last letter early this week. Miss Auricht also had your letter and thanks you. Her Mother seems to be brighter again now.*
> *Sybil and Geoff came over from Melbourne for their holidays, this time of course by train. Sybil rang and wanted me to stay with her a few days but it was not convenient for me to go, our busy period is starting now. Almanacs!*
> *Bert spent a day in town this week he was fortunate in getting a ride down, he went with Mr. Schmidt from the Hotel.*
> *Margaret Zerna is recovering from the accident, I heard it was her first day up last week, she suffered terribly from shock.*
> *Our Old Scholars Reunion is held again this month, but we shall not be going down. I believe they have cut down the functions quite a bit, I really don't think they will have the crowd now with the petrol rationing.*
> *Dulcie A. had word from Ross, he has enlisted in the Air Force but his eyesight is his trouble so he does not know if he will be accepted.*
> *Otto's (next to the Office) have sold their home and are shifting to Adelaide, it is more convenient for his work. The Tatts winners Reg Kleemann's have bought the place.*
> *It is a lovely place, garden and all, Mr. Otto showed Bert through last week, they spent quite a large amount in having it done up.*
> *Jack Corcoran (from Gramp's) was farewelled on Wed. night, he is in the Air Force and has only been training two months and*

has his call-up. You most probably remember him, he used to go out to Golf, was quite a fair player.

We had our tennis meeting this week and it was decided to try and keep going, but it depends what the Association Meeting decides.

Mr. and Mrs. Alan Howard are on holidays. He has given up his Wine Saloon in Pt. Pirie, and is interested in a Betting shop at present.

Annie is throwing a party for Mrs. Howard tonight.

I have some more sad news, too, Mrs. Liebich from Rowland Flat (wine people) died last week, she was under treatment with Mahomet Allum but was later taken to a specialist she had gone blind in one eye and also had a growth and in a very bad condition. Mr. ('Baldy') Liebich took it very badly indeed, the result was that he has been removed to a home, his mind having gone.

Our lemon tree is again loaded we are going to send a case up north to the Mission, as they are very plentiful around here now.

I wonder if you have received the rug yet? I s'pose you have had a picture show by now too.

We are still picking mushrooms from our patch. Bert picked over five pounds on Tuesday. Mum is trying to dry some now.

Vic Lindner brought us a nice hare this week, Mr. Obst gave us a fowl last week, and Kurtz's killed a pig and of course you know the amount of wurst etc. they usually send us, so you see we can live like a King.

We have had bitterly cold weather again, in fact it was so rough we could not wash this week.

Tante Anna is very poorly she is suffering terribly with Arthritis and is still living on her own.

Mrs. Klaebe (Albert's mother) has been very ill for some time now, and has been taken to Hospital.

Steve sends his regards to you, they have not started on the Power Alcohol yet at the Tarac Co. as they are held up with some of their machines.

Steve's brother Phil who was in Tobruk, has his birthday today and we have sent him a cable. He writes and tells us all about the mice, rats, fleas, dust-storms etc. and water rationing out in the desert.

Well Dad keep smiling, and keep well, and write if you want anything sent to you.

Regards from All
Your Daughter
Else xxxxx

18 September, 1941

The Rodney Shire Council's big roller arrives to roll our tennis courts and grade the Sports Ground.

A General inspects the Camp today. Australian born and naturalised internees are ordered to give their fingerprints. I was NOT called up.

It is Marie's Birthday today. I decorate her framed photo, fixed to the door of my locker, with flowers. I mentioned the date of her Birthday at the picture nights when showing her film, and receive many congratulations this morning as Grandpa of such a charming actress.

A letter from Bert arrives today dated 14 September.

Dear Dad,

By this time you should be in possession of the rug Cliff made for you. There should have been no delay in its reaching you, as I packed it carefully and sent the parcel at Commissioner's Risk rate. I also included 2 two-ounce packets of Fine Cut Tobacco and some papers. Cliff will be pleased to hear what you think of the rug. He wants you to particularly note the one 'blue' skin near the centre of the rug. He told me that the furrier who tanned the skins offered him quite a nice sum for just that one skin.

And while we're on the subject of skins and 'roos, etc., I was chatting with Alf Zander the other day. He sends his kindest regards, and said I should tell you that 'they're breeding the hares now, waiting till you get back.' They still haven't heard anything of Bob. It really is quite an anxious time for them.

Sickness has been taking a toll of Tanunda folk lately, too. Poor old Mr. E.E. Schrapel really does seem to be in his last days, and the doctor says, perhaps only hours. And Mr. Bert Hall had a stroke yesterday, too. He had been in ill health for some time past. Blood pressure, I believe. It never rains but it pours, does it not!

We have been having the strangest of weather during the last week, several days might have been from the middle of winter. And in midst of all this rain, I picked the largest crop of mushrooms yet – five and a quarter pounds. Can you beat that? Mum has tried drying some of them. Somebody had told me that used in soups etc., they add a lovely flavour. We shall see! That mushroom plot of ours has certainly been through all kinds of weather. And anything you want to know about growing mushrooms – well just ask me!

At the office we are still plodding and toiling on. It's not always easy, still we do our best. The Almanac has appeared on the horizon once again, so before we know it, Xmas will be with us.

Adelaide Electric are still about the town, and still we are on the local supply. There is a shortage of electric motors, and that is the main snag at the present moment, so we are told.

The time now is 2.30 p.m., and since 12.45 p.m. we have been listening to a recording over 5 C.K. of 'Handel's Messiah.' Wonderful!

You mention that the Taronga Park film was not amongst the 18 I sent over to you. Yes, I noticed that going through some of your movie material lately. I take it you wish to have this reel also. I *shall be making up another parcel for you soon, and will include it then.*

There is no place like home, but you apparently have ample opportunity for whiling away the time in many an interesting occupation. Wood inlay work must be an intricate art, and very interesting.

Mum wishes me to express her kindest regards, with those of the rest of us, and of course, of all the many enquiries after you.

Your son,
Bert.

19 September, 1941

Intensive work polishing my woodwork tray.

21 September, 1941

Church Service – Missionary Metzner. I showed pictures in the open last night and will do so again tonight. Great success, mainly because of the use of my screen.

22 September, 1941

I am putting the finishing touches on my tray today. There is much thunder and lightning and some rain during the day. Quite an electrical storm.

Helmuth Rothe and Max Abel are celebrating their Birthdays today. Some thirty of us sit down to Kaffee and Kuchen in Café Wellbech to help make this a special day for them.

A letter from Else arrives dated 18 September.

Dear Dad,

Well today was Marie's big day again, her Birthday. We all went up, in fact we nearly did not get there, I walked the last part of the journey.

First of all we ran out of petrol just near the Grape Growers, and was also a blockage somewhere which held us up quite some time but Steve and Mr. Maine and a man from the Tarac came along and soon fixed things up.

Bert took some snaps of Marie, the day was dull, but they should turn out alright and we shall send them on to you. Margaret will write all about the party in detail to you.

Mr. E. Schrapel is still hanging on, I spoke to Mrs. E. and she said the Dr. said it was only a matter of time. One of the employees from the shop usually sit up with him every night.

Mr. Hall is still very low, not improving at all. He had a kind of a stroke, one side of his body is paralysed and he has lost his speech. They have a trained nurse for him now. Poor Mrs. Hall has gone down again, she does not enjoy the best of health either, so Vi has come home to look after her. They are having a bad spin. Dr. Juttner goes to Schrapel's and Dr. Altmann to Hall's.

Hall's have not written to Frank as he is in the midst of Exams.

How is the tennis going and have you started bowling?

Claire Schultz has given up her job at Gramp's, she has accepted a position at the Renmark Hotel (the big new one) as secretary and receptionist. She said she wanted a change and I believe it is a very good job too.

Edna and Frank Fischer had quite a nice honeymoon I believe, Frank caught the measles and Edna had to nurse him.

Kath McGrath's (Tummel) little baby boy has a nasty illness, pink disease I believe it is called, similar complaint to Cliff's little lad, he is not a year old yet. She has had a lot of sickness, her husband is still in Tobruk and the two Tummel lads are over there somewhere too.

We are starting to get interested in Xmas Cards at the Office, Bert wants to get an early start this year, he is very keen. I am going to approach all the so-called 'society women' in the district, the cards etc. have really become very popular, during war time.

The lovely spring days are approaching now, and the gardens are very colourful again.

That is all the news for now. I am hurrying to catch the mail.
Love from all at home
Your Daughter
Else xxxx

23 September, 1941

I finish my tray and pack it to post home. Cost of postage and registration is one shilling and sixpence. With that one finished, I now start on a butterfly for Cliff Laycock, and by Saturday 27th I have got over the biggest part of the cutting out work. The fitting and polishing will take some time yet.

28 September, 1941

Our preacher at the Church service today is Wittmann. An inspiring address comes from this man who, yesterday and for weeks past, has worked on the Sports Ground stripped but for a pair of shorts and sandshoes. I admire the man.

Letters today from Margaret, Ted and Marie, and also one from Bert, both dated 24 September.

Dear Father,

Well, Marie's birthday has gone again. I gave her a little party and will tell you all about it. Firstly she wants to thank you for the belt you sent her, she was very pleased with it and I told her to put it nicely away in her drawer, but instead she went up to the wardrobe and hung it up with her frocks. We gave her a bike which she is greatly taken up with. It is a fairly big one, I think it is about the biggest of the three wheelers you can get. Now a bit about the party. Three girls arrived that I didn't know were coming. They told me that Marie asked them to come, trust Marie, and when one of the little boys arrived (Donald Kaesler it was) he didn't give Marie his parcel right away and that was too much for her so she went up to him and asked him who the parcel was for. Bert came up and took some snaps which all turned out very good. I am sending you three. Else is sending you some more.

Yesterday I went to Adelaide with Hastings and Marie went home for the day. El wanted to take her to the office in the afternoon but she wouldn't go. She doesn't like the machinery, too much like a tractor. But she is quite good with Grandma, only one thing, Grandma says she talks too much.

Sylvia Materne hasn't been too good again, she is in the Rua Hospital, but I believe she is improving now. Ted is kept pretty busy still, Miss Locking is on holidays so he is managing the whole shop.

Well Dad, I think this is where my letter ends. Hoping it finds you well as it leaves us.

Lots of love
From Marge, Ted and Marie.
(Keep smiling Grandpa xxxx)

Dear Dad,

Today has been quite a sad day in the town – Bert Hall died early Monday morning, and I attended his funeral today. The Schrapel family is certainly being hard hit just at present. Old Mr. E. was progressing quite nicely, and everybody expected him to be about again as usual. Then Mr. Hall had a second stroke which completely paralysed him, resulting in his death. This has upset the poor old chap terribly, and most people think he, too, will soon be carried to the grave. It was a large funeral, as you may well imagine.

We received your last letter on Monday, the 22nd, and are all pleased the rug arrived O.K. and that you like it. I saw Cliff at the funeral today and he was pleased to get your letter, he said.

Dad, there is still one matter I am not quite clear on. We have never heard from you whether there are any arrangements in Camp whereby you are able to purchase tobacco, etc. I expect you to say the word regarding smoking supplies etc. Remitting cash to you is of course the simplest way, I guess, but it rests with you. It's hard for me to know just how your tobacco stocks are. I've never heard from you on this subject. That means there are two possibilities – either you have plenty, or you won't sing out. If the latter is the case, well, you ought to know better!

Marie's birthday party last Thursday was quite an event! I took my camera up and I believe Marge has sent or will send you some of the snaps I took. I am enclosing four more which are also quite interesting. I have written an explanation on the back of each snap. I do hope they won't make you homesick too badly. I know how you must feel away from home!

We had another feed of mushrooms last Sunday evening, probably it will be the last picking, as the grass is taking the upper hand now.

We've had the most remarkable weather here lately, too. Dick Hentschke's prophesy of 4 inches of rain during September will certainly not be far off the mark.

I'll sign off now with kindest regards to you from all the many who are always asking after you.

Your son,
Bert

I have also included a copy of my letter to Mrs. Scheiner, dated 24 September, as requested.

Mrs. J. F. Scheiner

59 Cuming Street, Mile End S.A.

Dear Madam,

In a recent letter from my father he mentioned that your husband had done some work for him at Tatura, and that the cost was one pound five shillings. He asked me to forward this amount to you and I have pleasure in enclosing a cheque for that amount.

With best wishes for yourself,
I am
Yours faithfully
W B Schulz.

29 September, 1941

Things are getting hot in the Camp. Waldemar Weber had been allowed to go to Camp 4 to live with his wife. Refugees set to and gave him a hot reception because he apparently aired his Nazi views. A brawl ensued. Interned Italians came to Weber's assistance. One refugee was taken to hospital with a cracked skull and Weber was returned to our Camp with a wound in his head. While all this fighting is going on around me, I am busy working on Cliff's butterfly.

Next day, Weber's case is taken up by our Camp leader, Dr. Haslinger. After a conference with the Camp Commandant, the decision is arrived at that all Jews, Refugees, and Communists be cleared from our Camp. Dr. Haslinger announced this amid applause at the tea table. Personally, I am indifferent to what action is taken. I count some of the refugees I have met as my friends. Some consternation ensues at Haslinger's announcement that it is proposed to make No. 1 Camp a 100% NATIONAL SOCIALIST Camp!

1 October, 1941

Today I receive the photos of Marie taken by Bert at her 4th Birthday. All the Camp knows Marie from the film and talks about her. Herr Eckhard tells me that his little 9 year-old girl is not allowed to place kisses at the end of her letters because there may be secret codes contained!

2 October, 1941

An announcement is made at the tea table: Tomorrow 46 Jews etc. will leave the Camp. There is great excitement as to who will be included in the list. Our Hut leader, Jordan, is included. He is not a likeable fellow. Oskar Johannsen also goes.

All is excitement next day as the list of those who leave becomes known. I meet Herzfeld for the first time. He is a former teacher of German History and of Sport at St. Peter's College, Adelaide. He is also on the list to go. He says he is engaged to Hannaford's (Mayor of St. Peter's) daughter. Hertzfeld knows W. Hebart well.

4 October, 1941

I am spending most of today working on my circular swallow inlay. Also, news from home; a letter from Else dated 30 September.

> *Dear Dad,*
>
> *Thanks for your ever-welcome letter. Mum is anxiously awaiting the tray, which you are sending to her. I suppose it will arrive any day now. We are having terribly wintry weather again now with heavy rains.*
>
> *The golfing season has come to an end. Steve and I cycled out the other Sunday, on the closing day. They played a Tournament and presented the Trophies, and had afternoon tea. It was the first time we had been out this year. They have not made any alterations out there, and it was a glorious day, an ideal picnic day.*
>
> *Our Tennis opening has been postponed until a fortnight later as our courts are being top dressed but the wet weather has held up the workers considerably.*
>
> *Dulcie and Vic. and Steve and I are spending next weekend in Adelaide. It is the Final of the football. Sturt and Norwood are playing and Sturt looks likely to win, and we are hoping for fine weather as the last few matches have been a real washout on account of wet weather. Marion and Alf Cotton are also joining us, so we should have a nice weekend.*
>
> *Our pussycat kindly presented us with 3 kittens last week, two fat black ones and one skinny grey one which yells all day long. Of course, Marie just adores them. Something new for her.*
>
> *Bert sent the money to Mrs. Scheiner, and she also wrote back and thanked us for sending it along.*
>
> *Mr. E. Schrapel is still very low, he grieves terribly over Mr. Hall's death. Mrs. Hall has gone over to stay with Vi now at*

Keynton for a while. Frank is expected over shortly, it was terribly sad, he not being able to come over to his Dad's Funeral as he was in hospital with Mumps. We sent a lovely wreath from the Office, the flowers were beautiful and so many.

I heard the Bowling subscription has gone up to three pounds three shillings this season. I will write more particulars of the meeting next week.

Barbara Drennan and Derrick Trescowthick were married here last Saturday. Derrick is stationed at Parkes, NSW, he is in the Air Force and had a few days leave. Barbara is following in about a month's time and Connie John is carrying on after Barbara.

Today an Aborigine, David Unaipon, came around with books of Central Australia. I told him that you had been up amongst the natives several times and had also written books on natives and taken films. He was quite interested.

Annie and May have gone to Adelaide again today, Annie says she is not well and has to visit the Doctor. Her mother seems to be much brighter again, and they send their kind regards.

The Dan Hentschke's have a baby girl, and Adam has recently become engaged to some girl from Mannum.

Mr. Obst had quite a bad time with his hand. He will be away from work about another week. He was chopping down some trees in the Church yard (near main street) and a blister formed which he opened and then got some dirt into it. He went to Dr. Frank, who opened it, but next night it became worse, so on Friday he had to go to the Hospital and have a 'whiff' and have it opened properly. Poor old Chris. He was apologising all the time for not being able to come to work for a few days.

Mr. Gus Kleemann had a narrow escape on Saturday last. He was working on the new building (Gun and Teusner offices) when a plank hit his head and he fell to the ground. He was taken to Hospital and had six stitches inserted in his head, but luckily no other injuries.

We will see about some shirts for you in the near future. Bert was in the city yesterday, and sent you a half pound of Bauer's mixture for smoke-o.

Cheerio for now. Love from all.

Your daughter, Else xxxx

5 October, 1941

The preacher for our church service this morning is Rev. Meier, and today is Erntedankfest. Harvest Festival. Later, in the Mess, the speaker is Dr. Haslinger. He has composed a special Erntefest Cantate which is sung by his male choir accompanied by his orchestra. A beautiful sound indeed. Then an announcement is made: All internees who have not heard officially the result of their Appeal, to hand in their names. I hand mine in.

Today I receive my copy of the Tatura German Newspaper, Issue No. 1, printed in the Camp.

6 October, 1941

More information is given to us regarding the Appeal: date of internment, date of Hearing, date of arrival in Tatura to be stated. Spender has apparently got to clean-up and things are not 'all clear'.

7 October, 1941

Six Italians, including the giant Mario, receive notice that they must be ready to leave for Loveday tomorrow. I send greetings to Comelli, Capitano and Tony with them.

8 October, 1941

During the next two days Schombacher teaches me the finer points of treating inlay work, filling openings and polishing. He would have me remove all the chelac polish I have on my two inlay pieces and start filling in all the cracks and unevenness. This is more difficult than I had originally thought, but it must be done.

Our older pet Magpie amuses himself with a centipede and then swallows it alive. I spend an hour with Maggie No. 1 hunting for grubs and insects with him. He is very tame and seems to enjoy the company.

10 October, 1941

Dr. Brose has had an interview with the Commandant, Major Bligh, who assures Brose that the Military Authorities do not now look upon the inmates of Camp 1 as National Socialists. This is what we Australian born and naturalised British subjects have been hoping for, and now we have assurance.

I receive a letter from Mum today dated 6 October.

> Dear Dad,
>
> First of all I must thank you very much for the lovely tray you sent to me it arrived in good order. For your first attempt it is really excellent we could not find any fault on it, and it will look very nice when it is quite complete. Yesterday Bert and I spent the day at Nuri. El and Steve went to town for the weekend with Dulcie and Vic. Lindner. The weather was lovely, it was the first fine weekend for months. Marie enjoyed having us up there, she is growing up quite a big girl now and is very smart too. We sent you a parcel a few days ago, you should have it by now, the metwurst is from Mr. J. A. Pfeiffer who also sends along kindest regards to you, the cigarettes are from Steve, the sweets from Margaret and Ted, the

almonds from the Council Meeting, raisins and walnuts from us. Bert has gone back to work again tonight, as Mr. Obst is still away, his hand is still bad, and there is plenty of work waiting.

Alf Pfeiffer's little girl has had Bronchitis very badly, today they had the two doctors but there is no immediate danger. Mr. Schrapel is still the same. Margaret and I went to visit Mrs. Hahn last week she is very poorly nearly crippled on one arm, she seems to be going back a lot, she wished to be remembered to you. Minnie is not well either she may have to have an operation too.

Are you receiving the papers now? El will write later, Bert is a very busy man. I think this will be all for this time.

Love from us all
Mum

11 October, 1941

How different the result after Schombacher sits over me while I polish my Swallow and second Butterfly inlays! I am very grateful for his help.

12 October, 1941

Winkler is the preacher at church today. During the day, Hut 25 turns into a rough-house giving Kuhri severe handling. I don't know the reason but it's a pity all the same because we're all in the one Camp and should be trying to get along together. Issue No. 2 of the Camp Newspaper arrives today, and this evening the Commandant is attending Gruber's Symphony Concert.

13 October, 1941

Summer is on the way and I advance another slow step in the art of polishing.

14 October, 1941

Another warm, lazy day and I attend Dr. Erler's lecture on: The progress of the War in Russia, and America's participation in the War.

15 October, 1941

Today is Lagerdienst: Camp Duties. Drake and I are detailed for Lagersauberung (camp cleaning), thus being spared participation in the one and a half hour Kartoffalsschaldienst (potato peeling duty).

Today I receive from Bert a copy of the letter he has written to Makin in Melbourne, dated 11 October. It reads as follows:

> *Honourable Sir,*
>
> *I have discussed with the Leader of the State Opposition, the Honourable R. S. Richards, the question of further action on behalf of my father, Mr. J. F. W. Schulz, who is at present being detained at Tatura Camp, Victoria, under National Security Regulations.*
>
> *On Mr. Richard's suggestion I am writing directly to you. We at home feel that it may now be possible to investigate more deeply the evidence on which Mr. Schulz is being detained. We have always felt, and our counsel at the time of making our appeal was definitely of the opinion that upon the evidence which was tendered at the hearing, no British subject could be detained.*

The fact that Mr. Schulz's detention continued after the appeal, leaves us with only one conclusion to arrive at, namely, that he is at present being held on a charge or charges against which he has never had the opportunity, due to him in common justice, of defending himself.

I know that you will do what is in your power, to see that justice is done. I understand that you may be addressing a meeting in our section of the district in the near future, and I look forward to meeting you then. I have also written to your Canberra address, in order to reach you without delay.

Yours faithfully,
B. Schulz

16 October, 1941

There is great excitement in Camp today. Three men from the Camp, Lindner, Pentfield, and Stein, while at work outside cutting timber, have cleared out. There is a hunt on outside to recapture the runaways, who, by the way, are avowed Communists. Their bolt is interpreted as a political gesture. The Military pay for voluntary Camp workers outside is two pence an hour or one shilling a day for six hours. The basic wage is, of course, about four pounds and sixteen shillings!

17 October, 1941

No trace of the fugitives as yet and, interestingly, every reference to them in the newspapers, The Age, or The Argus, has been cut out.

Sturzen causes comment with his dictum on the Orderly Notice Board: 'Wir bluten für Hitler.' (We are bleeding for Hitler.) Someone added: 'Bis zu (up to) three pounds and fifteen shillings.'

A good day. Letters from Bert, and Margaret, Ted and Marie dated 12 October.

Dear Dad,

We were all very pleased and relieved to receive your letter dated 5 October. You have our sympathy in your 'teething' troubles. We can understand you wouldn't feel much like letter writing under those circumstances. At least you are rid of the toothache now. I am attaching a Money Order made payable to you at Tatura Military Post Office for the sum of five pounds. Mrs. Scheiner, also, will receive a cheque for two pounds.

Yes, Dad, we have received your first effort at wood inlay, and it has created great interest wherever we have shown it. They all say there doesn't seem to be any 'first effort' look about the job. We are getting Mr. Dernedde to finish it off as a tray when it should look wonderful. I have noted your suggestion re packing tobacco in cigar boxes, and shall enquire among tobacconists far and near.

It looks as though we'll be kept going fairly well between this and Xmas, as we've really only started on Almanac printing. Of course it shouldn't take as long this time as usually, on account of the off weeks, when there is no paper to put out.

(Tuesday, the 14th) Here I am again! I started this letter on Sunday afternoon, and all the time forgot the 8 Hours Day holiday yesterday. So I had to wait until today to get the Money Order. We had a wonderfully fine day for the holiday yesterday, and today the weather was just as nice.

While thinking of it, let me relate the sad tale of our friend, poor old 'Oscar.' For some time past it appears that he had been talking of a job he was getting up at Whyalla. Of course, nobody believed him. But it was true, for one day he went for it good and proper at the Club, so Otto asked him what it was all about and he announced that he was leaving next day for his new four pound and ten shilling a week job at Whyalla. That is the end of Scene One. Scene Two is played at Auburn. In the evening of the day that Oscar left for his new job the local police received a call from the Officer in Charge at Auburn: 'Did they know a man named Hoffmann?' Several. Which one? 'Oscar.' Oh, yes! We know him well, what's wrong? 'I've got him up here in a cell, he's full!' Poor old Oscar. He had apparently done himself well but not wisely on the trip up. In the back of the car he had eleven gallons of wine! I understand the whole joke cost him a cool twenty pounds. He hasn't been seen in the home town lately, so I don't know what happened to him.

Old Ernst Schrapel is still on the sick-bed. Most people think it is just a matter of time, and he, too, will be gone. What a difference all this has made to the business! I suppose Homburg will be in full charge eventually.

Well now, I will conclude and get this letter away to you. All at home, and the many other enquirers after you, send kind regards and sincerely trust you are well.

Your son
Bert

Dear Father,

We received your letter yesterday and were pleased when we received it as we always look forward to news of you. Today is a beautiful day spring weather at last it has also been very wet and cold here too. Your woodwork tray you made is quite a good piece of workmanship we are all greatly taken up with it and also everyone else who has seen it.

Tomorrow Marie and I are going to Adelaide for a few days we are staying with Ted's brother Herb and his family, they have just built a new home at Grassmere. Marie likes to go there as the *children are good company for her. I forgot to mention in my last letter that Mr. Heusler's two grandchildren are also on the snaps at Marie's party with Mrs. Tamke.*

Our garden is looking very nice all the flowers are out in bloom and present a nice sight. The creeper Lorraine Lee Rose over the front fence is just a mass of blooms. Marie is growing a big girl another year and she will be going to school. School won't be anything new to her as she marches and sings with them all now. Next week Marion is coming to stay with us for a while I'll be pleased of her company. The Ladies Hairdressing Saloon at Summertons is still without a Hairdresser and the prospects aren't too good of getting one either so I don't know what will happen there.

We are going down home presently and staying for tea. How lovely it will be when we are all together again which we hope will not be long. Marie still keeps asking about Grandpa and if he is still helping the soldiers.

Lots of Love from
Marge, Ted and Marie

18 October, 1941

Pentfield and Stein have been captured, but there is apparently no trace of Lindner.

19 October, 1941

Strauss is the preacher at today's church service and later on I receive the Tatura Newspaper No. 3. which gives me some reading for today.

20 October – 25 October, 1941

I am well on the way with my fourth piece of inlay work: Hut 28 and adjacent huts. Lindner is captured but none of the three are returned to this Camp. We wonder where they are? I spend time putting finishing touches on two of my pieces of work. Captain Junge asks me to fill in fifteen minutes at the Kammeradschaftsabend (fellowship evening), which I agree to. Dr. Erler gives a lecture on: 'Die Männer um Stalin.' (Stalin's supporters) Interesting. Wiech and I play in the first Bowls match at Tatura Internment Camp. Likewise, interesting! On the 25th we celebrate the opening of the Tennis Courts amid much jubilation.

Today I receive a letter from Else dated 21 October.

> *Dear Dad,*
>
> *We received your letter saying you received our parcel O. K. and were also pleased to hear the toothache trouble had ceased. I am also paying a visit to the Dentist tomorrow to have an impression taken for my set, as it is nearly three months since mine were extracted.*
>
> *Frank Hall was over from Melbourne on ten days leave and was looking quite well after his sickness. He thinks he will be finishing his course in S.A. so that will be nice for his Mother. Mrs. Hall seems much brighter again now and Mr. E. her father seems to be battling along again, although he is still in bed.*
>
> *Mr. and Mrs. Alf Zander have at last heard some news of Bob, after four and a half months of anxious waiting. They received a card signed by him and he is believed to be a prisoner of war in Germany. Poor Mrs. Zander was overcome and had to spend a few days in bed after all the messages and telephone calls and callers. The town was really very happy, it was really good news for all those who knew Bob.*
>
> *The latest weddings now are, Aubrey Wallent and Linda Woidt tomorrow (22 October) and on Saturday Clem Weckert and*

Elva Kretschmer. Clem is a Sergeant now and they will live in the city. Aub and Linda are living with her people, down our way.

Woidt's will have quite a house full, as another daughter who married an A.I.F. man is also living at home with her baby.

Steve left today for his holidays. He is going up to Gladstone again to his sister's place.

Lorna Schultz has been laid up with foot trouble, she has a germ between her toes and the Dr. says it will need some checking as it has advanced quite a bit.

Brian Anderson is still up at Darwin, he has not had any leave for fifteen months.

Mel Goers is a Reservist in the Air Force, and has passed his Medical and is doing some course now. He goes up to Nuri once a week at night for lessons.

We shall be sending you some clothing in a day or two, and hope you find things suitable, there is not such a wide choice in these shops, but if things are not quite right you can let us know and we can try in the city later on. Mum is also enclosing an extra pair of Pyejamer (her spelling) trousers, they were some old ones you still had here.

Are you receiving the papers now? Mrs. Auricht has been in bed for the past week, she is going back very much lately.

E.G. Hoffmann has been in a spot of bother again, poor old chap, I don't know much about it. It appears he was turning his buckboard in front of O. Klose's shop, and some kind motorist caught his front mudguard and bashed it in. No other damage was done.

Our kittens are one month old now they are all so lovely now, Mum does not know which one to kill, so we shall have to keep the lot, of course Marie would like to have the lot.

Last Sunday was Confirmation in our Church, eight children were confirmed.

By the way Dad, we are still picking mushrooms, certainly out of season, but still very delicious.

We are having our first Tennis Match on Saturday against Nuri. I do not know how we will get on for cars and petrol, we are playing two matches a month, one away. Angaston is not joining, so there is only Freeling, Greenock, Nuri and Tanunda in the Association.

The Bowling Club have also formed a Ladies Bowling Club of which Mrs. Hurst is captain.

Mrs. Geoff Russell and baby has been holidaying with Hetty and Helmi. Helmi spent a week in Melbourne recently, a business trip.

There is plenty of work now, the Almanacs have started, so from now till Xmas you will know what work there is.

Measles have been going around a lot, Bert Doering being among the victims, and was hardly out of bed when he got a nasty 'Flu attack and has been away from the shop for quite a while. Florrie Geyer helped in the shop.

Mrs. Hentsch is back again and seems to be quite well too, although she looks very thin, but her husband is delighted to have her back.

I think I have come to the end of my tether once again, hoping you are well and happy.

Bert is enclosing the letter he received from Norman J.O. Makin, Minister for Munitions in Melbourne, dated 16 October. He thought you might like to read it and keep it in your file.

Love from all at home
Your Daughter
Else xxxxxx

Dear Mr. Schulz,

Your letter of the 11th October regarding your father is to hand and I shall be glad to take this matter up with my colleague, the Minister for the Army.
  Later I shall advise you of the result of enquiries.
  Yours faithfully,
  Norman J.O. Makin

26 October, 1941

Last night we experienced heavy thunder, lightning and rain. Today Wittman is our preacher and later I attend the opening of our new Skittle Alley. Swallows have been building nests while labourers work on the alley and the building, and today we see there is a brood of four. The Tatura newspaper No. 4 arrives with more reading for me.

27 October, 1941

I am drawn for a four in tennis today. Schindler, Scherer, Max Abel and I play from 11.15 am to 12.15 pm. Despite the fact that the players are all novices, we agree it is good exercise.

28 October, 1941

Haslinger has apparently got it in the neck from someone. Among the usual evening's announcement, he promises an early reply to those who have implicated him somehow with the Authorities relative to his conduct as Camp Leader.

Krahwinkel, after about three weeks sojourn here, leaves for his Appeal in Melbourne.

My elbow and right arm are giving me considerable trouble after my strenuous tennis yesterday.

29 October, 1941

A slight drizzly rain prevents tennis which is now in full swing.

My letter to Margaret is returned with a note: 'No drawings allowed.' I had enclosed a lead pencil sketch of Marie! Bert has sent me the letter from F.M. Forde, Minister for the Army at the Victoria Barracks in Melbourne, to Makin, dated 21 October, which reads as follows:

> *My dear Minister,*
>
> *I acknowledge your representations of the 16th October on behalf of Mr. W.B. Schulz of Box 83 Tanunda, South Australia, regarding his father, Mr. J.F.W. Schulz, who is at present interned at Tatura Camp, Victoria.*
> *I shall be pleased to have this case reconsidered and will advise you further as soon as possible.*
> *Yours sincerely,*
> *F.M.Forde.'*

30 October, 1941

My arm is yielding to treatment, so, if I can get through tomorrow's tournament, I will be able to continue playing tennis.

31 October, 1941

My arm will not allow any more tennis for the time being. I regret this very much since I will miss very necessary exercise.

9

November, 1941. Pastime and Sport in the Camp.

The first six months of an internee's life in camp are interesting, always excepting the immediate reactions to the deprivation of liberty and freedom. Take the Tatura Camp 1A and B, whose several inmates are 'separated' by an open gate. Close up 1000 men intermingle in an area of approximately 20 acres. Ever and anon you meet new faces. Introductions, and new trains of thought are opened. You know that efforts for your release are definitely and earnestly being pursued 'outside', giving rise to hope that you are not condemned to be His Majesty's guest for the duration, or, keeping you buoyed up with hope. Later you patronisingly listen to recitals by 'newcomers' pursuing efforts similar to your own, long since abandoned as of no avail. You learn new games at cards, take a direct interest in music and song, or sit in silence listening to those at practice. A fairly comprehensive Library stimulates your flagging, sagging mentality.

The entire Camp is controlled by the internees under the supervision, of course, of the Camp Commandant and his staff. Work in the kitchen, the bakery, the canteen and the cafes provides a limited number with employment. Profits from the store, canteen, and café are used to pay a small amount to the men in charge of the above, as also to the men in the kitchen. Any surplus is distributed among the needy. Yet the great majority must simply remain at large. To distract the minds and stimulate the energies of these, the Lagerleitung (camp management) has set about evolving schemes and providing the necessary facilities in various branches of sport.

During August, 1941, a large area of vacant ground was provided by the Authorities to be fenced and got ready to build a Sports Ground. Here the younger athletic section engage in hand and football and conduct athletic events: running, putting the weight, etc. Men with financial means lay down tennis courts, a skittle alley, and initial preparations for a bowling green are even taken in hand. Weeks before the tennis courts are ready, players are busy practising at every point of vantage in the Camp.

The building of the Skittle Alley gives much scope for speculation, comment and criticism when in its initial stages. The slowness with which this work proceeds, and speculation relevant to the finished article evolving from the intricate foundations put down, justify the revised quotation: 'Es ist noch kein 'Bau'-Meister vom Himmel gefallen.' (No master builder has fallen from heaven.) When, however, ultimately the alley proper, with its cement foundation, ornamented with commodious café and small office is an accomplished fact and ready for the opening ceremony, the Lagerleiter's (Dr. Haslinger) congratulatory and commendatory remarks are entirely in place.

Engaged in this preparatory work of providing facilities to those ready to perfect their proclivities, incidentally giving an outlet to amassed superfluous energy, are men who when 'draussen' (out of doors) are engaged in many and varied occupations. Clad in shorts and sandshoes they are paid two pence an hour by the Military Authorities. At the head are men who formerly filled their lungs to capacity in woolbrokers auditoriums, outbidding one another at a quarter pence a time for the golden fleece of the quadruped constituting one of our staple industries, while others, speaking from a different rostrum, the pulpit, to wit, shear their lambkins at a revised rate of pay to that set by the Military Authorities.

And sport is taken seriously. Perhaps not so much in the Skittle Alley where, after numerous futile attempts at delivering the weighty ball scientifically, brawn triumphs over brain and the successive balls unmercifully crash into the assemblage of nine-pins with all the force at the players command, leaving the skittle boys, who have reappeared from the safety zone, to reconstruct another completely wrecked diamond-shaped diagram.

Athletics and particularly tennis are, however, taken most seriously. Novices at tennis are taken in hand and, for hours at a time, balls are tossed at them, which have to be played back according to instructions – always the absolute follow-through movement, forehand and backhand. At the outset, the Camp was fortunate in having first-class exponents of tennis; a quartet of players whom it would have been most difficult to defeat by any four in any Australian country association.

To recompense the promoters of tennis and skittles for their outlay, a small charge is made to players, and the playing areas are usually booked out weeks ahead.

Since the arrival in B Compound of Prisoners of War from overseas, men who had been rescued from the torpedoed 'Arandorra Star' and subsequently had fearful experiences on their eight weeks journey in the notorious 'Dunera' from England to Australia, there had eventuated keen rivalry in sports contests. In tennis they were weak with the exception of one player who had had A Grade continental experience. His forte was cutting and lobbing.

When the Christmas tournaments were scheduled to be played, B Compound had to all intents and purposes no doubles to try conclusion with A Compound. Herr von Zitzewitz, B Compound's player of note, giant in stature, decided upon strategy. A Compound concentrated on fast serves and forcing play. Von Zitzewitz schooled his team on slow but sure service and sky scraping lobs. This style of play, in its very nature, is exasperating. At first it intrigued our men, then it positively annoyed them. The B Compound players couldn't be inveigled into playing 'proper tennis.' B Compound ran out an easy winner in B Grade; comparative novices emerging as ultimate winners.

A Grade was a more difficult nut for von Zitzewitz to crack. He hadn't a player sufficiently able to back him up with a chance against our men.

The fact that the Camp is laid out on the slope of a small, stony hill, has not deterred the men detained here from turning comparatively waste land into flourishing gardens. Suitable fertile soil and manure is supplied by the Military Authorities. The gardens are a pleasing sight surrounding most of the huts in both grounds and the rockeries especially in B Compound. The layout of the gardens was left entirely to the inmates of the individual huts. Practically every known flower is represented in the gardens and here and there small vegetable plots are to be seen. Even at the end of July this year, large tomato plants loaded with green fruit were seen struggling to deliver ripe goods.

The Tatura Camp gardens are unlike many gardens you come across repeatedly where hardy perennials persist in drawing their blooms above masses of weeds which are doing their best to choke them, or some fruit gardens where you catch glimpses of pears and apples on trees which though they present a pathetic, drooping air, still keep on growing simply because no-one can stop them from growing.

At Tatura busy hands are found continually at work; digging, weeding, replanting. Here and there the original layout is being altered, even new gardens taken in hand. In the latter case good-natured banter that the war will be over before the work taken in hand comes to fruition, just makes the busy worker smile, suggesting that he will be quite ready and willing to down tools at the 'all clear' signal.

Films are hired from Melbourne and moving pictures are screened on three successive nights every two weeks. An orchestra and men's choir under the conductorship of the very able Dr. Gruber, the erstwhile conductor of the Viennese Boys Choir, practises assiduously. The periodical concerts given by these bodies are a musical treat.

Meals are prepared and served by a staff of volunteers from among the internees.

***

1 November, 1941

The men who worked over fifty hours at the Skittle Club building get a free afternoon at Café Westwall.

2 November, 1941

I attend the Reformation Service at Church today led by Pilhofer.
    Commencing soon after our midday meal, over 1000 men participate or watch Soccer between teams from A and B Compound. Three teams in relays play handball. Both tennis courts are continually in use, while Skittles, backed up by Café Westwall are in full swing. Few outside could picture life in an Internment Camp of this nature. And all the time Crucifixion goes on elsewhere.
    My copy of the Tatura Newsletter No. 5 arrives.

3 November, 1941

Quite surprisingly to many of us, Graf, Freund-Zinnbauer, Scherer and another are transferred to Camp 4, without notice to our Camp Leader even. The men concerned had apparently made application for this.

4 November, 1941

The running of the Melbourne Cup is relayed to our Camp. No comment about any increase or decrease of hard earned spending money!
    Today the Skittle Club, of which I am a member, has its first game.
    I send my inlay Butterfly picture to Mrs. Cliff Laycock.

A letter from Else dated 31 October arrives and it reads as follows:

Dear Dad,

I have just returned from tonight's mail by which your parcel arrived. My bike did overtime. I could not get home quick enough to see what it contained.

Thank you ever so much for the lovely gift, and I shall certainly treasure it. You are certainly an expert at that kind of work, you would not think it was done by an amateur. I am sure Cliff will be delighted when he receives his parcel.

Tomorrow we hope to play our first Tennis match against Nuri, last week was so boisterous we could not play, but the weather these last few days has been very pleasant and I think it will last.

Yesterday the death occurred of Mr. C.A. Jacobs, he used to live up Basedow Road, and this morning the sad news reached us that Mr. Ben Liebich from Rowland Flat has also passed away. He had been in ill health for some time now, and died from a heart attack. He was also very grieved over the death of his wife some two months ago.

Steve is still away on holidays but returns next week, we have missed him around the place, as he is the local wood chopper and lawn mower. Our garden is looking quite nice now and the roses are all blooming. We have been spring cleaning home here. The large shelf which was in the Lino Room at the Office, we have procured, and have it in the front room and have all the books etc. in it now and the small room is entirely a bedroom now. Bert and I had a lot of fun shifting the wardrobe into the little room. You know how large it is, well we just could not get it into the little room and after taking off all the 'fangly' bits, it was still three quarters too tall, so Bert said 'El we can't be beaten,' so we ended up by sawing the top off!! Bert said if it didn't go in then, well we would saw the whole thing up, but luckily it went in then.

> *An 'Echo', the College Magazine was sent to you today here, and amongst the Old Scholars who had enlisted was Ross's name in the Air Force, so he must have passed.*
>
> *Bert is sending you fifty feet of colour film shortly and we hope you receive it safely. It was his first attempt, it is not bad either, and he hopes his next attempt will be better, of course it is not as good as your pictures, but the idea is there.*
>
> *Mrs. Auricht is continually in bed now, she has kidney trouble too. She always asks after you, and hopes you are keeping well.*
>
> *Mr. Lake has been very ill again with his old complaint, he is suffering terribly.*
>
> *Mum sends her love to you, and says she will write to you next week. She and I are going to spend the day with Marie on Sunday.*
>
> *I will conclude now and hop up and post it straight away so it catches the morning's mail.*
>
> *Cheerio for this time, and thank you once again for the lovely piece of work.*
>
> *Love from all at home*
> *Your daughter*
> *Else xxxxx*

5 November, 1941

At midday today we experience very heavy rain. Although requested, I do not accede to Junge's wish for me to speak at the Kammeradschaftsabend (fellowship evening).

6 November, 1941

Hortze, Lutterby and I build a Laube (shed) adjoining our hut. The Laube was built in measurements to suit the timber.

7 November, 1941

Our second Choir Concert. It is a wonderful success. I imagine Dr. Gruber on a cold wintry day in his red overcoat among about fifteen others peeling potatoes. Half an hour before tonight's concert I saw him sitting on the steps of his hut shining his shoes. And just now I have returned from the concert conducted by him. What a man!

Today I receive a letter, dated 3 November, from Margaret, Ted and Marie and this one is written by Ted.

> *Dear Dad,*
>
> *We received your letter today which we are always eagerly awaiting, and were pleased to learn that you have regained your health, and find plenty to do to occupy your mind. So you have had your first game of bowls, well that is fine, I guess you find that a great relaxation, and with tennis, Skittles, woodwork etc. you must be a busy man. So far we all still have our health thank God, Marie is full of beans and growing like a mushroom, her latest is sewing lessons, she gets some of her mother's coloured threads, and then her 'Teddy's' dress, and does 'feather stitch' as she calls it, she amuses herself for hours that way, her bike she is quite an expert at riding, and usually comes with me as far as the corner when I go to work. We find it a great thing for her, especially when out walking she can get along much better and we too, she also takes great interest in school, in the mornings she goes up the yard, sings the National Anthem with the school children, and then marches into school as they do, I can assure you she is very grown up in her ways.*
>
> *The Barossa district is beginning to look a real picture now with all its orchards and vineyards becoming green and the crops are showing exceptionally heavy, so we are hoping for no frost which I think we have a good chance of escaping this year as the summer*

is drawing nearer. Saturday week we had a severe thunderstorm, although were fortunate enough to miss the hail part of it, but I believe some of the river districts suffered badly, damage amounting to the extent of eighteen thousand pounds so let us hope our district will be spared of that, however that is not for us to decide, at present it is very sultry, and a storm not very distant.

We are gradually getting all our Xmas goods to hand now, and getting the display Department ready as Xmas is not very far away and soon will be behind us again, seems not so long ago we were in 1940. Tomorrow the Melbourne Cup. I guess many will do the brass there. I wonder will there be another 100 to 1 winner turn up, I wish one knew.

We have at last been successful in obtaining a lady Hairdresser, until three weeks ago we hadn't anyone, then all at once we had three applications, so then we had to contract to choose the right one, however that task was easily overcome as two of them were only four days a week, so we gave the full-time one the position, and I think the choice has been justified as she seems very capable, and has a good business knowledge. She started last Wednesday week and has been kept very busy indeed, and by work she has done I think we were fortunate in getting her.

Trusting this letter will find you well and happy.
Your loving children
Marge, Marie and Ted

8 November, 1941

Preparations are in full swing for tomorrow, the day on which Hitler's sixteen comrades fell in the Munchen Putsch (the Munich Riots). Also today, Tournaments between A and B Compounds commence.

9 November, 1941

Our Church service is led by Metzner. Today is a big day consisting of a huge sports programme. The continental champion, von Zitzewitz beats our tennis champion Luyken 6-1, 6-0. There was a big torchlight procession this evening, led by Hemrich, to the shrine erected in memory of Hitler's sixteen fallen heroes. I and a number of others did not take part; instead I read the letter from Bert dated 5 November.

> *Dear Dad,*
>
> *A few lines from me once again. El has more or less assumed the role of chief news writer, and I leave that job to her mainly. Still I know what it is to receive letters when away from home, and you probably feel that more than ever.*
>
> *I have posted on to you fifty feet of Colour Film which I took on Marie's birthday and later. You, as an expert photographer, will soon note the mistake I made. The exposure is fairly O.K. for a part of it, but the latter part, taken in bright sunlight, is rather over-exposed. Anyhow, I hope you will like it. By the way, I posted it addressed to you as a registered packet, so it should reach you safely.*
>
> *Another Tanunda identity has passed into the beyond – Mr. Clem Lake. I understand he suffered terribly right to the last. It was a sad case, as even when Mr. Hall passed away, and that is some time ago now, he wished it might have been he.*

> *We have received your gift to El and you sure are an expert at inlay work now! As regards the cigar boxes, I have chatted the hairdressers and Clarry is getting some ready for you. I hope to be able to send them along to you soon.*
>
> *We have not been forgetting you, I have been interviewing certain people lately, the right people, I hope!*
>
> *Cheerio for the present, and keep smiling,*
> *Your son*
> *Bert*

The Tatura Newsletter No. 6 comes to hand today also.

10 November, 1941

Haslinger makes another of his famous pronouncements concerning those who did not take part in last night's procession. His Gestapo must have been busy. How nauseating the whole management business is developing.

11 – 12 November, 1941

Reading, writing, and working on covering my first cigar box with inlay.

13 November, 1941

Together with a number of others, I am asked into the Orderly Room to sign a receipt for receipt of the following notice:

> *Re Internee No. S3077 – J.F.W. Schulz.*
>
> *With reference to the recent appeal by the above-named to the Advisory Committee in Adelaide, will you please advise this internee that after consideration of the recommendation of the Advisory Committee, it has been decided that his detention is to continue.*

So that's that.

14 November, 1941

Bert sends me correspondence from Makin, dated 8 November, which includes a letter from Forde to Makin, dated 5 November. All of which confirms yesterday's notice. The correspondence reads as follows:

> *Dear Mr. Schulz,*
>
> *Further to my letter of the 16th October regarding your father, as promised, I took his case up with the Minister for the Army, and I am now attaching a reply to my representations.*
>   *I am very sorry to see that the Minister can see no reason to reverse the decision of his predecessor.*
>   *Faithfully yours,*
>   *Norman Makin*

> *My dear Minister,*
>
> *I desire to refer again to your representations of 16 October, 1941, on behalf of Mr. W.B. Schulz of Box 83. Tanunda, South Australia, regarding the internment of his father, Mr. J.F.W. Schulz.*

> *Following an appeal to an Advisory Committee in February last, Mr. Schulz's continued detention was ordered by my predecessor. On examination of the file I regret I can see no reason why that decision should be reversed, and Mr. Schulz must, therefore, remain in internment.*
> *Yours sincerely*
> *F.M.Forde*

Despite this upsetting news, we enjoy a wonderful Kino (cinema) programme today. Also, our gardens are a beautiful picture, and our Laube (shed) nears completion. All is not lost.

15 November, 1941

What a wonderful day for me; Margaret, Else, and Marie visit me unexpectedly. I had written advising no visiting, yet, what a joy to see them and they come again tomorrow and Monday.

16 November, 1941

I am busy all the forenoon getting ready for the afternoon's visit; collecting things for Marie and something for Margaret and Else. A thermos of coffee and plate of cakes, and we have to hurry with Marie's Zoo, but by visiting hour everything is ready. We spend an enjoyable and informative one and a half hours. Later on, I read through the Tatura Newsletter No. 7.

17 November, 1941

Today is the last visiting day of my Margaret, Else, and Marie. We spend a wonderful time and finally a number of friends and others who had learned to know Marie from the film, assemble at the gate to bid them farewell.

After they leave, I sit down and begin working on the first draft of a letter to the Minister for the Army in Canberra, F.M.Forde, requesting a review of my internment here. I must be allowed to return to my home and family soon.

I receive a letter from John H. Biar, I.C.O.S.A. Secretary, dated 12 November, forwarded to me by Bert, and addressed to MRS. J.F.W. Schulz, re the Annual Sports Day donation. The letter reads as follows:

Dear Madam,

After another year's happy play together we must again choose those who have rendered excellent service to their school in the Sports Field. Your husband has given us an Annual Cup and despite your position with which we heartily sympathise, we felt that he would hardly leave this honour go out of the family so I again turn to you depending on your generosity to be the donor of a Cup. Usually he pays us one pound and we go ahead and purchase the Cup we need. As heretofore your Cup will be presented to the winner of the Handicap Championship in Tennis, which is annually conducted at the College. Your favours are much appreciated and do much to encourage students to put forth their best efforts.

Owing to an oversight on my behalf this letter has been left rather late, so would you please reply at your earliest convenience.

Thanking you already in anticipation for your favours,
I am, dear sir,
Yours respectfully,
John H. Briar
Secretary, - I.C.O.S.A.

Bert's reply, dated 22 November, reads as follows:

Dear Sir:

This letter is in reply to your letter of the 12th instant, addressed to Mrs. J.F.W. Schulz. Regarding the Cup usually given by Mr. J.F.W.Schulz, we are sorry that you did not write before going ahead with the usual arrangements.

However, we have discussed the matter here, and I am therefore pleased to foreward herewith the sum of one pound to cover the cost of the Cup. Will you please note that this is from Auricht's Printing Office, who take this opportunity of wishing you every success on your Sports Day.
Yours faithfully,
W.B. Schulz
for Auricht's Printing Office

18 November, 1941

I call at the Orderly Room and ask for particulars relative to my intended letter to the Minister for the Army. The Commandant, Major Bligh, says I shall write my letter in triplicate. He would send it further but could not promise that the letter would reach the Minister.

19 November, 1941

I was present at last night's Sports function when it was announced that the result of Spende-Woche (donations) for Christmas Cheer would be one hundred and thirty five pounds. Today I have my letter to the

Minister typed in Haslinger's Office and contribute five shillings to the Christmas Cheer for the work done. This evening I speak Schlessich (in the Silesian dialect) at the social function and cause much merriment.

20 November, 1941

I hand my triplicate letter to the Commandant. In reply to my question whether I would be advised if my letter did not go on to the Minister, he replied, 'If the letter is not returned to you it will leave here and go to the Minister.'

Here is the final draft of my letter dated 17 November, which reads as follows:

> *Dear Sir,*
>
> *On the 13th inst., just eleven months after I was interned I received a reply to my appeal which was lodged immediately after my internment and was heard during the last week of February of this year. The reply states, that I am to be further detained.*
>
> *Permit me, Sir, respectfully to state the following additional particulars in relation to my appeal and detention:*
>
> *The evidence taken down at the appeal, covered, I think, twenty five typed sheets of foolscap. This was never read to me for verification, but a duplicate was later made available to me by my counsel.*
>
> *I desire to state, that some of the evidence tendered by me is inaccurately recorded, and in one instance at least it is recorded that I replied 'Yes' to a certain question, when my reply was in the NEGATIVE. Much of my evidence is not recorded in detail.*
>
> *With reference to my film shows; for instance, the report simply states that I had given a number of shows for Red Cross and Soldiers' Comfort Funds, and that I was unable to say what amount*

of money was collected. This is correct, as far as it goes, I kept NO records of the moneys actually collected at the shows. All the arrangements: Sales of tickets, money taken etc. was the work of the Committee, which had engaged me. Though I am unable to state the exact total, I knew that I raised just on two hundred pounds in my district and beyond for patriotic purposes, and I asked for less than seven pounds for expenses. When the price of films rose and I found that I was no longer able to buy films for film functions and stage further shows, I appealed to Mr. W. Seppelt of the firm of B. Seppelt & Sons, whom I knew well. Consequently Mr. Seppelt purchased ten pounds worth of films for me.

Soon after the outbreak of war, the Defence Department at Adelaide Headquarters organised Civil Defence Committees in country centres. I attended a meeting convened for that purpose in my home town Tanunda, and was elected Chairman of the Tanunda Civil Defence Committee. At the second meeting of my committee it was decided to draft and forward a circular to every rate-payer listed in the Tanunda District Council Books. This circular was duly sent out with my signature. It asked every householder to state on an appended form how many evacuees he or she could billet in case of an air raid in Adelaide. Within two weeks Tanunda had its quota of two hundred people billeted and I was able to personally hand this list to Lieutn. Col. Bice, Adelaide, within that time. I was complimented by him on the excellent work done.

When preparing for my appeal I naturally produced particulars in reference to my activities as chairman of the Tanunda Civil Defence Committee. Then I learned to my greatest astonishment that the same document had been used by a former internee, Mr. Fritz Homburg, when appealing against his detention.

I might state here, that at the last District Council Elections, I replaced M. Homburg as Councillor for Tanunda.

The minutes and documents in connection with the local Civil Defence Committees work were kept in the Council's safe in the

Council Office, situated in one of Mr. Homburg's office building rooms.

Mr. Homburg was interned some time in October 1940 and through his counsel he must have secured the documents from the Council clerk without my knowledge and consent. You will readily understand how dumbfounded I was to hear at my appeal, the documents referred to as 'Mr. Fritz Homburg's documents.'

Mr. Homburg was a member of the Defence Committee and much of the work tabulating particulars was done by his office staff, but I have a prior right to these documents, which were used by him without my knowledge.

My appearance at the last S.A. elections as a Labor Candidate, when I had been a supporter of the Liberal Party before, should not be misconstrued. The soldier, who answered the call and offers his life's blood, offers his all – he is all-in, and I honestly felt that the government of the day was not making an all-in effort.

The fact that I actually contested this election, though interned, was not a presumptuous or impudent act. The Labor Executive asked me to nominate since, from information gained, they believed that I would be released in time for the election campaign. When it was learned that the Advisory Committee's recommendation was not favourable to my release, Mr. Richards, Leader of the Opposition, who visited me at the camp, saw the Chief Electoral Officer to have my name removed from the list of candidates. The electoral regulations, however, did not allow this after nominations day.

I respectfully ask that my case be reviewed.

Anything that I might have done, which in the eyes of the Military Authorities was deserving of censure, I respectfully submit that my term of nearly twelve month internment might be considered sufficient atonement.

Thanking you for an early review of my case.
Yours sincerely
J.F.W. Schulz. Int. No.3077

Today I have my second game of tennis, but my arm does not like it overmuch. Thinking of home, as I often do, I realise my visitors will have reached there by now.

21 November, 1941

I weigh myself and turn the scale at thirteen stone three pounds against fourteen stone four pounds on my arrival here. But I feel all the better for the reduction in weight.

22 November, 1941

Rather an important day today. The Minister for the Army, Mr. Forde, visits the Camp on a tour of inspection. Dr. Brose, Mr. Burkard, and two or three Queenslanders manage to have a word with him. I also line up but fail to get an interview. It was not the Minister's fault.

23 November, 1941

Church Service, and the preacher is Wittmann. The day is very hot but with a sudden cool change, to our relief. Am reading the Tatura Newsletter No. 8.

24 – 27 November, 1941

My tennis arm continues to trouble me and during this time the weather is exceptionally hot, especially on our regular Skittle day. The Kino machine refuses to function; the lamp has fused so we have no show. I donate horse hair for the doctor to sew Hohnemann's severed and profusely bleeding vein.

28 November, 1941

Second washing day with Helmuth Rothe. I get letters from Else and Margaret, dated 24 November, saying they have reached home safely.

> *Dear Dad,*
>
> *Well, we arrived home safe and sound after our trip, a little tired of course, but nevertheless very happy after our trip. Marie was an excellent traveller, she enjoyed every minute of it. Bert was at the station to meet us, and we had to wait a while. As he had an appointment with Mr. Ward. We met about an hour later and Bert was in high spirits, he had a very successful talk and everybody feels very confident and expect to hear a reply shortly. Tonight there is a Labor meeting in the Lodge Hall. Bert and Steve have just gone, I believe there were some men coming up from Adelaide.*
>
> *Everyone was anxious to hear news of you when we arrived back and are all hoping to see you back soon.*
>
> *We managed to keep the tarts till we arrived back here, they were still quite tasty.*
>
> *Steve has been notified of a move back to Angaston, this time in charge at Yalumba, he is quite pleased about the appointment. There are quite a few changes in the district and Steve most probably will take over early in December.*

Today I started full-time at the Office, there is plenty for me to do now.

We were unfortunate not to get the Cookery Book after all, Bert was quite upset, but he says, 'All right if the Barossa News can be tough so can we.' Anyhow, Bert says they certainly will not make too much on it, as the blocks are ours. The minute the Almanacs are over he says, then on his bike for jobs.

Mum said they had to smile when your letter arrived here and we were well on our way to see you. I pressed some of the flowers and was able to bring them home. I hope they will keep, as a souvenir.

The Adelaide Electric Supply is here in full force, things are beginning to take shape now and the change-over is expected within a very short time now.

Mrs. Auricht is still about the same now, but she seems to be getting weaker, I noticed the change in her after only a week's absence.

Gus Niejalke from Matt's shop goes into camp next week for the duration, he had an interest in poultry and has to sell the lot now. Mum is thinking of purchasing a few younger fowls and kill off the old ones.

Mrs. Hentsch is quite well again, and she is out with her 'hubby' quite a lot now, and she is looking extra well too.

Well I think I have run out of news, so will say 'Cheerio' for now.
Lots of love from all at Home.
Your Daughter
Else. Xxxxxx

Dear Father,

Well here we are home once again and quite pleased to get back after our long journey. We were not so fortunate coming home our carriage was booked out. Fortunately when we arrived in Melbourne from Tatura El went and booked our seat for our return journey and luckily got the last three seats. I tried to book a sleeper going back but no hope, was just told I'd have to book about a month ahead for that, but anyhow Marie had quite a good sleep, she slept from nine o'clock to four thirty next morning so she did have a bit of a sleep, but nevertheless I enjoyed the break and furthermore were pleased to see you again and to find you well and that we were able to brighten your outlook again.

Ted is quite well and was pleased to see us back again. Our garden is looking lovely now. It is surprising how it went ahead in the short time I was away. We have been picking a tremendous lot of strawberries this morning. I picked a quarter dipper full again. Marie just loves them especially with cream. Well Dad this seems to be all I'm able to write about this time hoping this finds you well as it leaves us.

Lots of Love
from Marge, Ted and Marie.
Keep smiling Grandpa.

29 November, 1941

I had to spend an hour outside last night on account of Franz Drake's snoring. A very hot, windy day today; the hottest so far and it neared the century.

30 November, 1941

At last, a wonderful cool change. The Free French have a second fight. More reading for me; the Tatura Newsletter No. 9 arrives.

1 December, 1941

Cold and wet today for the opening of the gate to B Compound. I am surprised at the amount of work which has been done on the Tennis Courts in B Compound.

2 December, 1941

I decline Junge's request to speak at Kammeradschaftsabend (fellowship evening) for reasons I have stated before. I start work on my second cigar box, and this evening, once again, I sleep outside to escape the snoring.

3 December, 1941

A huge change in the temperature and woollens are required against the cold. We now have a wireless in Mess 4 and Café Wellblech. Sorry about Jacky Wilson on Sunday.

4 December, 1941

A very cold, wintry night. The day is also cold and I need to resort to covering myself with blankets during the day. I receive letters from Mum and Bert, dated 30 November:

> *Dear Dad,*
>
> *It is quite a while since I wrote to you.*
> *Last week we had a heat wave it was very hot for a few days. The heat made Mrs. Auricht very weak, the Doctor calls nearly*

every day to see her, she has been laid up for six weeks now, and the rest has completely healed her wounds on her legs. The girls enjoyed their trip over to you very much and we were all pleased to hear all the news from you, Marie looked very tired and grubby after her long train journey. Our garden looks quite nice now the flowers all blooming we hear you have very nice gardens too. El pressed some of the flowers to show us. Helmi's mother came to visit me and I gave her the toys for the little boy.

Marie loves her animals and she plays with them such a lot. This year I have no chickens as there is plenty other things to see to. My vegetable garden looks quite nice now, we have quite a lot of our own vegetables now. We had about four cases of lemons they are very useful.

Tomorrow night the choir is having a concert at Geyer's. Bert, Helmi, El and Adeline, are singing a quartet, they were here last night at our place to practice. Hope these few lines find you in the best of Health as they leave us.

Love from
Mum

Dear Dad,

It is quite a time since I last wrote to you. You have had visitors and all. We at home didn't know what to think when your letter arrived saying that you didn't want anyone to come and see you. And we knew all along that a day or two later Marge and El and Marie would be with you. And from their reports you didn't mean what you wrote, which was as we had expected. Apart from them coming to see you, both El and Marge were in need of a holiday, so they decided to come and see you.

As you have no doubt thought, when wondering about things in general at the Office, we are in full swing with Almanac work.

And El is certainly a wonderful help. She really takes an interest in the work, and that means everything. We are somewhat later this year than last, with the Almanacs, but we will have them completed in good time, we expect. Last night, (Saturday) at 10.30 p.m. I finished packing away, ready for the Post Office, the twelve hundred Queensland Almanacs. And here is our programme regarding this lot, showing what a help El is. Thursday morning: All Qld. Almanacs had been glued ('eingespannt') and Alfred had only about two hundred to staple. At 10 a.m. El and I started binding in earnest, with Alfred handling the presses, and at 6 p.m. we had bound one thousand and twenty. Now that's not bad going, you must admit. Next morning (Friday) we finished the binding, and after lunch I started trimming the Almanacs. That night the whole twelve hundred Almanacs were ready for packing. Starting Saturday morning with the packing, I went back to work in the afternoon and evening, and the Qld. Almanacs are now ready for posting. About five hundred were taken to the Post Office Saturday morning. As I said to one of the others, we've only got another three thousand to bind and pack, and they're finished! But how thankful we are for such work. As you will no doubt realise, it's not all beer and skittles nowadays.

I fancy El mentioned the Cookery Book to you while she was with you. Well, we didn't get the job. I did my damnedest, but it was no good. George, the Secretary, was on our side, and one or two others, but there was no hope. Our price was cut in a, well, low-down is the only word, manner. I rammed the fact for all it was worth that right back at the time when the new Cookery Book was put out, you did all the slavery as far as the get-up of the book was concerned. But that meant nothing to the bulk of the present Institute Committee. You see, since that time, the Committee has been entirely reformed, and now includes three, yes, three members who are financially interested in the 'B.N.' Two guesses why they are on the Committee.

Anyhow, little affairs like this are not necessarily forgotten in a hurry. Until Xmas we will have almost more work than we can handle, and after that, well, it won't be our fault if we're not in on anything that's going. For a fair while now, we have been trying to get people out of the habit of thinking that the only people who can do their printing are in the city. Happily, it seems that one or two are gradually waking up to the fact that not every country printer is just another country bumpkin.

Regarding malley stumps for making up pipes, I must confess that I still haven't sent anything along to you. I have discussed this matter with Alf Zander. He knew all about the job the minute I mentioned it. He told me he had made two pipes for Bill Bietz to take away with him. Bill had promised him the world in return, but Alf had never received anything from him. Alf reckons the white mallee is the best for the job. Red stuff is too brittle. And another thing he used to do was to turn out the holes while the wood was still in block or rough form, as he found it was usually rather brittle. I hope to be able to let you have some suitable pieces of wood within a day or so.

And now the latest newsflash: we are working on Adelaide Electric Supply current! It was turned on for us on Tuesday last, at 10.30 a.m. And jolly fine too! One certainly has to hand it to them when it comes to organisation. When we turned on the power our machines ran at just the right speeds, all of them. But there is one little hitch, the little half h.p. motor we used on the platen press in the hand-composing room. Some weeks ago our own motor conked out, you know, the one we purchased from the Institute. Well, Ad. Electric maintain it's our funeral, and that we've got to fix it up before they put a new A. C. motor in. I maintain that we shouldn't stand the cost, as they should have changed over back in August last. It's not our fault that they were unable to. Anyhow, the argument is still on. If they want to be tough we can be too! As a final resort though, do you think you could suggest seeing one of the heads of the A.E.S.Co. who came to see you while the proposition of Adelaide current was still being discussed. Some of those chaps ought to remember that you did quite a lot to help them. I have been told that each of the fellows that was about the place while the change-over was in progress was a little boss on his own, so I've said no to them all. I will wait on your early reply and any suggestions. As far as we are concerned there is no hurry to put the motor into commission. Goodness knows we've put enough thousands through under foot power!

Old Ernst Schrapel is certainly a miracle man. A few weeks ago he was at death's door. Nobody held out any hope for him, often his brain failed and he was quite childish. And yet last week he was over at the shop once again! However, he was taken over in a wheel-chair, but for all that it does seem a miracle.

The day I called at the Adelaide Railway Station for the girls on returning from their visit to you, that is, last Thursday week, I posted on to you, or rather, I had the tobacconist post on to you a half pound pipe mixture. Unfortunately, I was unable to secure the mixture you used to have. I hope you will like it though. Skinny Winton stopped in the street the other day and said he reckoned he had a mixture that you would like. I got him to make up four ounces, which I will be sending on to you within a day or so. Please let me know how this last lot suits you, or both lots for that matter, so that I know just what you like.

A local branch of the A.L.P. has been formed at Tanunda. Quite a lot of interest has been aroused, in certain matters particularly, and though one may receive a setback along one line of action, one doesn't despair. Lots of things give us ground for hope.

My committee instructed me to approach Mr., or rather the Honourable, N.J.O. Makin to see if he would consent to open our next Show. He has accepted, so we will have quite a newcomer at our next Show.

> *Nobody seems to know anything at all of the fate which befell our Oskar! He hasn't been seen in the home town since his tragic trip to Whyalla which ended at Auburn or Watervale, I forget which.*
>
> *Lots of people send their kind regards, nobody forgets you! Helmie and Cliff, and Clem, Aug. and Theo. Even Otto Klose was asking after you the other day. My letters may not be as frequent as the others, but I feel you will understand. It isn't as though I forget you. I have been kept going all along and am pleased to say that I haven't felt better for a long time. Sometimes one gets a bit down in the dumps, this crops up and that crops up, but we just carry on. Everyone does his best. There's always something funny cropping up. The Annual Club meeting was held last Thursday night. I didn't attend, but they tell me there were nearly some fireworks. Somebody brought up the suggestion that a member having liquor interests should not be a committee-man. (This was obviously aimed at Fritz Basedow). Imagine the uproar! Someone yelled out: 'What the hell does it matter, Bassie's Claret is the best,' and so on. Other complaints came in that about the only wine served if you didn't specially ask for something, was Bassie's. I understand it all blew over, but there were plenty of hard words. By the way, Artley is out of the Committee (he resigned voluntarily). The new President is Charlie Hurst. I must close now; it is 11.45 p.m.*
>
> *Love from all*
> *Bert*

5 – 6 December, 1941

The weather is still cold and we also have rain. To ward off a cold, I spend most of the day under my blanket reading. I receive a letter from Mrs. Laycock, dated 2 December:

Dear Mr. Schulz,

I was surprised and delighted to receive a parcel from you. The tray is lovely and, I guess, you spent a lot of labour on it; thank you very much.

Cliff had another trip, with the Brocks, earlier this year, and sincerely wished you were with them. They had quite a good time, although the weather was not so good on their way home, and nearly left them bogged by the wayside.

No doubt you have heard that both Os. and Stan are married. Os. has built a new home, near his Orange Garden, and Stan has the old home, which has been renovated.

Cliff is very busy, he has a long job at Seppeltsfield, painting all the Winery Buildings, and usually does any work in the shop, at night and over the weekend.

The Hentsch's are living across the road from us. Mrs. Hentsch was very sick for months, and was eventually taken to town, where she made a rapid recovery, and now appears to be her old self again.

It is blowing a gale here today, almost like a winter day, as it is so cold. We have had marvellous weather for the vines this year, no frosts and plenty of late rains.

Only another three weeks to Xmas; we intend spending a week or two at the shack, mainly for the Kiddies' benefit. Coral had her tonsils removed recently, and has not fully recovered, so needs the holiday.

Both Cliff and I send our very Best Wishes for Xmas and the New Year, and hope to see you back home soon.

Yours sincerely,
Malie Laycock

7 December, 1941

Rain but not cold. We receive news of tension between Japan and America. More reading of the Tatura Newsletter No. 10.

8 December, 1941

Japan attacks American possessions in the Pacific; Philipines, Guam, etc. Now the world's all-in. God protect us! A disturbing letter from Else dated 4 December arrives today:

> *Dear Dad,*
>
> *This is just a hurried note to tell you of Mrs. Auricht's condition. She has been very low for the past few days and the Dr. has said to be prepared for her end anytime. She has been having injections and the Dr. did not expect her to live through last night, but she rallied early this morning and today seems to be more composed. She has not taken any nourishment for the past two days, she is too weak. I stayed with Annie last night and again tonight as she does not want to be in the house alone now. Meta Graetz has also been helping she is excellent help at a time like this.*
>
> *Mrs. Auricht spoke clearly for the first time in a week this morning after we had called our Minister and she prayed a few words together with him. He calls in every day and has been very good to Annie too.*
>
> *We received your letter last night and I was pleased to hear once again that you received the mug.*
>
> *Our Choir had a social evening on Monday night at Geyer's, it was a huge success. Addie, Helmi, Bert and I gave a quartette, 'The*

Long Day Closes,' which was much appreciated. Then on Tuesday night, the Committee of the 'Queen of the Navy' in the recent Queen Competitions gave Steve a surprise farewell in the Supper Room. They thought it nice to give him something for all the work he did, and presented him with a nice reading lamp. It was a great surprise for him.

Steve's brother Phil is now in Palestine from Tobruk.

Annie said would you please convey the news to Willie and he to his wife please, as she does not feel like writing at the present.

I must conclude now and will write more over the weekend.

Love from all at Home.

Else xxxx

9 December, 1941

The wireless room is packed daily for news from the Pacific. Today I receive a telegram from Annie Auricht in Tanunda informing me of her mother's death. It's not clear from the wire, but it seems that Mrs. A. died on Monday.

10 December, 1941

Mrs. A's funeral is probably today. I'm satisfied that Bert and the other men at the Printing Office will do the right thing. I will perforce have to let the future look after itself.

Sensational news today of the loss of two ships, the Prince of Wales and the Repulse. Please God, be with the families of those lost.

11 December, 1941

A hot day. Japan meets with phenomenal success in the Pacific. BUT, may he never step on our shores! I receive a letter dated 7 December from Margaret, Ted and Marie, written by Ted:

> *Dear Dad,*
>
> *I guess you have received Margaret's letter, and learned they have arrived home safely. Today she is busy packing and getting prepared for tomorrow. As we had an opportunity for she and Marie to go through to Renmark for several days, I thought it a good idea, as I have a sister living there. So far we are all well thank God, Marie is full of beans, at present she is singing the Song of Australia to the top of her voice, which of course does not help letter writing very much, but as long as she is well and happy that is all that matters. Just now she is not very happy, as she has just fallen from her bike, and the melody is very much different to what it was a few minutes ago, however the fall was not serious. The past week the weather has been very cold, almost like winter again, and today we had some nice rain, which is very nice for the garden. Xmas very near now.*
>
> *On Tuesday Margaret went to town with Hastings, so she took Marie to see Father Xmas, but Marie wasn't having any, she is still afraid of him.*
>
> *No doubt you are an expert on woodwork, that box you made for Margaret, and the animals, is indeed a fine piece of work. Marie is very thrilled with her animals believe me, she has them displayed in her room, everyone that has seen the work you have done, think it a wonderful achievement.*
>
> *The Nuri bowlers are going strong this year, the green is perfect, like a billiard table, and easily the best in the district in fact one of Adelaide's bowlers, Mr. Hogben, said it is quite the best in the State. I don't know if you know of him he plays with Eldrige in*

the pairs I understand. We are about to take a run home now. Trusting this brief note will find you well. Love from all.
   Your Children
   Marge, Marie and Ted.

12 December, 1941

Very hot and tiresome all day. Not much enthusiasm.

13 December, 1941

TWELVE MONTHS since my internment. I receive a letter from Else dated 9 December:

Dear Dad,

I wonder if you received the telegram we sent you yesterday (8th) afternoon informing you of Mrs. Auricht's death. She lingered for five days, we expected her to go any time. I was down there most of the time with Annie, and Sister McGrath (Kath Tummel) was there the last two nights. She was unconscious all the time and had no nourishment the last days and she passed away quite peacefully at a quarter to one p.m. on Dec. 8th. Mrs. Auricht was seventy two years old. Mrs. Weckert made a wreath from our family, quite a nice one for five shillings, and one from the Staff at the Office from Spooner's at fifteen shillings, with a lovely sash on which Bert printed in Gold --- 'Mrs. G. Auricht – Always remembered by the Staff of Auricht's Printing Office'. It was pink and mauve and looked beautiful. Annie has made no plans for the immediate future. She is going away for a while first to Mrs. Daly and then to

Sabel's. Quite probably she will rent the house and keep a few rooms for herself, but she has said nothing definite yet.

We have been working day and night at the office. I am going back in a few mins. There has been more work coming in so we are quite happy. I had intended going fruit cutting at Plush's starting Jan. 2nd, but Bert informs me I shall be on full-time again after Xmas.

Steve started at Yalumba today, he is very pleased of his transfer there.

Margaret and Marie have gone to Renmark to Ted's sister's place for a few days. They had the chance of a ride both ways, so accepted.

It was very warm again today, I suppose you are having it now too. Mum is well and sends her love, she will be sending you a Xmas parcel later on.

Bert hopes you enjoyed his letter, he does not get much time to write, but when he does it is ten pages!!!

I must conclude now,
Lots of love from home.
Your daughter
Else xxx

On 13 November, 1941, I received the official reply to my appeal which was heard in February: Further detention. Today I receive the following in reply to my letter to the Minister dated 20 November, 1941. (This is not dated or signed and apparently does not emanate from the Minister for the Army's office.)

Re Internee No. S.3077, Schulz, Johann Friedrich Wilhelm. Appeal for Review of Decision of Advisory Committee / South Australia.

It is advised that after consideration of the above application, it has been decided that as no new evidence has been produced, Schulz's application for a review of the decision of the Advisory

Committee cannot be granted. May the internee be informed accordingly.

So that's that, AGAIN!

Today is the hottest day so far. I sleep outside on a form, and sleep well.

14 December, 1941

Very hot and windy, but I am told a weather change is in the offing. I have coffee with the Meiers when Missionary Martin of the Gold Coast, South Africa, relates his experiences. The Tatura Newsletter No. 11 arrives for my perusal.

15 December, 1941

A cool change sets in, and how welcome it is.

16 December, 1941

I take part in a route march to the Waronga Water basin in a party of about one hundred. Most of the men go in for a swim though it is somewhat cold. I decline the offer. Ern Pohl and Adamers leave for the Refugee and Jews Camp. He says his Solicitor, Howard Vaughan, is responsible for the change-over.

17 December, 1941

Another camp inmate, Henzel of Hut 20, goes out of his mind. God preserve us our health.

18 December, 1941

Another very hot day. I get a wonderful parcel from Mum. Later I go to see the Official Visitor.

19 December, 1941

Parcels from Ted and also from Bert arrive for me. The bent-stem pipe I asked Ted to send me yesterday has arrived today. I sleep outside overnight and in the early hours of the morning, have to hurry inside because of rain.

20 - 21 December, 1941

The temperature finally recedes to agreeableness. Missionary Baer takes the Sunday service this week, and later we begin our Christmas celebration activities.

22 December, 1941

I receive two letters from my family today, dated 18 December; one from Else and Bert, and one from Margaret, Ted, and Marie:

Dear Dad,

'A very Happy Xmas' Dad from all at home. We hope you received the parcels O.K. and with it went our very best wishes for you, we shall be thinking of you during the Xmas days and hope there will be no more away from home. It seems hardly possible that a year has gone by, and things certainly look dreary now, but we must all face the future bravely now.

It has been hot here, no doubt you have had it warm too, it is a pity we cannot bring you nice cool bottles of lemon squash this Xmas, but I daresay you can get drinks.

Well, we managed to get through the Almanacs all right, my first experience of 'Almanac time'. We included a Qld. Copy in your parcels, as the various times given in the calendarium will be O.K. with Vic. time and you will know best when the moon rises, and when it is time to put in your seeds etc.!! (This is Mum's idea so it must be O.K.)

At present the main job here is printing beer labels, we have an order of eighteen thousand labels in all, for the various Hotels in the district. They seem to like our work. Bert gets pretty dry by the end of the evening!!

The Evacuation scheme for which you worked so hard, and which was so highly praised by the heads in Adelaide, is now being put into actual practise here. The Chairman of the Council is now at the head of the scheme.

Annie is spending Xmas at Freeling and then intends coming home again for a while.

The Choir has been busy practising for Xmas again, and this year we are practising some Chanting, introduced by our Minister. It is fairly hard to sing as we have never done anything like it before.

By the way, I nearly forgot. I went out selling Almanacs this year, and sold fifty five in a day and a half. It was a bit strenuous as the weather was pretty hot, but I managed to 'snaffle' a few bob.

I am writing this at the Office so must close now and get it into the post, once again, 'Wishing you a Happy Xmas and New Year'. From all at Home.

Dear Dad,

Just a few lines in the midst of all the heat and bustle of a real 'scorcher,' to wish you an enjoyable Christmas. That is, as far as circumstances will allow.

Nobody is having a very easy time at present, but while we are well, and able to take up our share of the burden nobody will grumble.

I am attaching a M.O. for five pounds, made payable to J.F.W. Schulz at Tatura Military P.O. We trust it reaches you safely and that it will help to bring a little cheer to your Christmas. When this letter reaches you, the various parcels we forwarded should be in your hands. Various well-wishers have helped with different items, and Gert and Steve, who also wish you the best.

With love,
Bert

Dear Father,

We received your letter today, and believe me we can never open your letters quick enough when they arrive.

On Tuesday we posted a little Xmas parcel for you, and included a pipe for you but unfortunately it's not a bent-stem one, Ted knows you like those best but didn't have one in the shop. Another few days and Xmas is here again, my word a lot has happened in the last twelve months, hasn't there? There is not much Xmas spirit about this year the world is not too bright. Ted's two men left to go into camp this morning for the duration so he is only left with two lads so will have to manage the best they can, there are certainly not the lads about either as those most of them have gone to camp. No more night shopping either all shops closed Xmas Eve included.

We have had some very hot weather this last fortnight and very hot again today, but a change is in sight. Marie doesn't seem to feel the heat she never complains. She is still scared of Father Christmas, on Tuesday there was a Xmas party in the hall for the school children and I took her along to see Father Xmas. She told me she would go and tell him what she wanted for Xmas (which happens to be a pram) but it was a different tale when we got there. I told her Father Xmas wouldn't bring her one if she didn't ask him but she calmly told me he didn't have any prams, so that was that. If anybody asks her whose little girl she is, she tells them Grandpa's little girl.

We came back from Renmark last Friday, had four days up there and my word was it very hot up there. But it was nice to see Ted's sister again. Marie was only sixteen months when she last saw her. We went up with a Mr. Hogben he is a superintendent of the A.M.P. He really wanted Ted to go with him which unfortunately was impossible, so Ted asked if I could go along instead it was too good an opportunity to miss so we went.

Well dear father I think this is all the news for this year I'll end my letter, hoping the next year will have brighter things in store for us all. Good luck to you for the future and may your Xmas be as happy as possible is the sincere wish of Margaret, Ted, and Marie.

Keep smiling Grandpa xxxx.

P.S. You will note Margaret said I had no bent-stem pipe but it is one, she must have been too excited to notice the stem as she packed same. Hoping you will enjoy pipe and two tins of Vice Regal, nuts and raisins, Campie etc. Again wishing you the best. Ted.

***

Christmas Preparations and Celebration

Days before the actual festival of Christmas, preparations were going on apace to create an atmosphere providing the Camp inmates with a 'merry' Christmas. Hundreds, if not thousands, of small stars cut from thin cardboard, containers of cigarettes and other articles of merchandisable value saved at the canteen and covered with silver and gold paint, were being got ready by willing hands.

Around the twenty second of December, pine trees and pine tree branches, addressed to Internment Camp 1A, Tatura, arrived at the large double gates leading from freedom to us. The smaller branches and twigs were cut from the larger branches and, after having been steeped in a lime solution and nailed to the rafters of our three large Mess rooms, were then adorned with myriads of shining stars swaying with every breeze. This vista transferred us to scenes similar to those cherished in the memories of many of the internees.

The fact that we had, of necessity, to partake of our meals under this festive canopy a day before Christmas Eve actually arrived, of course, robbed the glorious event of that expectant surprise unequivocally associated with it. But there were still surprises in store for us.

To begin with, those of us who have their dear ones here received parcels from home, in most cases days ahead of Christmas. Surprises! Many a tear fell unabashed onto the wrappers of the smallest parcels as they were taken from the larger container and unwrapped.

Possibly never before have I prayed so fervently that God grant my dear ones a glad Christmas and that He bring Peace on earth and restore a feeling of Good-will of man towards man.

24 December, 1941

Christmas Eve arrives in the Camp and I also receive the Tatura Newsletter No. 12. Programmes had been set out by the Lagerleitung (Camp Management) for the entire festive week. Under trying weather conditions there was an assemblage in Messe 1. Musical numbers by combined orchestra and choir, including the Hallelujah chorus, were conducted by Dr. Gruber. An address was given by Dr. Haslinger and then all were asked to assemble in the three large Messrooms where tables were laden with good things for everyone, including a plate holding fruit, cakes, nuts, as well as a quart pot of steaming hot delicious cocoa.

There were no electric lights, but numberless candles in sets of three flickered on the long tables. The Christmas tree, also, had its candles ablaze. The tree was of a different species of pine than the kind we know in South Australia. Not only was it different in appearance, but when occasionally, by accident or design, a branch singed or caught alight, the smell of burning pine was different; it didn't assimilate with our reminiscences of our childhood days.

Nevertheless, we were enjoying ourselves like children. In due course Father Christmas arrived. Having said his piece in original verse, he called up the Hüttenfuhrers (Hut Leaders) one at a time, and with a further short rhyme and the accompaniment of much cheering, the hut leader received the big parcel containing individual parcels for the inmates of his hut. My parcel contained: a pound tin of tropical salad, two-ounce Campion Ruby cigarette tobacco, two rolls of sweets (Steam Rollers and Thirst Quenchers), a block of cheese, and fruit. We went to bed late (or was it early?) on Christmas Eve. I slept outside.

25 December, 1941

Very, very hot weather. Christmas Day is duly observed: Church Service and orchestral music were the morning's programme. Relative to the

Church service and speeches made in the Camp during Christmas, I feel constrained to say that they conveyed nothing of the essential Christmas tidings. They spoke of and looked to a potentate of this earth to free mankind of all earthly ills and right all wrongs, instead of to the lovely child in the manger.

On the eve of Christmas Day, the Camp was promised a surprise. It came in the form of a picture show featuring the German film, 'Der Bettel-Student'. ('The Surprise Packet') A surprise packet it was indeed for which the Lagerleitung deserved in full the applause that greeted the appearance of the film. Once again, the film showed the marked difference between Hollywood and Continental productions. 'Der Betel-Student', apart from lacking nothing in the way of acting, portrayed simple, realistic love scenes, dialogues of original wit and humour; clean, wholesome, devoid of morbid, sensual chapters of sex appeal.

26 December, 1941

Hotter still. Another man, Grunow, becomes unbalanced. Early in the morning he is at the gate with his things ready for home. It is interesting to note the remarks of other 'half-wits' in reference to poor Grunow; remarks which I will not lower myself to record.

I have my own dinner in the hut – Crab, followed by Fruit Salad (ex Christmas present). Today I receive a card from August Geyer incidentally advising that Darwin evacuees have reached Tanunda.

27 December, 1941

I shifted my sleeping gear outside again last night. Soon the wind sprang up and dust, pebbles, and cinders gave me an uncomfortable half hour. But I persevered and soon the wind died down and, after a round with the mosquitoes, I have a better night than those inside the hot huts. Toward this evening a welcome cool change sets in.

28 December, 1941

A comparatively cool and pleasant day.

29 December, 1941

The thieving in this camp is terrible. My quart pot disappears overnight. There's a dog fight and our camp dog, Schnapps, wins.

30 December, 1941

Worked almost all day on tree inlay. Windy, dusty, but cool weather.

31 December, 1941

I receive a Christmas surprise packet from home: five pounds. The hut opposite ours is using flame throwers to exterminate the bugs in their beds.

New Year's Eve Celebrations.

New Year's Eve also brings its surprise: A pint of beer for each internee! At a cost of ten pence per man. I have been detained fifty four weeks. A pint of beer!

    The weather is warm. We sit at our accustomed table in the Mess Room. There are twenty tables in the room. The tables are called up in turn. Our table is number seventeen. Will the supply hold out till it's our turn?! We finger our mugs nervously, happy in the thought that by the time our turn comes, the mugs on table one will be empty and the fortunate ones seated there will cast anxious eyes in our direction. Eating sausage rolls, bread, and Pfannkuchen, we watch one, two, three nine gallon casks slowly but definitely giving out their last drops – like drops of life-giving blood. We finger our mugs.

The mugs used daily at meal times are guaranteed to hold just one pint. When on a recent visit to Tatura, my daughters had brought me an enamelled mug. During the fateful Christmas Eve day, I measured the enamelled mug against the table mug. The former held slightly more than the latter. When finally our table lines up before that blessed barrel, I produce my enamelled mug and have it filled to the brim. There was enough and even a little Frei-Bier (free beer). Soon everybody is speaking with an affected hiccup, and when later we see the Old Year out and the New Year in, small parties with a final handshake vow they have 'never spent celebrations like this before!'

So closes 1941.

10

1 January, 1942

A new year starts. What has it in store for the world? Each nation? For the individual? For me? It's a depressing day generally.

2 January, 1942

Hot day. 'A' Grade semi-finals supply entertainment. Athletic sports first heats are interesting. Competitions can go on to almost 9 p.m. now that our clocks are put on an hour. I receive a letter from Else dated 29 December:

> *Dear Dad,*
>
> *Well, here we are once again and Xmas gone too. My word we did have it hot, it really was an effort to eat our Xmas dinner, it was the hottest Xmas Day on record, 108 degrees. We thought of you all in your tin huts and how hot they must have been too.*
>
> *We had a nice tree in the Church as usual, and the School children recited little verses and lighted little candles which they carried. We sang several songs out of the 'Adoration' and Bert sang the bass solo of 'Break Forth', which you no doubt will remember.*
>
> *We had cards from all the folk at Mt. Gambier and Willunga. Melva has had another transfer she is now nearer home, she is*

teaching at Kuitpo, only eleven miles from Willunga and Aunty said they were pleased she was nearer home.

Mum thanks you for the lovely Xmas card it came as a nice surprise, and also your last letter which came on Saturday.

You wrote us some time back about writing to Mr. Wilson. That was not his son on the 'Sydney', Mr. Wilson's son was Ron and he was on board the 'Canberra'. Bert enquired from Harold Meyer so we did not write. A lot of people thought it was he.

One of our kittens 'Sandy' was run over, and now we have only Pussy Pattercakes whom Marie still adores.

Mr. Guerin has finally been moved. He starts the new year at Lockleys, on the Henley Beach line.

Splinter and Audrey and the little lad Jimmy, spent Xmas at home. We hear Splinter is still the big man about the place, or tries to be.

Oscar H. was home from Whyalla where he has been employed and looks a real Frenchman. He is terribly burnt in the face and has grown a black moustache – which does NOT improve him and is still as crazy as ever. E.G. had a fall at home and hurt his back. He is very shaky, so has not been about the place lately.

So many of the lads are in camp now, even Dan Hentsche was called up. His wife had to leave their nice home and with the young babe is living with her parents.

Steve had his Birthday on the 27th, he is registered but has not heard any further if he has to go into camp. He was exempt first time.

Annie has been spending most of her time at Freeling, and very a gay time too I believe, so she has told her friends. She tells us that she spent an exceptionally quiet time, she is beginning to tell me a few too many lies for my liking, she treats me like the mug about the place. She expected me to water her garden while she was away and I did it (she wouldn't ask May) but Bert wouldn't let me do it anymore, so I don't know who does it now.

Marie thinks the 'Jumping Aunty El' is great.
Lots of love from Home.
Your Daughter
Else. Xxxx

3 January, 1942

Still hot. The threatened rain last night did not materialise.

4 January, 1942

Messedienst. Heat persists. Finals of the athletic sports and tennis. The unsportsman-like action of Thiermann and Herr B. is so embarrassing, I choose to not write about it. Luger wins 'A' and 'B' Grade Tennis Doubles. Little Mayer of 'B' wins the 100 and 400 metres flat races. A little feeling appears to be developing between the two Camps. Our glamour boys seem unable to take bumps. I receive the Tatura Newsletter No. 2/1.

5 January, 1942

I slept outside last night. Today, planes continuously roar above us. We look at them more closely! Are they ours? We hope.

6 January, 1942

I am writing and reading more intensely and find much pleasure in reading 'heavier' books.

7 January, 1942

What a day! Wind and dust all day long and throughout the night.

8 – 9 January, 1942

A welcome drop in the temperature. No rain but it is delightfully cool. H. Rothe helps me wash: 8 pairs of socks, 1 hat, 10 pieces of underclothing, 4 towels, 5 shirts, 1 pair of pyjamers, and 3 handkerchiefs. A letter arrives from Margaret, Ted, and Marie dated 4 January. On the top left hand corner of the first page, a small slip of paper has been glued, with this wording written in pencil, 'No photograph enclosed. Censorship Office':

> *Dear Father,*
>
> *First of all Marie wants to thank you for the lovely Xmas present you sent her it arrived the day after Xmas day she was very pleased with it and Aunty El was amused too. I've hung it up in the dining room and when anybody comes Marie shows it and naturally they have a pull at it and then Marie gets excited and tells them not to pull too hard. At present we are having a real taste of summer weather. Xmas day was the hottest Xmas on record 108 was the temp. We went down home but it was too hot for anything even to eat.*
>
> *The week before Xmas I was confined to my bed with a severe attack of the 'flu' my goodness I didn't know it could make one feel so ill, but am fully recovered again now.*
>
> *Marie is outside with Daddy at the present moment and is she talking, she isn't quiet for a minute, the heat doesn't seem to affect her she runs around in her singlet and panties only. Father Xmas*

brought her a pram and dolly and she is very pleased with it. We had a real job with her Xmas morn she wanted to go to church and she wanted right or wrong to take her pram and dolly but she finally gave in.

We will be getting new neighbours soon you may know him, Mr. Roy Braun, one time captain of the West Torrens Football Club he is the new School master to take Mr. Lord's place.

The fruit season is approaching fast especially with this hot weather the Apricots are ripening fast but everywhere there is a shortage of labour which is difficult to get.

The photo I'm sending you of Marie is the one we had taken in Melbourne. May the New Year bring peace and happiness.

Love from Margaret Ted and Marie.
Keep smiling Grandpa
From Marie xxxx

10 January, 1942

Delightful weather. Reading and writing again.

11 January, 1942

I attend Pastor Meier's Church Service, and then play Skat during the afternoon and evening. The Tatura Newsletter No. 2/2 arrives today.

12 – 13 January, 1942

The weather is warming up. I am currently writing about our Camp pets.

14 January, 1942

A warm to hot day.

15 January, 1942

I witness the best tennis play seen by me ever: Zitzewitz and Ekels beat Theirmann and Herr, 7-5, 6-2. A long, welcome, uncensored letter from Else, dated 12 January, arrives today:

> *Dear Dad,*
>
> *We were pleased to receive your last letter, as we had not received one since just before Xmas, and we always look forward to your letter. I daresay it was too hot to write over the holidays, it certainly was a very hot Xmas and New Year here.*
>
> *I am home from the Office now for a few days, as there is nothing for me till the weekend when it is paper week again.*
>
> *The Show had a meeting on Thursday last, and the Show this year has been cancelled, which also means we have no book to print. There was only one man for the Show, and he was Kuchel, of course he wins a large amount of money at Shows with his pigeons. At the close of the meeting there was a surprise social for Mr. Guerin who has been transferred to Lockleys. It was a great surprise for him and he was presented with a very nice Reading Lamp on a stand. The new teacher's name is Mr. Dack.*
>
> *Uncle came up this weekend from Willunga, and was of course interested to hear all the news of our trip. He sends his regards and*

hopes you will understand him not writing, and will be pleased to hear news through us.

Ross is expecting his call-up for the Air Force in February. Uncle and Auntie have been spending their holidays at Semaphore and Auntie's father is not enjoying the best of health at present.

You said Mr. Geyer wrote and told you of Darwin evacuees arriving here, yes they were supposed to have arrived on Xmas eve, but there was some hold up and they never came, and now the people here are waiting to receive women and children from New Guinea, but who are still held up in the city.

Bert is kept very busy still, we can't get anyone to trim our hedges, so he has had to tackle them and is making a very good job too, they were left too long and now are certainly a bit out of hand, but Ted thought he had done an extra good job.

Annie goes to and fro to Daly's but is home again now. I had a few words with her, and feel much better now that it is off my chest and we understand each other better now. She had been giving people the idea that she was a wealthy young lady, and was not going to sit back now that she was free to have a good time. She said she was not quite responsible for different things as she had been living under such a terrible strain, but in the future things would be different (we hope). May very seldom goes down to her now, she is suddenly realising that Annie is far too old for her now.

Frank Hall is home on final leave I believe, and off he will be going too.

Audrey and young Jimmy were home for Xmas. I went over one evening to Schulz's, they all send their kindest regards. Young Myra is home from College now and is working in Schrapel's Office. Mr. E.E. is about again, although very weak, he occasionally goes over to the shop for a while.

Yesterday afternoon Steve and I, Winnie and Eric went out to Doreen's place in Mrs. Schulz's car. Doreen and Ern have a lovely home, it is an old place renovated. We went out 'yabbying' in one of the creeks, it was good fun, and then stayed out for tea. They live near Steele's place and Ern has mostly sheep. Doreen still comes in two days a week to her 'Salon,' and Elsa is still with her.

Quite an interesting case opened at the Court today. Peter Mayr insulted some of the workmen at Hage's Garage and they wanted him to apologise through the 'B. News' which he would not, so these men have taken it to court. I am not quite sure of the men's names, but I know Mr. Ed. Juttner snr. is urging these men to go on with it. There are quite a few 'rats' in the town who want to be cleaned up.

Mum is I think getting the 'Flu so I am pleased I am home again for a few days.

Bert was in town again last week and he had various important calls to make, and we are still hoping to hear good news in the near future.

Ora Gersch was married early in the New Year in Adelaide, to Ira Oink. I believe he is in the new call-up.

Tomorrow is another med. Examination day for married men, up to 35. All the chaps, Vic Lindner, H. Wallent, B. Tuesner, and lots of others are in this call-up.

Werner has a job at last, and is quite thrilled. He is a resident Master at King's College, he never expected quite such a high position, I believe.

Our Pattercakes presented us with another family of five this time. Two have mysteriously disappeared, we think Mum is to blame. We are hoping one to be a Persian to replace our lovely 'Sandy' (1st litter) who got 'ironed out' on the road, like most of our pets.

How are you off for clothing, still O.K.? and how about sheets etc.

We still play tennis although our matches are finished on account of petrol rationing.

The Hurst's also send along New Year Greetings to you.

> *The swimming pool is always crowded these hot days, and is always blacked out at night same as the bowls, and no Friday night shopping, and no shoplights at night. Things seem much quieter now.*
>
> *I think I have written all the news for this time so I will say 'Cheerio' and keep smiling.*
>
> *Love from all at Home.*
> *Your Daughter*
> *Else. Xxxxxxx*

16 January, 1942

We've had an extreme change of weather overnight. It is quite cold today.

17 January, 1942

A wonderful cool night and pleasant day.

18 January, 1942

I am on Tischdienst (table duty). The Tatura Newsletter No. 2/3 arrives.

Today is the official opening of the Tennis Courts in 'B' Compound. The Commandant and his staff witness the match of Thiermann and Herr versus Zitzewitz and Luyken. The result: Thiermann and Herr win 4-6, 6-4, 6-2. It was as good tennis as I have ever witnessed.

I am sorry to have to record that the Cabaret Concert given in 'B' Compound in the evening lowered the prestige of the inmates of that compound and particularly that of its leader, Dr. Erler, in my humble estimation. Every item announced by the latter was introduced with some 'spicy' anecdote or deprecatory reference to theology or the clergy. This both pained and surprised me. Is not Hitler and Nazism 'professedly' the embodiment and personification of all that is good, clean and worthy of emulation! So we are led to believe, particularly by some of the inmates here. If so, then its disciples here are considerably cruelling its pitch.

19 January, 1942

The announcement by Dr. Haslinger at tea that inmates of the Camp might be asked to volunteer for fruit picking creates a good deal of excitement, comment and argument. The prospect of activity outside the barbed wire enclosure fills me with glad anticipation. Probably the scheme will come to nothing. Today we experience a terrific dust storm.

Today I receive a letter from the Official Visitor, dated 19 January, which, like all the other official letters from the powers that be, fills me with despair:

Dear Sir,

We are in receipt of the following communication from the Military Authorities:-
'The enclosure submitted from this internee making application for a further appeal to the Tribunal has been referred to the intervening authority, and it is advised that the decision of the Advisory Committee to the effect that SCHULZ must remain interned is final.'
Yours truly
OFFICIAL VISITORS.

20 January, 1942

The 'Fruit Picking Scheme' gave me much food for thought before falling asleep last night, so immediately after breakfast I sought out Dr. Haslinger. In case our camp does not come into consideration, would he intercede on behalf of the men who never participated in Geldspenden (money donation): Australian born and naturalised British subjects, giving them the opportunity of earning some money to enable them to buy such comforts denied them to date. Dr. Haslinger was all with me.

21 January, 1942

A delightful day weather-wise. Reports tell us the Japs come ever closer with intense bombing at Rabaul and Kavieng. I receive two letters today. The first is from the Official Visitor, dated today, re my discussion with Dr. Haslinger about paid employment:

> Dear Sir,
>
> We are in receipt of the following reply from the Military Authorities:-
> 'As many internees as possible are employed under the Paid Employment Scheme and it is desired to inform you that priority of employment is offered to indigent internees. As all the inmates of this Camp are being held for security reasons, it is unlikely that they would be released for employment.'
> Yours truly,
> OFFICIAL VISITORS

My second letter of the day, dated 17 January, is from Bert:

Dear Dad,

According to the time that has passed since I last wrote to you, I should really write a book, not a letter. So here goes.

We received your letter addressed to El this morning. We were all glad to hear that some of the good old Xmas customs and Xmas spirit had not been forgotten in Tatura. Your previous letter had made no mention of the festivities, and we were wondering whether perhaps one letter had gone astray. But now of course we know that none is missing.

One of the first items I am sure you want to hear is regarding the Office. Recent events have made things difficult in many ways, but we are thankful that the staff remains unaltered. We are glad to be able to make ends meet, so that the various families interested are assured of a livelihood, which in these times is all we have a right to expect.

There is to be no S.A. District Synod this year, petrol rationing and the shortage of labour on the land being the main contributing causes. However, a Synod Report is to be printed. The Almanac seems to have met with a good demand once again, as we have very few on demand.

Mr. Aug. Geyer wrote you saying that the Darwin evacuees were to be billeted in Tanunda (or at least some of them). Well, none have arrived as yet. The next thing everyone got ready for then was the arrival of the New Guinea folk in Tanunda, Angaston and Nuriootpa. These folk, also, have not reached here. They are still at Immanuel College, and nobody seems to know just exactly what's going to happen in their case.

Next newsflash is an interesting case heard in the local Courthouse last Monday. Vic Schulz, Dud Gursansky and Eddie Juttner 'went' Peter Mayr for allegedly saying something like this: 'You are Nazis.' To Vic he is supposed to have said: 'You, Schulz, you've got a three inch yellow streak up the middle of your back. You bought a house to invest your money. You'll lose that alright. The Japs will get that.' When Juttner said: 'You've played your trump card, Peter!,' Mayr is supposed to have said: 'You're a cold-footed, six-footed b------. I'd put you all in front of a machine gun. You're all yellow. You've got no guts.'

Schulz, Gursansky and Juttner were represented by Gun & Teusner, and Clem Gun was up here for the case. The case finished that day and left Peter with about sixteen to eighteen pounds in fines and I don't know how much his solicitor, Abbott, will want. So much for that newsflash.

As I mentioned before, labour is hard to get. Nowadays, if you want the hedge clipped - do it yourself! That's the cold, hard fact. It's hopeless to try to get anybody in to do such work. Well, you know how many hedges I've clipped in my time! But I've had a go at the long Carob hedge and Ted thinks I'm doing quite well.

The present time is Apricot cutting time. Workers are hard to get. You'll understand this when you hear that Mrs. Moran, the banker's wife is a fruit cutter. So is May Goers, Mrs. Erwin Hoffmann, Mrs. Leon Allchurch and so on. And 'Spuddy' Lindner is in charge of operations in 'Monty' Ellis's Orchard. (El has just told me Mrs. Moran is not cutting, but she had intended doing so.)

Show matters: No, there will be no 1942 Show. This was decided at a meeting held on Thursday, the 8th January, when the Show Committee gave Mr. Guerin a send-off. We presented him with a pedestal reading lamp. Angaston is not going on with their Show, and Freeling also will probably cancel arrangements. Our Committee had quite a lengthy discussion before deciding to discontinue for this year.

To come back to your request for Mallee stumps, Alf Zander tried to get some suitable material for me from Jack Pfeiffer's woodheap, but there was nothing doing. I therefore don't know where else I can try. Perhaps you have been able to get something suitable *from one of the men over there? Or would some other kind of wood do the job? Let me know if you wish me to send something else.*

Have you received the half pound of Pipe Mixture I got Bauer to send you on the 9th *January? He was able to let me have perfumed Rhodesian, so you should find it the dinky-die brew.*

Dudley Goers is home from camp. I understand he has been discharged, on account of a recurrence of trouble with his neck. You will remember he had a nasty scar there, and it appears that this has opened up. Hase Helling is in khaki now, too. Young Colin Hueppauff has taken over his job, and this has given the wags another opportunity for wise-cracking. They congratulated Colin on getting Hase's truck so cheaply, and when he asked, 'how do you mean, cheap?' they said: 'Well, you got it for sh--, didn't you?'

Frank Hall was home on final leave for a few days, and left Tanunda yesterday. He was a fine lad and often asked after you. The Zander's received five letters in a batch from Bob last week. He is well and makes the most of the situation. I am told he plays in a Camp Band at weekend concerts.

I don't know whether I have mentioned it before – I don't think I have – but Gert has given up sewing at her shop. It is just as well, for it was too much for her. She had hardly shifted her machines and things home when she had quite a run of petty sickness. It was probably the reaction after so long a stretch of nerve-tiring work. Now she is well on the mend again and we are looking forward to the day when we can settle down together.

I had intended disposing of the 'Singer', so as to have the use of a few more shekels just now when they are needed. But at present-day prices one would not be wise to sell out. I've got to have something for the business, and it is the cheapest running. So we are endeavouring to set up with just what we have, hoping to add to our possessions as we go along. Eric Schulz and his wife made such a start and have got on marvellously. Those, however, are our fond hopes. We must never forget, though, that man proposes, but God disposes.

With love from all of us and the hope that you are well and in good spirits,
Your son
Bert

22 January, 1942

I order coffee and three Pfannkuchen (doughnuts) at Café Wellblech and get three man-sized Plinse (pancakes). Grumow's bed plus other belongings are placed outside his hut, No. 79. Snoring?

23 January, 1942

The weather is warming up again. Disquieting news from New Guinea. The Japs seem to have landed after much bombing.

24 January, 1942

More disquieting news from New Guinea. I think back to the time I worked up there.

25 January, 1942

A terribly windy day. Dust as only Tatura can supply it. The Tatura Newsletter No.2/ 4 arrives. I receive letters dated 21 January from my family. One from Else, and one from Margaret, Ted and Marie:

Dear Dad,

I received your very welcome letter last weekend, and we were all very pleased to hear of your Xmas festivities.

The weather is lovely now, not so very hot, I hope you are having cooler days now too.

You remember Bert Spaeth who used to live here? Well he passed away recently, he had been in ill health for quite some time, and had been living up the River.

We have had another nice big job from Gramp's, and Bert is going down tomorrow to discuss different things with Mr. Lawson, and also some other little jobs. Bert is very pleased of course and he gets on extra well with Mr. Lawson.

I am going to try my hand at Grape-picking in the coming season. Mr. Artly Nettelbeck is looking for pickers, so I have let them know I will come. He is paying one shilling and six pence an hour and they are mostly trellis vines, which will not be too bad.

Elva has had word from Frank Hall, he has been sent to Sydney. Schulz's had a party last week, just before Frank left.

Ora was home for a few days, her husband is still in camp at Largs Bay, but may be off any time. She has a position in Adelaide.

Mum made Apricot jam today from our Apricots, they were not too bad this year, much better than a lot we saw, although some were fairly spotted. Mum is keeping fairly well, she usually leaves the writing to me.

There has been a rumour that the New Guinea evacuees are arriving this week, in Tanunda.

Inge is home now with her mother, she has given up her position in the city for the time being.

Dud Goers has been discharged from the Army, he has always had a scar on his neck, which has again opened after many years and later on has to have an operation on it. He is back at the Chateau again.

Everyone is looking for help these days, there is such a shortage of men everywhere, and girls are nearly all going grape-picking etc.

Frank Fischer is in Palestine now, and Edna is still home with her people.

The Frank Munzberg's have another baby son.

Things will certainly seem quiet this year with no Show. Bert is quite pleased of the break as he has ample to see to at the Office etc.

I went round and said 'goodbye' to Mr. and Mrs. Guerin, they were very sorry to leave here, and hoped to see us down their way some time. He also enquired after you.

Well news has run out so will say 'Cheerio'.

Love from all at Home

Else. Xxxx

Dear Father,

Today is a beautiful day and when I've finished this letter I and Marie are going for a walk out to the park, Marie loves to go there to the playground she loves the swings and seesaws. The weather here has been perfect the last few days which is welcome after the heat we also have had. I often thought of you Dad and wondered if the heat played up with you at all. Your teeth no doubt seem to be giving you some trouble, but hope they are O.K. again. Ted's brother George has been with us for a few days. He has had a stiff neck for quite a while so came up here for treatment at the Willows Hospital for it.

Now Marie has some news for you, she is going to Sunday School this year and is very excited about going too she can't await the time to go, probably the Sunday after next classes reopen for the New Year. Ted or I will always have to take her and get her again.

I think she's a bit too young yet to go on her own. Just a week ago today we had a terrific dust storm, the worst the state's experienced, it blew all day and nearly half the night, the poor garden suffered which resulted in a shortage of fruit and vegetables, and what is to be got is terribly dear. Last year this time we were picking tomatoes more than we could use. This year I don't think we've picked a dozen. Ted's got a nice lot of beans in but they don't seem to be setting either.

Well Dear Father this is all the news hope this letter finds well as it leaves us.

Keep smiling says Marie.

Love, Margaret, Ted and Marie

26 January, 1942

I join the Carpenter's gang and assist in making tables for Internment and P.O.W. Camps at two pence per hour and work half a day.

27 January, 1942

I work a full day at the Carpentry and earn another shilling. I receive a definite warning: 'Don't break that half inch chisel. It's the only tool we have.' I work carefully.

28 January, 1942

Last night was not one of my better ones. I passed a bad night suffering from acute dysentery and practically all day today without food. Morphia pills finally bring relief.

29 January, 1942

Preparations are on for tomorrow's German National Holiday: Machtubernahme (assumption of power) on 30th January 1933.

30 January, 1942

National German Holiday of which National Socialists (German) are participants. During the morning's Official Ceremony, which took place 'unter der Linde' (under the Linden trees), I with other Australians or naturalised British subjects were in our huts reading or writing. The Sports Programme later in the forenoon and in the afternoon and evening was interesting.

31 January, 1942

Received from the Kantine Board: 'Gutschein (credit note) No. 463. Gegen diesen Schein konnen waren in werte von acht schilling in der 'A' Kantine bezogen werde. Tatura 30-1-42. Die Kantinenleitung. L. Mueller, J. Bitzer.'

For my eight shillings I bought three packets of cigarette tobacco (seven shillings and six pence), a packet of cigarette papers (four pence), and matches (two pence).

1 February, 1942

Pastor Martins of the Gold Coast is our preacher today. In the evening I play 'Augenzeuge' (Kruger) tennis and beat him 6-3. The Tatura Newsletter No. 2/5 arrives. I receive a letter from Else dated 28 January:

> *Dear Dad,*
>
> *Well, another week has slipped by, so it is letter writing day again. It was a nice surprise getting two letters last week.*
>
> *At the present time our house is rather upside down. We are busy renovating and calsomining the rooms. Bert is doing all the work in his spare time. He mended the roof where it always used to rain into Mum's bedroom and has plastered up all the cracks etc. and has calsomined it cream and it is beginning to look really good now, he is making an extra good job too.*
>
> *We had our Annual Meeting of the Choir on Sunday night, in the Church Hall, and the ladies made supper later. The Choir is not very strong now, owing to different members leaving and also Military duties.*
>
> *The evacuees have still not arrived, they have been coming three times now, and something has always cropped up the last minute.*
>
> *Our lawn is looking better again now, Bert clipped it and is now going to top dress it too, during the heat we could not give it much attention as we were so busy at the Office and to try and get a workman now is like looking for gold.*
>
> *I want to write to the Mt. Gambier folk today too, they want to hear of our trip etc.*
>
> *No, Annie does not do any work in the Office at all, she has not helped since months before her Mother died, although she always says she wants to help, but there is usually an excuse. Her work (when she did help) was always unsatisfactory, so we really get on better just as we are. Mr. Obst and Alfred always work well and*

we are quite a happy staff. We are working the new forty four hour week too.

The days have been ideal lately but the nights have been bitterly cold.

Our bonus at Farmer's was nearly six pounds, so we have been buying up sheets etc. and several other necessary things. It came in quite handy.

Dulcie was expecting Melva to come up for a few days during the hols. But she didn't come so Dulcie says she is going to strike her out of her 'will' (ha ha).

News is a bit scarce today, Bert will no doubt be writing in a day or two so 'Cheerio'.

Love from all at Home.

Else xxxx

2 February, 1942

Lugging and stacking timber with the Carpenter's gang. It's tough work, but I earn another shilling – always enough for smokes. Maybe it's a preparatory school for the future.

3 February, 1942

At work outside. Krugge and I cut the ends, twenty pieces of three by two. We didn't quite finish the job. The ways of a Carpenter's gang!

4 February, 1942

Half a day at Carpenter's gang. We do not go out in the afternoon, until more satisfactory arrangements are made re tools and we get definite instructions as to whether we work on tables only or shall do casual work and repair work.

Twenty new arrivals from Gaythorne, Brisbane, Queensland. I don't want to witness their arrival. I feel sick at heart (for security reasons) when the first man arrives and later drops his straw paliasse on the floor of our hut.

5 February, 1942

The Carpenter's strike is still on.

I receive Bert's letter, dated 29 January, re his and Trudi's future and their desire to live at home:

> Dear Dad,
>
> I received your letter last night, and we were surprised at the short time of transit. You had written it on the 24th. In a previous letter you wrote of receiving a package of tobacco, the address of which had neither Tatura nor Victoria on it. Next time I go to the city I must tell Alf Bauer about it and ask him who addresses his parcels. Anyhow, the main point is – you got the goods.
>
> Marge and Marie were down today and Marge read your letter to me. She will tell Ted about the tobacco pouch. No doubt he will be able to do something about it.
>
> El has written you saying that I had something to write to you about. Well, it's this. Regarding Trudi and myself settling down, we have done a lot of thinking this way and that way. Right at first we considered taking a house. Then we thought: why go to a place when there are vacant rooms at Auricht's. In fact, Miss Auricht made that suggestion to us. Of course, you know the condition that place is in, and it would have needed a lot of repairing and renovating. Where were the funds to come from? I might have considered committing myself for those expenses, but after some consideration

we felt that we could not live as harmoniously together as one would naturally wish to. And then, if any place needed doing up, then ours at home does. If this were done, Mum and El would enjoy the comforts, and not outsiders. The suggestion came from Mum that in these uncertain times it would perhaps be best to incur as little expense and as few responsibilities as possible. Would we perhaps like to share the house with her and El? I said it would depend on Trudi. She said she would be pleased to, but would Mum and El be willing to give up a part of the house? So we discussed the matter thoroughly one night after tea, and everybody seemed pleased with the idea. It will certainly give Mum the rest she so badly needs. The girls would look after the cooking and housework, and all expenses would be shared. Trudi and I would pay a weekly rental for the use of the kitchen and bathroom. The benefits seem obvious. If we went into another place, the womenfolk here at home would never be able to look after the whole place and I would have my time cut out looking after my own home. I forgot to mention that we would use the rooms at present used as the dining room and the front room. So you see there would be plenty of privacy. Mum and El would share Mum's room as bedroom, and El's room would become their private sitting room. Their rooms are well on the way to completion as I write. I have taken upon myself the job of interior decorator, plasterer and general handyman. You won't know the place again! It means a terrific lot of work, but it's worth it. What do you think of the plan?

You ask about the business; finances, and so on. Well, it hasn't been an easy year for anyone. I don't think we were an exception. But while we can meet expenses we won't grumble.

I started this letter on Thursday, and today it's Sunday, so I'll have another shot at finishing it.

On Friday evening the New Guinea Mission evacuees reached Tanunda. As I understand, not all are at Tanunda, as the other surrounding towns are also taking some of them. It was the third time the arrival had been announced and this time they really arrived. The previous attempt was cancelled owing to the Health Department wanting them in the city for a further week's observation or something. Mrs. Flierl and young Hans, and Mrs. Maurer and little girl are staying with Miss Auricht. That is, in the Auricht home, as Miss Auricht is spending the weekend at Freeling! Still, I suppose the good ladies are quite pleased to look after themselves.

I am told that Helmie Wallent has enlisted in the A.I.F. His brother Aubrey, who was in full-time service with the Militia, has been discharged. You will remember he never did look well, but now the poor lad looks really sick. I fancy it must be his stomach, as he often used to complain of it.

Reverend Hebart is in bed once again – stomach or heart trouble I believe. Werner has been fortunate in securing a position at King's College. He had been up at Brinkworth for the harvest.

Rev. Albrecht is down from Hermannsburg on his holidays. He is really in need of a rest. They have decided that nobody may ask him to lecture without the consent of the Mission Board. This should give him a well-earned rest.

In December last the Jay Creek Church, for which Borgelt had been showing his films, was dedicated. Rev. Heidenreich made the trip up specially for the occasion. There were about four hundred people at the opening.

Rev. Theile advises that he is able once more to resume his work back home in Brisbane.

I don't know if we've mentioned it before, but power alcohol production is in full swing in our district. Tarac at Nuriootpa were the first to start on the job. Seppeltsfield are on it too. Sugar is the raw material being used. They were going to use wheat but that presented too many difficulties I understand.

Well, that seems to have cleaned me up for news, so keep your pecker up and keep smiling. With a cheerio from all of us,

Your son, Bert

6 February, 1942

Special attention is given to the huts in readiness for an official Inspection by General Stanke. Rothe and I have another big washing day.

7 February, 1942

Murky hot weather all day.

8 – 9 February, 1942

Another hot and sultry day. The Tatura Newsletter No. 2/6 is to hand.

An announcement is made that a Tribunal is to sit at Tatura. I get in touch with other Australian borns here to appear before this Tribunal. I write a short letter asking for release and offering services.

Dr. Brose writes a letter re the present Attorney-General's statement when still in Opposition; viz. that Australian internees should receive an open trial etc.

In the Orderly Room I ask the Commandant if he could arrange for my appearance before the Tribunal to plead the cause of the Australian borns, or could a letter be handed in. The Commandant replied that he would let me know through Dr. Haslinger.

10 February, 1942

A fairly cool and welcome change overnight, but very hot during the day.

11 February, 1942

A very cool change has arrived now, in fact, it is actually quite cold. A celebration of some kind took place in one of the Mess Halls 'in commemoration of two years occupancy of Camp 1A, Tatura.' I did not partake.

12 February, 1942

Today it is two years since the first internees came to Tatura. It's Bretag's Birthday and the party relates stories of its trip over from S.A. in a boat. Cast and Henke try to escape. Result: Roll Call at 5.20 p.m. Schnapps was the Verrater (traitor).

Reading 'The Argus' today, with its articles regarding grave news from Singapore, I write a comment as follows: Singapore Naval Base and floating dock – It took twenty years to build and cost sixty million pounds. 'Like the Maginot Line, the base has never been fully in action,' says a paper correspondent. Oh, the tragedy of it all! While Rome was burning, we sure have been fiddling. Later on I ask permission to cut out most of the articles from the page and include them in my 'Political Pellets' booklet.

13 February, 1942

Lightning, thunder and rain overnight. Sultry again throughout the day. I received a lovely tobacco pouch and tobacco from Ted yesterday as well as a letter, dated 8 February:

Dear Dad,

So it is my turn to write, I thought this afternoon most suitable as I have little time during the week. So far we are all still in good health, and we hope and trust you are too.

Marie went to Sunday School this morning for the first time and she was very pleased with herself after it was all over, she brought home a card with her lesson on it, being the first time Margaret went with her, also called for her again, as traffic on the road one cannot be too careful.

On Tuesday past we all went to town, probably my last opportunity for some time, as my third male assistant went into camp on Wednesday leaving myself and one boy, five girls in the shop. You see one does not have many so idle moments, however we hope to get help that was my intention on Tuesday to engage a Hairdresser, but no such luck they are very scarce, nevertheless one never knows, someone may turn up, but until such time arrives we can only do as best we can. After we had finished our business, we took Marie to the Zoo, where she had a very enjoyable time, the monkeys in particular were very amusing, diving and swimming exhibitions were main features, as the day was fairly hot, conditions were favourable for that type of thing.

Marie is sending a Tobacco pouch for Grandpa today and we hope you will be able to keep your Tobacco nice and moist, as the packets dry out very quickly.

The past week the temperatures have been rising and at present it is very sultry, with rain not very distant, which at present the vineyards are much in need. The Apricots have almost finished, and Peaches coming in now. Apricots throughout the district, very good this season, even Monty Ellis had a good crop. We are very busy in the garden these days, as vegetables are a scarce item at present, we have been putting lots of seedlings in, although we have quite a lot we can use out of our garden, at present, there is always *room for more. Bert is getting very garden minded and getting into practice of home life, he is a real hard worker, believe me.*

We went down home last night for a while, and I was surprised to see what he had done, such as top dressed the lawn, trimming Hedges etc. The latter end he had help with Hedge trimming but what he had done, a real good effort.

The late Gus Schildt's daughter-in-law, (nee Florrie Laucke) passed away suddenly this morning thirty four years of age she was. On Tuesday the burial takes place, and I am one of the Bearers.

We are enclosing with your pouch some Smoking mixture, it is not the best, however I hope you will get some pleasure out of it. I will now conclude. Hoping you are well.

Your loving Children

Marge, Marie and Ted.

P.S. I have packed Tobacco in vine leaves so as to keep it moist. Should it get dry, pat some moist blotting paper over it. Ted.'

14 February, 1942

Terrific thunderstorm and cloudburst last night. A definite cold change overnight. Shorts are conspicuous by their absence and warm guernseys are in evidence.

In the Orderly Room, with others, I sign that the Authorities still hold a petrol lighter taken from me when I arrived here. To my question: 'What about the ointment and medicine taken from me?' The reply is: 'Oh, that would be no good to you now!'

15 February, 1942

Today's preacher is Walther. Tennis this afternoon: Zitzewiz beats Thierman 6-2, 6-1. The big fellow does represent 'A' Grade. The Tatura Newsletter No. 2/7 arrives.

16 February, 1942

Quite a winter's morning and a pleasant day.

17 February, 1942

Camp 'weighing' day. When I came here my weight was fourteen stone, four pounds: two hundred pounds. Today I turned the scale at twelve stone, ten pounds: one hundred and seventy eight pounds.

18 February, 1942

I have to go to the dentist. An abscess has formed on my gums where I lost the gold tooth. Seith says it will be dangerous to try and replace the tooth. The roots had better come out – and out they did come. Seith's nerves seem to be completely unstrung. I underwent a real 'Pferdekur' (drastic treatment), and appear to have holes in my face structure right up to the eyes. I feel I am getting old.

19 February, 1942

Our position in the World Armageddon appears to be worsening from day to day. Malaya and Singapore gone. The entire Philippines, Java, Sumatra, Borneo, New Guinea, and Burma in dire distress.

The successful, audacious sailing of the Gneisenau, Scharntorst, and Prince Eugen through the Straits of Dover from Brest to Heligoland. We appear powerless and impotent. What of the future?!

And our Intelligence authorities continue to hold natural born British subjects behind barbed wire! Is it thinkable that the latter would rejoice in the Japs landing on the soil of their birth?! Even at this stage, who should perform the act of setting the unjustly interned free; the Japs or the Intelligence?! Is the moment arriving when those whom the Gods are about to destroy have been made sufficiently mad or blind?! May God give us wisdom!

I send a letter, dated today, to the Intelligence, Melbourne, per the Camp Commandant, that I don't want the Japs to liberate me, but that I make a final appeal to the authorities to release me:

Sir,

The midday broadcast announces that Darwin has been bombed by Japan. Camp inmates assure one another that Japan will soon get us out of here. I don't want Japan to liberate me. I am almost sixty years old and want to place what strength I still possess at the disposal of the country of my birth, Australia. I make a final appeal for my release.
    Respectfully yours
    J.F.W. Schulz – 3077

20 February, 1942

Radio news: Seventeen killed on first Jap raid on Darwin. And I am still being held for security reasons!

21 February, 1942

What a delightful spring day. I receive a letter from Mum dated 17 February:

Dear Dad,

It is quite a time since I have written so it is my turn. We are having a very dry spell of weather just now, we hope some rain will come now. We were pleased to read that you are occupying your time with other work now. I am having bad luck with my fowls lately. I have lost quite a few. We are going in a lot for vegetables now they are so scarce and very dear. Last Sunday we had Mission festivals in all the churches morning and evening.

In connection with Bert and Gert settling down here I think it will be quite suitable and will save quite a lot and it also means that Bert is here on the place. We will come to arrangements later on about sharing expenses. Next Sunday we are going up to Margaret's it's Ted's Birthday on Monday.

Ross and Melva are coming up to Dulcie's for the weekend this will most probably be the last time Ross will come up here for some time as he expects to go into the Air Force any time now.

Mrs. A. Geyer paid me a visit last week it was nice to have a talk with her. The family all wish to be remembered to you. Marie is quite proud now she goes to Sunday school.

With love from us all.
Mum

22 February, 1942

Weather perfect. On Tuesday an announcement was made that the Canteen would have to close. All purchases are now to be made through the Military Canteen. Haslinger is furious about this. The Tatura Newsletter No. 2/8 arrives. I also receive a letter from Else dated 18 February:

Dear Dad,

We were ever so pleased to receive your last letter, and Bert was very pleased you approved of all the arrangements here.

He has made quite a lot of improvements to the place and it looks really nice. He is quite a handyman. Mum and I are in the one room and my bedroom we made into our sitting room, it is small but, very cosy and quite large enough for us. At present Bert is on the bathroom, he has done up all the cracks and is now on the painting. After that we shall be on the kitchen which will take us a fair time as we want to paint all the cupboards too.

Bert and Gert will occupy the front room as their bedroom and the other room as their sitting- dining room. I think the arrangements this way will be O.K. as it will cut down quite a lot of expenditure and things are so very dear these days and are certainly getting worse.

It also means Bert is here on the place, which always needs a lot of looking after.

Bert and Gert went to town today to have a look around in general. Quite probably the wedding will be soon after Easter. Linda Zerna and Benno Keil, Steve and I will be in the wedding and of course Marie will be flower-girl, she can hardly wait the time. She is terribly thrilled because she can have a 'dancing dress.'

Last night was a choir evening for Hilda Raethel who is being married today to Aircraftsman Ed. Leske.

We had 'the Pasha' (Paschke) in to do our hedges again, he was not working for a while.

Mum is saying I shall stop as she wants to write tonight and won't have any news left, so will say 'Cheerio'.

Love from all at home.
Your Daughter
Else. Xxxxxx

25 February, 1942

I start a labour of love: inlaying Marie's photo drawn by Zanker for me from a recent photo. I am told that I am starting a hopeless task. But Zanker says, 'You can do it.' It will take me at least two months, but I am right on with the work.

Today bugs have also been found in our hut and the hunt is on.

26 February, 1942

Bug hunting is the order of the day.

27 – 28 February, 1942

The heat continues accompanied by strong wind and dust.

11

Camp Pets.

Schnapps, so I am told, was smuggled into the Camp when quite a pup. What breed of dog is he? I can't say, but would designate him as a canine cocktail, somewhat bigger than the average cattle dog with just a streak of greyhound in him. Reared in the lap of luxury and petted by all, he shows no outward signs of vice. Unfortunately for him, the readiness with which he understands and applies action to the command 'Fass ihn' (bite him), on the approach of the khaki-clad individual very nearly led to his earthly pilgrimage coming to an untimely end. Following on from numerous frights and sudden unpleasant surprises occasioned to guards on duty outside the Camp, and also those who enter our hallowed precincts for inspections and other duties, an order was issued to the effect that all dogs, for hygienic purposes, will have to be removed from the Camp.

The announcement that Schnapps will receive a good home is little consolation to those who hold him most dear. Leading about on a chain henceforth has failed to satisfy the 'health' authorities, and in due course he had perforce to disappear. When fricassee meat or 'Falscher Hase' (false hare, a German meatloaf) was next served at mealtimes, someone remarked facetiously that he could hear Schnapps' faint bark.

However, the powers that removed Schnapps had not done so with malice aforethought. Having rather inhibited the milk of human kindness they had apparently placed him so that he was continually brought in contact with soldiery. Treated well, he soon became more kindly disposed to those whose presence he had formerly been taught to resent, with the result that in due course he reappeared in the camp to find favour with all.

Schnapps' favourite pastime and recreation is to participate in foot and Handball on the Sports Ground. He is the self-appointed first reserve and 'helps' both sides before casualties are reported. It is interesting to watch him follow the ball up and down the field, uncannily anticipating its immediate next direction.

Next to come under notice among pets in the Camp is Jakob, the pet Magpie, who lives right up to the traditional cheek, drollery and mimicry that his species are noted for when in captivity. Jakob is hardly held captive, though he had to suffer a clipped wing early in the piece. He always appears hungry and it is amusing to watch him in his endeavours to attract the attention of anyone near him whose assistance he needs to turn over a stone or a piece of timber in order to get at the worms etc. that he is sure are harboured underneath.

The stones forming the borders of the many flower-beds in the camp are his favourite resort. Underneath these is dampness and here are sleek earthworms and crawlies in plenty and Jakob, in his eagerness to get at his meal is ever-ready to lend a bill, pecking vigorously while the stones, more often than not firmly bedded, are being moved, and he minds not if your fingers get the worst of his 'help'.

On one occasion, Jakob positively shocked me. I had turned a large flat stone for him and uncovered a centipede. For a moment Jakob eyed this many-footed new find in surprise. The centipede sought cover, but Jakob, guided by instinct, made one peck, caught it fair on the head and brought the loathsome, writhing tid-bit back into the referee hold. Every attempt at escape was treated in a similar cavalier manner until, without warning, Jakob momentarily held the squirming thing in his beak and with two or three gulps and lazily blinking eye, he finally stowed the centipede safely from sight, the last to disappear being a vigorously protesting tail-piece adorned with its many pedes. I left Jacob to hunt alone for more breakfast on this occasion.

Many a captivating moment have I spent with others at early morning listening to Jakob perched on one of the guard railings enclosing the many gardens surrounding the camp huts. About to preen his feathers, someone will prompt him with a whistle. Automatically his head will be pointed heavenwards and a glorious warble, defying all melody, will fill our hearts with delight. Ever and ever again, sometimes suddenly interrupting his toilet work, he will respond to our call. We forgave Jakob much for these regular and wonderful treats!

Another interesting pet is a Murray Magpie, belonging to the same species as Jakob, though smaller and less wily. This fellow had been brought into the camp by our wood-cutters when very young. He had never been kept captive nor had his wings received attention. He gave many people a frightful surprise. Pursued by one of his species he would invariably seek safety on the head or shoulder of anybody nearest to hand. In the moment of surprise, the haven of rest was unconsciously seen to react strangely. If attacked during meal times, with nobody sitting at leisure or wandering about, our little magpie would suddenly sail into one of the mess huts, perch on one of the crossbeams and commence preening his feathers. After an experience or two similar to that of Tobias asleep under the swallow's nest, the magpie's position on the crossbeam was carefully noted and he was soon persuaded to seek more open spaces.

One day the wood-cutters brought a barely fledged rosella and grass parrot into camp. An inmate of Hut 32, who had had experience in rearing and training birds, took charge of these. It was an education to watch him feed the birds. He would take a mouthful of suitable food, carefully crunch and munch it and, carefully holding the bird in his hand, present his mouth to it with the prepared food between the lips for reception. It didn't take long and the birds knew where to look for food. Had they been able to add expression to their face, you would assuredly have noticed them often looking expectantly into the face of their keeper.

Soon the birds were given a little freedom on the lawn adjacent the hut, where they hopped and chattered and fed at leisure. Unexpectedly, one tried its wings and succeeded in reaching the telephone wires. It took a fair amount of persuasion to entice the delinquent back into the cage.

Right from the outset, it might be mentioned, the intention had not been to keep the two birds as captives. The inmates of a Prisoner of War Camp know what deprivation of freedom means. It was attempted to rear and train them, that when given their freedom entirely, they might not altogether forget the place where they had been tenderly treated and had eaten in fullness.

Anxious eyes followed the first flight of the birds into the trees that fringed the southern boundary of our Compound. They had followed the call of their mates from leafy boughs where during increasing chatter, honey bearing blossoms were being ransacked of their saccharine contents. Long sustained whistled demands for their return, at first, were unheeded. Was it that undue and unkind attention was paid the strangers from captivity, by those who had only moved in freedom unfettered, or was it that the call from 'home' was irresistible? The rosella suddenly alighted on the head of his keeper, soon, in his inimitable way telling him all about the bad world outside. The green parrot also returned. They were well fed and carefully housed, the door being left ajar later that they might 'go as you please' in the morning. They were away early the following day and failed to return at night. Great was the delight, however, when next day they came 'home' again.

Though they could hardly be placed in the category of pets, a pair of swallows gave the camp inmates much pleasure and opportunity for nature study. During the latter months of 1941, the Skittle Alley was under construction, a café annexe forming the northern end. Hardly were the walls of the café in position and the rafters placed in position, when a pair of swallows began building their nest on one of them. Masons and carpenters were loth to disturb and disappoint the blithesome little co-workers and with much precaution, operated round the swallow's reserve. The building having been roofed brought the swallows in through the door and window openings, and when doors and windows had finally to be placed in position, one door or window was always left ajar. When the day for the official opening of the Skittle Alley came round, four little swallows sat wing to wing along the crescent of the nest greeting with wide open large yellow fringed beak, the frequent arrivals of their dutiful parents carrying dainty morsels of food.

How sorry I was that filming was prohibited in the Camp. I felt like appearing on bended knees before the authorities begging for permission to get my film camera so I could record all these birds.

Of course the Camp had its colony of cats which, however, aroused little interest. Ferdinand, the big bull-headed tomcat possibly received most notice. After occasional retirements to some secluded spot he would reappear to partake of a little nourishment, adorned with a slit auricular appendage and sundry other damaged parts of his anatomy. All of these sustained, no doubt, while engaged in mortal combat with another Thomas over rightful ownership of this or that female species of the genus felis catus.

Speaking of cats reminds me of mice. Yes, we also had a colony of these destructive rodents caged as pets. During my first weeks of compulsory retirement at Tatura, I spent many an idle moment in front of the large mouse cage, watching these tiny quadrupeds at work and at play. Feeding time was the best time for observation. White mice, grey mice, yellow mice, mice striped and spotted flitted hither and thither, picking up a morsel here, sipping a little water there, carrying wisps of straw or strands of twine upstairs along a little ladder where cosy nests were in course of preparation to house additional families of an ever multiplying colony. But you derive little pleasure watching these little malodorous rodents. Even the camp Cats would sit at a little distance and blink lazily at the hurry and bustle in our mouse cage.

One whole week! Why no daily record? My first and last thoughts daily are centred on my work - the work - wood-inlaying Marie's portrait. The hair, the bow in her hair, are practically finished. The difficult part, the features of the face, must be tackled now. How I do hope that when I am finished, those who know her will say, 'Why, that's Marie!'

Little of moment has happened. The Camp complement has been augmented by seventy odd additional arrivals, mostly Queenslanders. A further twenty are promised for tomorrow. All our huts now have twenty inmates. – Gisar's case.

The temperature has changed from heat to absolute cold so I stay inside and read the Tatura Newsletter No. 2/9. Four letters arrive for me, one from Else dated 26 February, one from Annie Auricht dated 2 March, another from Else and dated 3 March, and a letter from Bert which he had received from Villeneuve Smith Harford dated 5 March. Much reading ahead:

Dear Dad,

Well we are nearly at the end of another month, the time just simply flies here.

How are you progressing with your carpentry? You will be an expert soon.

The weather at present is very hot, so this will ripen the grapes, I saw several loads coming through in the last few days.

Artley N. grapes only ripen in April, they are the later kind and I will mention about sending you a case.

If we are slack and I can arrange my office work in between, I thought I might ask Ted Jenkins or someone with a vineyard handy around here, and try my hand too. The folks here think I won't be able to stand it, but I am going to give it a go.

Marie spent the day with us yesterday as Margaret, Gert and Bert went to the city. She loves our kittens and spends all her time playing with them.

At present we have a nice lot of work again at the Office. Gramps and Seppelts have given jobs again.

Dr. Frank Juttner has a brand new Oldsmobile car from Ed Hage. I daresay he wants to use up some of his surplus cash.

Bikes are very much to the fore in Tanunda, practically all the ladies are cycling now.

Steve says they are very short-handed at Yalumba, and don't know how they will manage during vintage. I wonder what will happen in the next few months, there certainly does not look to be a very bright future for we younger generation. Freda Gehling has joined the W.A.A.F.'s. She gave up a lovely job, she feels she wants to do her bit too.

We are doing a lot of gardening, vegetables, we have put in every seed and plant you can imagine, we are doing our bit to 'Dig for Victory'!!

Bert said he told Mr. Bauer to send you some Tobacco so no doubt you have received it by now.

I noticed Murray Ellis home on leave and also Garth Offe.

Steve's brother is in Palestine and letters are very irregular now. Aubrey Schrapel and Dr. Colin Juttner were in Malaya.

Re Bert's page 7, it was nothing important at all, we were amazed as it was Steve's work mainly, when he was at Tarac in Nuriootpa.

I made Tomato Relish last night, we bought some lovely tomatoes from Alfred P. and he also gave us a lot of passion fruit. They are great gardeners.

Ross and Melva were up last weekend they are both very lively. Ross has a girl and of course was very love-sick and asked Dulcie if he can bring her up next time he comes. Melva is broader than ever, her figure, I mean, but she seems quite happy for all that. Her boyfriend is a farmer on the west coast.

Well news has spun out once again so I will say Cheerio.

Love from all at home.

Else xxxxx

70 Burnside Road, Kensington Gardens

Dear Mr Schulz

By the above address you will see where I am living at present. Mrs. Tolley has had an operation and I have been housekeeping and looking after the children while she was in hospital. At the same time it has been a break for me as well and I feel that I will be able to take up my duties at home again.

Luckily they have been able to manage in the office without me which saved me from a collapse after mother died. You will have heard from your family that Mrs. Flierl and son and Mrs. Mauer and daughter are now sharing my home with me. It is quite a good arrangement for the time being as it is quite impossible for me to live by myself and it saves me from making any other final alterations before you come home and can advise me about same.

Mother's sickness and passing away took more out of me than I thought possible and am only now beginning to feel normal again. Thank you so much for your nice sympathetic letter at the time of mother's death, and believe me although everything was done for me that was possible, it was much harder to go through such a sad time without your kind and thoughtful help, as you have been such a staunch and reliable stand-by in all my previous sorrows.

I will take this opportunity of wishing you the very best and many happy returns of your birthday, this may reach you a few days before but as we say 'better never late' and I don't know how *long this will take to reach you. I want to make quite sure of you getting it in time.*

Please accept my deepest gratitude and thanks for all the help and comfort you have been to Mother, the girls and myself all the years you have been in our business.

Hoping you are well,
Very sincerely yrs,
A.H. Auricht

Dear Dad,

Your last letter arrived just after I had posted mine, so of course I could not tell you the colour of Marie's eyes. Well, they are blue, with a slight touch of grey, but mostly blue, not light blue, or dark blue, just in between, I hope you will understand, but they certainly are not brown. It sounds like a surprise to us?

We are having another very hot spell. If it is as hot as this for grape-picking I shall certainly pass out!! I would certainly prefer it a little cooler.

I had today off from the Office. Mum and I have been busy preserving and pickling etc. Next Monday is Bert's Birthday on the 9th.

Basedow's machine across the road is busy and it sounds as if vintage has started. Nettelbeck's grapes will be ready for picking at the end of this month.

We hope you are not having too much hot weather, as I can well imagine how trying it would be over there. We often talk about our lovely trip over to see you, and wonder when we shall all be together again.

The flower gardens have suffered badly through the heat, things are terribly burnt. Vic Hoffmann is in camp at (name of camp cut out by Censor) we have heard. He joined up with the R.A.A.F.

Alfred and his wife and Eunice spent last weekend in the city, it was a break for him too, he has had a nasty cough left over from the 'Flu, although he is over it again now.

Groceries are becoming more and more rationed every week, some lines are right off the market, and we have to use things very sparingly or do without.

Aubrey Wallent still looks a very sick man. Ralph Eckermann was telling us he took fits and collapsed in camp and was only just getting about. He has been home several months now, but still looks very seedy.

Bert has started on the Kitchen now. He has calsomined the top half and tonight will go on with the lower half and I will do the woodwork etc. We are beginning to get a little more straight now.

The Frank John's have bought Cliff L. house the one up Helmi's street over the railway line. Mrs. Frank is working in Gramp's Office and Frank is helping his Dad.

The Clem Eckermann's (garage) have a baby son, and Roma Schubert (nee Schulz) also has a son.

The Butchers are only allowed to call three times a week now, and the Bakers I believe are having a meeting this week, for one baker to do one half of the town, and the other baker the other half.

The Betting Shop has also been closed, likewise all in S. Aust.

Are you playing any sport now? What colour are your creams? (ha ha) You are having bad luck with your teeth, since you have been away.

Well news has run out again, so I will say Cheerio for now and keep smiling.

Love from all at home.
Your daughter
Else xxxx

Villeneuve Smith & Harford

Barristers, Solicitors, and Notaries

Dear Sir,

RE YOUR FATHER

We acknowledge receipt of your letter of the 4th inst. and should be glad if you would direct any further communications to the firm and not to the writer personally. The cheque for twenty five pounds was requested as a further payment on account of costs and disbursements and to cover witness fees and not expressly as you say namely to cover witness fees only. We duly requested witnesses to let us have a memo of the fees and all who did forward any memo have been paid. Others preferred it otherwise. If you know of any outstanding, please let us know of them.

So far as Messrs. Gun & Teusner's account is concerned, we requested Mr. Teusner to let us have a memo of his fees and undertook to pay them. We have not to our recollection received any account. If and when it is received and is in order it will be paid. We have this day written to Messrs. Gun & Teusner for a memo thereof.

The Local Civil Defence and Evacuation Authorities if asking for the return of the black-covered Minute Book should apply to the Military Authorities. The book was tendered in evidence and although we pursued the matter to its limit, we have not received any satisfactory explanation of its whereabouts. We have therefore done our utmost to obtain the book. If there is anything further which you think we should do to assist and within our power we shall do so.

We would add that in all the circumstances the fees and charges in this matter were fixed extremely low, including the fees of Mr. F. Villeneuve Smith K.C., the writer's counsel fees and the special

attendances at Tanunda as well as numerous attendances at Wayville Camp and upon you at all hours. Whilst our undertaking to pay any witnesses who should send in their claims stands, no refund is in any way available in respect of the payments made.
   Yours faithfully,
   Villeneuve Smith & Harford

I make a note on this letter to jog my memory: the first Hearing cost approx. two hundred pounds, and the second hearing fifty pounds. In my mind I think: at what cost and to what end?

7 – 13 March, 1942

Intensive work on Marie's portrait. Dr. Haslinger's wife is interned and there are speculations made regarding the Camp leader's future in the Camp. The Tatura Newsletter No. 2/10 is to hand, a few days later a letter from Margaret, Ted and Marie, dated 8 March, arrives:

Dear Father,

We received your last letter and were pleased to hear you received tobacco and pouch. Today is a beautiful day as have been the last few days, but last week we had very trying weather the temp soared over the century for four days, and we did welcome the cool change, but no rain, which is badly needed. So Bert and Gert are going to be married too after Easter and good luck to them but if only you were home and we could all be together how much happier we would be. Marie is going to be Flower-girl, she only said yesterday, I wish Grandpa could see me as a Flower-girl but never mind she said we'll send him a photo, because I'm his girl aren't I the dear little thing.

> *You wouldn't know the place at home now. Bert's working hard and fast at it and he's not making a bad job of it either. We are going down to tea tonight. It's his birthday tomorrow so we'll wish him happy birthday today. Ted's brother George came up from Adelaide last night but is going back again tonight. Marie loves going to Sunday School she wouldn't miss it not for anything. She has four little cards now pasted in a little book and she is proud of her little book too.*
>
> *Ted is very busy in his vegetable garden at present trying to keep up the supply of vegetables, which are scarce and going to get still worse I believe. The vacant block alongside our place I believe is going to be dug up and an Air Raid Shelter made for the school children. Ted has volunteered to help. Last Friday night there was a big A.R.P. meeting held here to prepare for air raid precautions.*
>
> *Well dear father hoping these few lines find you well as it leaves us.*
>
> *Lots of love from*
> *Marge Ted and Marie.*
> *Keep smiling Grandpa xxxx*

14 – 20 March, 1942

I have recently found out that American flour is being used in this Camp. Have our own supplies dwindled to such an extent that we must now import it?

I write to the Camp Commandant because if internment in Camp 1A identifies the individual as a Nazi, I desire removal to a South Australian Camp. My draft of the letter reads as follows:

> Sir,
>
> *On the date of the first Japanese attack on Australia I wrote to the head of the Intelligence Dept., asking that I might be released thus*

being enabled to help a little in the defence of the country of my birth. No reply has to date come to hand to my note.

Every additional success of the enemy meets with much approval by the majority in this camp. To this I cannot subscribe. Further, the arrogant behaviour of the camp leader, Dr. Haslinger, is designed to make this camp a definite Nazi camp. If internment in this camp is considered that the individual is in agreement with Nazi ideals, I ask that if it be possible I be transferred to a South Australian camp.

Yours respectfully
J.F.W. Schulz
P.O.W. 3077

Oh, what wonderful parcels and fruit I get for my Birthday, also a letter from Bert dated 11 March:

Dear Dad,

With your birthday but a week hence, we have got a package ready for you, and trust you receive everything safely. May your birthday be as happy as the circumstances allow. The thoughts of all will be with you on that day. May your next birthday be celebrated under more cheerful circumstances, and we hope, with everybody in the best of health.

If you were home now, you would hardly know your own place – that is, as far as the interior is concerned. I have still not nearly finished the work that has to be done, as one doesn't get very much spare time in the task of looking after the Office. We are still struggling along, although believe me, I get a headache at times. However, I am very happy to be able to do my bit to keep going. Trudi and I are hoping for our great day to be on the Saturday after Easter, that is on the 11th April. It will, in the circumstances, of course be restricted to the two families only. We are very sorry that the occasion should be marred by your absence, but we know your thoughts will be with us. Marie has even said she is sorry Grandpa will not be able to see her in her 'flower-girl dress'. I believe Marge has written you about this. As you say, we are making a small start (even that hasn't been easy) but both Trudi and I feel happier to have it this way.

I believe El has told you about the censoring of my letter. You remember? One whole paragraph on page 7. I was surprised that such an item should be cut out, as I thought, my other letters having reached you O.K., that my judgement was pretty fair. Anyhow, I will try not to transgress again.

Re sending Grapes. Our vines at home show promise of a record crop, you know the ones – black prince, or blue crystal, or something. I must get Bert Doering to advise me how to pack grapes, and we'll forward a sample lot along. If they reach you O.K. we can follow up with a lot of the later sorts, perhaps Muscatels. Did you receive the last half pound of Pipe Mixture quite safely? It should have reached you about a fortnight ago. I told the tobacconist about the incomplete address. He promised to be more careful next time. Please tell me are you able to purchase cigarette tobacco at the Camp. (Second thought! – I am reminded that El told us you couldn't get your favourite Capstan.) I guess we will from time to time be able to get hold of that blend for you up here.

A money order for five pounds accompanies this letter. It is made out, as usual, to J.F.W. Schulz, Military Post Office, Tatura, Vic. I guess you'll be needing some when the dentist is finished with you. Let us know whatever you require.

I am enclosing, also, a form which the Telephone people desire to be completed. We have shifted the telephone at home from the dining room to the passage, where it will be more convenient for both families. When the position was made clear to them they required the subscriber's account to be in my name. It seems a lot of unnecessary bother, but there you are. Your signature is required where marked with a cross on the form.

Vintage is about to begin, and as El has told you, she will be well in it also. It will be a good change for her, I think. Most of the young girls in the district will be in the vineyards. Some of the growers are complaining about the condition of their vineyards. They needed rain badly early in February. Now, any rain might do more harm than good.

Now, I will close this letter, with best wishes and birthday greetings to you from all of us at home.

Your son

Bert.

The Tatura Newsletter No. 2/11 arrives on 15 March and a few days later I receive two letters from home, one from Margaret, Ted and Marie written by Ted, dated 15 March, and one from Else dated 16 March:

Dear Dad,

Just a few lines to let you know we are all still enjoying fairly good health, and we trust you are too, but with weather conditions so changeable there are many colds etc. in our town and I guess you find it the same. Marie is very well and full of beans on the go all day. She has just returned from Sunday School, and is full of information. She just loves going, it would break her heart should she have to miss a lesson. Yesterday there was a busy bee at the school digging A.R. Shelter where quite a number took part. Marie certainly had a good time as numerous children were there so she had a grand time, but her father didn't fair quite as well, he has some blisters on his hands which are not so good, however another day will finish the job. Marie her mother and Mrs. Brown served afternoon tea which was a good let up, especially after a while on the pick and shovel.

Our garden is still going strong, and we have had some good results particularly with Tomatoes, Potatoes, and Cabbages have been excellent. The Vintage is now in progress, began on Wednesday last, I believe it is a little early, but owing to the last heat wave, practically all the vines lost the foliage which exposed the fruit to the sun and naturally burnt it badly. Some varieties there will not need to be picked as they will not go the test.

On Friday 12 March we packed a small parcel for you with the following: 1 Palmolive Shave Cream, 2 Packs Minora Blades, half ounce Papua (Bafra), four ounce Capstan R.R., 1 tin sweets and nuts assorted, we hope these will help to make your birthday a happy one, and we all join in wishing you a happy birthday and many more to come, when I hope we will be together again.

My pen I had dropped at the beginning and somehow affected the nib which you will notice has given quite a lot of trouble. The best for the 19th.

Your loving children,
Marge Marie and Ted
Kisses from your little girl xxxx

Dear Dad,

By the time you receive this letter you will no doubt have also received your birthday parcel and enjoyed some of its contents.

The question of fruit is at present rather a problem, the greengrocers have hardly had any apples or pears, and one cannot get them privately as you have no doubt heard of the apple and pear board.

Anyway, we have had a few peaches for preserving, from Kappler and I have sent you a few, and you will notice they are not very choice, but we expect to get a few better ones later on. Grapes we shall send you in the near future, and I have also asked the greengrocer to see if he can procure a half case of decent apples and he said he *thinks he can, so we shall know in a few days, and will forward them on to you.*

I should have started grape-picking today with the others, but we are on the Synod Reports at the Office, so I am not going until Wednesday, so you can imagine me the next few weeks hard at work!!

Mel Goers has left the B. News, as he is preparing to go into the Air Force anytime now.

To our knowledge Erwin Thiele will be manager, and they have a young girl Barbara Hoffrichter in the Office, and also in different towns they have appointed people to collect the news etc. and send them into the B.News.

Things are certainly looking black aren't they? I wonder what will happen to all of us. Women have to register too now, and we also have to state another job we would like to do next to our own now, I think I shall put my name down as a driver.

Bert is going to do some A.R.P. work. Mr. Alf Schultz had asked him to join up and Bert is quite pleased to do work of that type, we have to try and do our bit now too. I think we shall make our Air Raid Shelter in the creek!!!

Your work will certainly be a masterpiece when it is finished.

There have been two more deaths in the town, Paul Schmidt, and old Mr. Vorwerk from Goat's Square, both men had been in ill health for quite some time.

Mr. Heutz. sends his regards and says to 'keep your chin up'. He is giving me some of my favourite bulbs – daffodils.

Next Sunday is Harvest Thanksgiving in our Church.

Sabels are coming to live in Tanunda. They are going into the house next to Dulcie's, where Ben Wilkoch's used to live. Les Lehmann, the boy who married Pat Walther just before Xmas, is returning from Pt. Moresby, he had an accident and had to have his foot amputated. Vic Lindner is in camp now, so no doubt Mr. Riedel has quite a lot of work to do now on his own.

Are you having cooler weather now? I can imagine how trying the hot weather must have been.

Helmi W. has gone on another Business trip to Melbourne, as he cannot buy enough here. Old Mr. Schrapel is often out in his chair and is of course very shaky.

'Seedy' Nietschke's have a baby boy, and also Clem Eckermann's from Leditschke & Jansen's Garage. I met Winnie Schulz's father (Eric) on Sunday and he said he knew you from the time you used to travel around up Eudunda way years ago.

Peter Seppelt was on the 'Perth' which was lost, and also one of Clem Eckermann's brothers from Eudunda. Peter is Mrs. Camillo's son, and they haven't heard any word from Pat's husband either, Dr. C. Juttner who was in Malaya.

What a terrible time these poor families are going through. Jack Corcoran, Connie John's boy spoke from England recently, quite a number of folk here heard him.

News has spun out once again so I will say Cheerio and we all hope you enjoyed your parcel.

Love from home.

Else. xxxx

P.S. Don't ever think it is too much for us to send things we are only glad we can send them to you, you have only to say the word.

21 – 27 March, 1942

Dr. Haslinger applies for removal to the Family Camp. His request is granted. During these days I work intensively on Marie's portrait, but allow time to read the Tatura Newsletter No. 2/12.

28 March, 1942

Fireworks today when the new Camp Leader is elected. Dr. Haslinger nominates Herm. Junge as his successor as Camp Leader. Someone nominates Dr. Becker. Haslinger refuses to accept the nomination and charges Becker with having acted in a way to the detriment of camp inmates. He cites the case of the deceased Degen, that the kitchen staff had not done their duty, that Dr. Becker had communicated with the Camp Commandant on matters affecting the leader, that he had written privately to the Swiss Consul and the Official Visitor and to the German Authorities on the Camp Leader's conducting of the camp etc.

Dr. Becker mounts the platform and states that what Haslinger has said is 'erstunken und erlagen' (a pack of lies); th*at* Dr. Haslinger was never entitled to the title 'Dr'; that he had never fought in the war nor served in the Army; that he is a 'Schwindler und Hochstapler' (swindler and imposter).

Things were just reaching a climax when on the initiative of Dehnel this unsavoury washing of dirty linen was abruptly terminated and Herm. Junge was elected leader.

29 – 31 March, 1942

I enter the 'C' Grade Tennis Tournament and am successful through four rounds. The 'B' Compound entrants contest the finals in 'B' and 'C' Grade tennis.

A lovely box of grapes reaches me from home. I send Bert a box and two serviette rings for the day of his wedding.

Dietrich escapes from Hut 36. One other inmate of the hut gets a week's bunker for complicity. We (the camp) are deprived of radio and daily paper. Dietrich is captured and returned to the bunker.

The Tatura Newsletter No. 2/13 is to hand and I receive letters from home. One from Else dated 24 March, and one from Bert dated 26 March:

Dear Dad,

Just a few lines to say 'hello' once more. Did you receive the parcel O.K.? We hope you enjoyed it, as we thought of you that day.

Well I daresay you are wondering how grape-picking is going. Well, it is going great, of course it is fairly tough work I will admit. But I haven't packed up yet. Last week we picked several days at Willie Schulz's and then one day at Cox Heinemann's (he bought a garden out next to Percy Lindner's place along the Adelaide road). Today we picked at Artley N.'s garden down in the flat. We start at a quarter to eight and finish at five, and take our lunch out with us. Of course by the time I get home at night I am a real pig, but after a bath and rub down, feel pretty good again.

Marie and Margaret were down to see Mum today, Marie is growing up so now, she is quite a little girl.

(Half the page has been cut out by the Censor here.)

Steve has just arrived with the news that he is being sent to Coonawarra down the south-east to Milne & Co. Distillery, leaving Easter Monday for about four months so it looks as if Bert will have to find another groomsman.

Bert sent some peaches off today for you. We hope the other fruit arrived safely. The grapes will be sent soon too.

Excuse the short note as I still have some work to do before retiring, and I am always up at 6 a.m. these days.

Cheerio and keep smiling.
Love from all at Home.
Yr. Daughter, Else xxxxxxx

Dear Dad,

Just a short note this time.

Your welcome letter arrived today, and we were glad to hear that all our parcels reached you O.K. We trust that the half case of apples were in good condition also. Bert Doering packed these for us. By today's train I forwarded to you one fruit-case of grapes, and we are really anxious to hear how they reach you. Please reply immediately, as now is the time they are just right, and we could send you another lot next weekend, (including Muscatels, I hope). The grapes you are receiving in this first case were by favour of Mr. Art. Nettelbeck, and were picked by El. Alwin Zerna has offered me some Muscatels and Black Malagas, and these we hope to send to you as a next shipment. Railage per fruit-case, irrespective of weight, is three shillings and six pence. Per half case: two shillings. Really not expensive, is it!

Love from all,
Your son,
Bert

1 – 11 April, 1942

Dr. Haslinger has received news that he leaves for the Family Camp on the 11th. Bert's Wedding day is on the 11th. I receive my second case of grapes from home during the week. The Tatura Newsletter No. 2/14 arrives on the 5th for my perusal.

I receive a letter from Else dated 1 April:

Dear Dad,

We received your ever-welcome letter yesterday, and were glad to know that you had received all the parcels and fruit O.K.

You would hardly know our little town now. In the last few days (remainder of sentence cut out by Censor).

Most of the men have been billeted to the different homes, some people taking as many as six or more. Of course we were exempt, and where there is no man on the home also.

They are a decent lot of soldiers and quite often call at the vineyards to have a chat. Some of them think they will be able to help grape-picking, they certainly would clean-up a vineyard in double quick time, as so many women have had to leave work to cook for them. (Next two lines cut out by Censor.)

They have pictures every few nights, the butchers, bakers etc., don't know whether they are on their heads or heels.

Bert has asked Werner H. to be groomsman in Steve's place now, so that difficulty has been overcome. They have also had to change the time from 7 to 5, as no church service is held at night anymore on account of the black-out.

Our usual Thurs. night communion service is being held Good Friday afternoon. We have been holding our Choir Practices at Theo. Geyer's. Theo. celebrated his 69th birthday last Sat. He is still hail and hearty.

Next week will be a busy week. Steve leaves on Easter Monday, and in the evening the Choir is giving Bert and Gert a social.

Tuesday night the girls are giving Gert a surprise gift evening, on Wed. night the crowd at 'Cookies' are giving them an evening. Thursday night (up-to-date) is free, Friday, tin kittling and Sat. wedding.

This week we have only picked eleven hours as the weather has been wet and cold, and the cellars don't take grapes every day.

We are only six pickers now, where just we were eleven to twelve, so if we don't get help, we shall still be picking for a few weeks.

My hands are almost black, and not to mention the plasters!!!

We thought Fred. Johnson might be back with this lot and also Steve's brother, but so far have not heard.

Bert Doering must have included those cigs. We shall thank him.

I don't know if I ever told you Artley N. put down a lovely lawn tennis court, in front of their house. It was started last November, and is ready for playing now, the garden has been laid out beautifully too. (Section missing because it was written on the reverse of page 1.)

Gretchen Sobel has been ill again since they have shifted up here, poor girl she is always on the sick list, and Pastor is very shaky too.

News has run out again, so once more will say 'Cheerio.'

Love from all at Home.

Your daughter

Else xxxx

On 4 April I write to Bert.

Dear Bert,

The question asked by you in your last letter, namely how your first case of grapes had stood transporting, was already answered in my letter which was on its way Home while yours was coming to me. Today I am having the last bunch of that case and how lovely they were! And I am still eating of the apples which are keeping well. Thank you for your trouble with these consignments.

And now dear Trudi and Bert! Soon upon receipt of this letter a big day in your lives will be near at hand. I am sorry that I cannot be present on your wedding day. The main thing, however, is that you live happy. Bear one another's short-comings as you will share each other's joys. The future appears dark and uncertain; but there will assuredly also be bright days ahead. I wish you both God's blessing and am happy in the thought that I may find you both in our home when I return.

I am getting near to the completion of Marie's portrait. The work is giving me much pleasure and delight.

I entered a tennis tournament and struggled into the round in 'C' Grade. The finals in the three Grades are being played now. It is tennis as I have not witnessed it before.

I hope that with the cold weather approaching Mum and you all are keeping well.

Love, Dad

6 April.

Dear Bert,

Directly after I had posted my letter of yesterday's date I remembered that a few days ago I had sent you a small box and two serviette rings. It is intended for Trudi as a small wedding present. Unfortunately I couldn't obtain the material to give the case the final polish. Still you will, I am sure, appreciate the fact that during the hours of wood-inlaying and polishing my thoughts were with you both – Good luck!

Dad.'

Bert's letter dated 6 April arrives a few days later:

Dear Dad,

I trust this letter finds you in a better mood than I am at present. Everything that could possibly happen to make things harder for us, has happened. Or so it seems to me. Wrong furniture arriving, changing time of wedding, and a general upset of arrangements, such as having to look for another groomsman. And so on, Gert *comforts me by saying that if everything goes right before the wedding, there'll be trouble later on. Well, if there's any truth in that saying, it seems that our married life will be very happy.*

The date of the wedding is still next Saturday, the eleventh. But we have had to alter the time from 6.30 p.m. to 5 p.m. on account of lighting difficulties. Pastor Held will, of course, officiate. Linda, Gert's sister, is 1st bridesmaid and El is second. Benno Keil is best man, Werner Hebart, Groomsman. Marie is our little flower-girl. I think we have given you this information before. The reception is to be at Mrs. Zerna's – just the family circle, so to say.

The Choir is giving us a social tonight, the girls are giving Trudi a surprise evening tomorrow night. And on Wednesday night the folk round at Dulcie Auricht's are giving us an evening. And on Friday I suppose there'll be a little tin-kettling, so you see this week is going to be rather rushed.

We are all sorry that you should have to be absent, it will certainly rob the occasion of some pleasure for us both. But we know you will understand. And we will be thinking of you on the 11th.

I was pleased to know that the case of grapes arrived in good condition. By this afternoon's rail I am dispatching another case to you. Good appetite! They are from our own grapes. I haven't got any from Alwin Zerna, yet. Apparently, he hasn't got as many muscatels as he thought. But I think you will agree that ours are good eating.

I will close now and let you know more about us in the next letter.
Love from both of us,
Bert

12 - 19 April, 1942

The Tatura Newsletter No. 2/15, dated 12 April arrives for my perusal.

I receive a letter, dated 11 April, from Johs. J. Stolz, President of the U.E.L.C.A. whom I have known for many years:

Dear Brother Schulz,

Today the wedding of your son takes place, I have just sent a wire to him and his young wife. This forcefully reminded of you and your present situation. You will feel it very much that you are not with your people today. May it be of some comfort to you that you and the other members of our Church are not forgotten by us.

A better comfort, however, will be the text which I included in my message to your children, (The Censor has cut out the Biblical text reference here) 'Great peace have they which love thy law: and nothing shall offend them.' May this peace help you through until the day of liberation.

As to your son, he is doing well. You may thank God that he has developed so finely. You will not find anything amiss in your business when you return.

Sincerely yours,
Johs. J. Stolz

A letter from Mum dated 13 April:

Well now the excitement of the wedding is over. Everything went off perfectly and Trudi made a very pretty bride it was a beautiful spring day the bridesmaids and Marie looked very pretty too. El will write more details about the wedding, the reception was held at Mrs. Zerna's, and there were about thirty present just the two families.

I have just packed a tin with Wedding Kuchen from Mrs. Zerna for you and hope you enjoy it.

Pastor Held and others spoke very nicely of you at the reception and we did not forget you, they received a lovely lot of presents telegrams and letters from relatives and friends.

Bertha sent over a pair of socks for your Birthday and I will send them shortly on to you, Paul and Maggie are still with Bertha.

Harry called in to see us the other day he is in camp here. For the past week the weather has been very hot and people are complaining of water shortage we still have plenty. El has finished grape picking as there is plenty to do at the Office, she earned over five pounds. In today's paper was Melva's engagement to a farmer from the West Coast his name is Donald Wake.

Bert and Trudi have gone for a few days honeymoon, they will be back by the end of the week, hope this letter finds you in the best of Health as it is leaving us.

With love from

Mum

A further chapter opens. On Friday morning, the 17th, the Commandant at our Tatura Camp 1 called Materne and myself into the Orderly Room. Eime should have come also but was out working in the garden. We were informed that we had to be at the gate with our luggage on Sunday morning. On Monday we would leave probably for Camp 2 and thence probably for South Australia. All was excitement, of course. The 'probably' kept us in suspense. We had asked to be transferred from Camp 1, which is admittedly recognised by the Military Authorities as a Nazi Camp, but we wanted also to go to South Australia, the state of our birth, nearer our families. The possibility of transference to Camp 2, Tatura, was disconcerting, to say the least. All doubts as to our destination were set at rest when we learned on Sunday that our Bank account had been transferred from Tatura to Loveday, South Australia.

All is hustle and bustle. What a load of junk and impedimenta accumulates in ten short months even in an internment camp!

A Glad Birthday. Commit thy way unto the Lord; trust also in Him; and He shall bring it to pass. Psa 37:5.

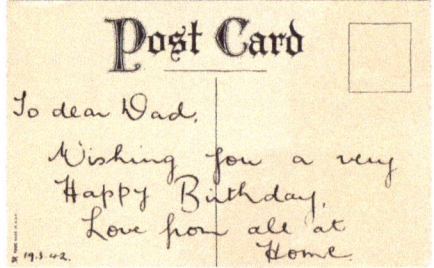

To dear Dad, Wishing you a very Happy Birthday, Love from all at Home.

3

LOVEDAY INTERNMENT CAMP

20 APRIL 1942 – 5 JANUARY 1944

12

20 April, 1942

Seven o'clock Monday morning found us at the 'One Way' gate, four of us, all excitement. We did head for Camp 2 but only to join a second lorry bound for East Murchison.

The train was considerably late at East Murchison and apparently filled to the last seat. In addition to our party of thirteen there were many soldiers on the platform. The Porter's appeal to the passengers already seated to make room fell on deaf ears. Only the Station Master's announcement, 'Under a Military Order, all passengers in this carriage must vacate their seats,' had effect. Soon we were seated and travelling to Broadmeadows. Feelings of relief and thanks manifested themselves within me; I was still a P.O.W. but I was homeward bound.

Upon arrival at Broadmeadows we found a further six internees on the 'waiting list', to accompany us to Loveday. At Broadmeadows I was impressed with the changed attitude of the guards as compared with the behaviour of some of them when we were upwards bound in June, 1941. We were treated more as victims of circumstance than as criminals, and right here I would like to put on record the considerate and gentlemanly behaviour of the Lieutenant in charge of us and directing the youthful guards who did sentry duty. Lieutenant Crewes, I am told that was his name, showed us every possible consideration. He was firm, yet whenever it was possible to spare our feelings from curious crowds, he acted in our interests. Our bodily requirements received punctilious attention. The few words of thanks that I addressed him when we reached our destination came from the bottom of my heart.

Thus, a party of nineteen boarded the Melbourne Express about 7 p.m., changing at Murray Bridge on Tuesday morning, the 21st, and we eventually reached Loveday at about 7 p.m. that night. A very tiresome trip.

21 April, 1942

What a denouement when we reached Loveday! Rain fell slowly. Together with such luggage as we carried we were separately called into a room to be searched. And a thorough search it was, stripped to the skin. Yet it was according to regulations no doubt, and there was no undue harshness. Emerging from the search I placed what I was carrying slap-bang into a large pool of water, due to the faulty glasses I had perforce to wear.

On to the Compound proper! Former inmates of Tatura 1 greeted us. 'You'll get a shock!' We sure did! Compared with Tatura the conditions at Loveday are disappointing. But I'm near home!

I had never been reared and never lived in luxury, and providing my health does not give out entirely, I pray to God that he gives me strength to pull through. On my short walks every morning now, I look in the direction of Tanunda. Vineyards are within sight, a homely atmosphere pervades the air, and please God, this is the final stage to home. Today, Saturday 25th, I already look more hopeful into the future. I have written home and look forward for news.

26 April, 1942

Church Service – Pastor Zinnbauer. At last Sunday's service at Tatura there were prayers for the success of Hitler's Arms, by the Reverend gentleman officiating. Today we have prayers for our King. May God grant us a victory with lasting peace.

27 April, 1942

There is unrest in the Camp owing to compulsory vaccination. I receive my second inoculation at fifty-nine years of age. Later I go to the dentist in an adjoining Camp in an ambulance drawn by two draught horses. I meet Phillips, former photographer at Tanunda. It was good to meet a soldier whose friendship extends into the Internment Camp.

28 April 1942

The vaccination has affected me adversely and I passed a bad night. I was called to the Post Office and find a parcel has been returned to me from Tatura, and I receive two letters – all from home. I leave my inlay work and Marie's watercolour with the Commandant at the Post Office who has promised to forward them to the address left with him – Bert's address.

29 April, 1942

My arm is swollen from the vaccination. Rev. E. Stolz visits Doehler and Zinnbauer and brings oranges and watermelons. Doehler's first job is dividing the fruit. In reply to the interrogation by an inmate: 'Pastor, I am your friend,' Doehler replies, 'The Scripture says, if your enemy hungers, feed him.'

30 April, 1942

The weather is ideal, warm with occasional showers. When we arrived here not two weeks ago the ground was completely bare, now it is almost covered with green.

1 May, 1942

Today Willie Zuzz, Dr. Gruber's protégé, is eighteen years old. We have a little celebration and present Willie with a Birthday cake. The Thiele boys bring their guitar and banjo and we have quite a happy sing song.

2 May, 1942

News reaches us that the inmates of Camp 10 had burrowed a tunnel thirty seven yards long before the enterprise was discovered.

I get my first letter from home since I am here. I am glad that my films, screen, and bowls have arrived home safely.

3 May, 1942

We experienced very heavy thunder and lightning during the night and probably even an inch of rain. Though we are compelled to camp and sleep cheek by jowl – thirty-seven in a portion of a Mess hut – we are at least spared the drenching that many of the other hut inmates suffered.

Our church service today is led by Pastor Materne.

4 May, 1942

Around about the middle of January I handed in my spectacles at Tatura for repairs. They were promised me back within a week, or at least a fortnight. It is now almost four months since I handed in the glasses. The old pair that I am using have played up with my eyes and cause me much suffering.

5 May, 1942

I write a rough draft for a letter to the Commandant here at Loveday re my spectacles:

> *Sir,*
>
> *About the middle of January, I handed in my broken spectacles (broken rims) to the military optician at Tatura. He promised to repair and have them returned to me within a week or at latest two weeks. I paid six shillings in advance for the repairs. Repeated applications to the hospital orderly as also to the Camp leader, who, I understand, passed the complaint on, that the spectacles be returned to me, have been of no avail. The spectacles I am forced to use now for almost four months, were discarded six years ago as unsuitable for my eyes. I am suffering continued headaches and am almost unable to see anything in bright sunlight. Is there a camp optician here who can do something for me?*
> *Yours respectfully*
> *J.F.W. Schulz, 3077*

7 May, 1942

There is a General Meeting today re the liabilities of Tatura 4 – one hundred and forty pounds apparently. Financial chaos generally.

8 May, 1942

Today's General meeting is about the Canteen. Eime and myself ask for a competent declaration that internees, other than those from Tatura 4, be not held responsible for liabilities incurred by the Tatura men. There is general approval and agreement to this request.

9 May, 1942

There is no letter yet from home and I spend most of the day reading.

10 May, 1942

Rev. Doehler is preacher in the Lutheran Service and approximately twenty inmates attend.

11 May, 1942

I join the outside wood-gang as cook. What a chapter I could write on my first attempt to cook for a gang of sixteen men! But, judging by the remarks of those who had perforce to eat what I cooked, I passed the test with credit.

12 May, 1942

Stayed 'at home' to interview the Official Visitor, who, however, did not put in an appearance.

13 May, 1942

Out cooking again.

14 May, 1942

At last I get a letter from Else dated 8th inst., and am relieved to learn that Marie's photos have arrived safely. I did not go out with the wood-gang as I object to the 'sit down' method of working. Every member of the gang knows that he is required to do a certain amount of work for stipulated pay before signing on. Enough said. Instead of working outside I write to Else and Margaret.

15 – 16 May, 1942

I draft a letter to the Intelligence Department, Adelaide, seeking a second Hearing. I also send a copy to the Official Visitor asking if the letter has reached its address and if I will be given a second Hearing before the Advisory Committee:

Sir,

In June of last year, I was transferred from Wayville, S.A. to Tatura, Vic. Internment Camp. It soon became evident to me that the internees at this Camp were with few exceptions Nazis. I approached the Official Visitor and asked him if internees who remained in Camp No.1 Tatura were considered Nazis. He gave me no satisfactory answer. On Feb. 19th of this year when Darwin was bombed for the first time the inmates of Camp 1 rejoiced and proclaimed: 'The Japs are coming and will get us out of here.' On that date I wrote the following short note to the Intelligence Dept., Vic.:

'The midday broadcast announces that Darwin has been bombed by Japan. Camp inmates here assure one another that Japan will soon get us out of here. I don't want Japan to liberate me. I am almost 60 years of age and want to place what strength I still possess at the disposal of the country of my birth, Australia. I make a final appeal for my release.'

Respectfully
J.F.W. Schulz

On the same day (15th) I also write two notes to the Commandant here; one about my films and the other regarding my inability to work with the wood-gang. I have kept a copy of each one:

Sir,

Both at Wayville and Tatura I showed films taken by myself to camp inmates, and I hereby seek permission to screen my films in this camp. I am, of course, quite ready to run these films through for you before screening them in camp, or your good self or a member of your staff could be present at the first screening. At the screening here I would like to make a charge of one penny for admission to cover expenses incurred in transporting the films, screen and projector.

Thanking you in anticipation of a favourable reply.
Yours respectfully
J.F.W. Schulz 3077

Sir,

Weather conditions and age have forced me to resign from the wood-gang (outside). I would be deeply grateful for any job that you could offer me, clerical or store work.

I wish to thank you for dispatching my portraiture work which reached its address safely.
Yours respectfully
J.F.W. Schulz 3077

17 May, 1942

Steiniger preaches on 'Prayer'. He tells us to not only 'ask' but to 'listen' to what is required.

There is an incident at breakfast over eggs 'commandeered' by one table from another. I have never thought it possible that 'humans' could behave as individuals do in this Compound. We are prone to look down upon the Italian section in this Compound. They are noisy; they are argumentative, but I have yet to experience at their hands treatment similar to the treatment handed out from one to the other among the 'cultured' in our section.

18 May, 1942

There is trouble in the hut over beds built, presumably, with stolen timber. Passing my place in the hut, Sergeant Major Battams remarks, 'How is it you haven't pinched any timber yet?' My reply, 'Let me go out and get some bush timber and I'll build a bed for myself.' The Sergeant Major gives me permission to go out with the wood-gang to get timber.

19 May, 1942

I go out for the day to collect timber for my bed.

Bob Nielsen, the arch blasphemer in the Camp, gets two weeks in the bunker for stealing timber for his bed.

20 May, 1942

After about five months delay, I have my glasses returned to me with repaired frame. What a relief for the eyes!

I build my bed. To be honest, I sit on a log and watch the Thiele boys at work on the bed!

Else writes me yesterday that I can expect visitors on Sunday!

21 May, 1942

I get two parcels containing the good things that were to be brought to me personally. What a delight to unpack the eats! During the day I get a clothing issue from the Authorities.

ELIZABETH M. SCHULZ

22 May, 1942

Bert writes me how the intended visit miscarries. Well, I still have a visit in store! His letter is dated 17 May:

Dear Dad,

Today is Sunday, and if things had gone according to plan we should have been with you by now. You will no doubt have received El's letter telling you that we had made enquiries in Adelaide, and at Barmera, and as a result of these enquiries had made all arrangements to make the trip to Loveday today. But by yesterday morning's mail, we received notice from Camp 14D Headquarters to the effect that no visitors are allowed on Sundays. So that is that. As I mentioned before, all arrangements had been made – cake baked, biscuits baked, fruit purchased, etc. So, we are getting these goods ready and they will leave here tomorrow, Monday.

So, we cannot say when we will be able to get away to come up to Loveday. You may be sure that it will be at the first possible opportunity, and we will let you know in good time.

It is quite some time since I have written anything regarding the Office. Well, it isn't just fun nowadays, as you will readily understand. The paper question is always presenting fresh problems, and there is a continual search for substitutes. What a godsend it is that there are Australian mills, even though they have a somewhat limited output. Newsprint as we use it will most likely gradually disappear entirely from the market.

At home we have settled down comfortably, and are all very happy to be together. Our vegetable garden is gradually undergoing a rebuilding process, and even now some beds extend as far back as Ellis' apricot orchard. The heavy rains we have had during the last weeks have been ideal, and conditions for sowing and planting are wonderful. We have been keeping our own mushroom patch well under observation, but so far have picked none, although a basketful was given us last Sunday. In some parts they seem very plentiful.

You may be interested to hear that Gus Braunach's mother passed away recently, as also Herm Schild's wife. Mr. Obst, Alf, the Zerna's, Hans Hartmann, Frank Heinrich, Mr. Presser, and lots of others send their greetings, which we would have given you personally, had things gone according to plan today.

Love from Bert and Gert

23 May, 1942

I receive a supply of tobacco – the dinkum mixture! What matters as to whether our kitchen rations are supplied according to regulations?! I have my tobacco! In the parcel, Bert includes a copy of the brief letter he wrote to the Camp Commandant accompanying the Money Order sent for me. It reads as follows:

Sir,

Herewith please receive a Money Order to the value of one pound ten shillings, made payable to my father, Mr. J.F.W. Schulz, P.O.W. 3077. I would thank you in anticipation for making this available to him at an early date.
Yours faithfully,
W.B. Schulz

Vernon R. tells me of the death of old Mr. S. A life full of energy, ambition, resolve, ended. Barry H. has the job of entering particulars of parcels in the Post Office.

24 May, 1942

Pastor Materne preaches the Pentacost sermon.

25 May, 1942

Cold, drizzling weather. A wonderful season is promising in the district.

26 – 27 May, 1942

Continuance of wet, drizzly weather. I contract one cold after another. It almost looks like bed from morning till morning. What a life. Inactivity drawing in its wake morbidity, despair, and attendant consequences. Living in a cosmopolitan community, including the dregs of society, calls for its toll.

28 May, 1942

I have visitors from home: Bert, Trudi, Margaret, and Marie visit me. I take a new lease of life. Marie recites to me her Sunday School verses. Oh, and what a lot of good things do they bring me! How much reason for thankfulness I have! May I never forget! While they were here, Bert showed me the telegram they received yesterday: 'Permission granted 1p.m. Thursday.' This news brought much joy to them also.

29 May, 1942

What a glorious sunshine day! And out between the two Compounds are being loaded tons upon tons of galvanised iron and hundreds of thousands of feet of timber for the building of more huts for internees!

30 May, 1942

I have a good night. Cliff's horseradish, which my family brought with them on their visit, finds general appreciation. Pahnke, the boiler-man, is served a 'Messerspitze' (small taste) of the delectable appetiser and the strong man presents a ludicrous picture when tears roll down his cheeks. An apple from my larder appeases his anger.

31 May, 1942

Zinnbauer gives the Trinity Sunday sermon. There is a jocular affair with the corpulent Sergeant later at Inspection, and tonight we have another concert on Graf's electric gramophone.

1 June, 1942

Six men start work on building huts for our accommodation as the majority of the internees are in tents and the rest in the unused Mess huts.

2 June, 1942

Twelve months ago today I arrived at Tatura. What a wealth of experiences are crowded into the past short year! What sufferings the world has passed through! How much nearer to human happiness has Armageddon brought us? Armageddon: The scene of the battle between the forces of good and evil which is to precede the millennial reign of Christ on earth, according to Revelations 16. May God grant that the peoples of the earth soon arrive at an understanding!

3 June, 1942

Mitchell returns to the hut from the bunker.
    The newspaper reports of Japanese submarines in Sydney Harbour. The submarines are reported to have operated with negative results. Their presence is disturbing. Has the result of the Coral Sea fight lost us the protection of our own and the American fleet? The paper reports that there were nineteen killed and ten injured suggests that the submarine's incursion into the harbour was not a haphazard one.

4 – 5 June, 1942

Typical winter's day – bleak winds, clouds, and sunshine.
    The Italians are busy building huts. The necessary tools are brought into the Compound and again delivered at the gate each day. Italians working on the huts attend to the work of transporting the tools. At 9 a.m. all workers go to work. Those working outside line up at the gate, those working inside go to their jobs. The two men transporting the tools also attend at the gate to bring the tools through the gate. The tools are in a box to which two long handlebars are attached. From the

gate to the scene of action the transporters have a walk of about fifteen chains. They carry their box about five chains, sit down on the box, roll a cigarette and enjoy a restful smoke.

The rest of the way to the huts being built is broken by a similar rest, and all the time the workers on the huts are 'anxiously' awaiting the arrival of the tools.

Many interesting discussions take place among the internees of the various huts, the internees representing all walks of life: refugees, once in affluent circumstances and moving in influential circles of society. They recount their experiences, and the future, in most cases, is designated as hopeless. Particularly that of the refugee who was brought to Australia as his haven of refuge only to be ultimately interned and refused a hearing before an Appeal Tribunal.

Over against these, I do not lose faith in my country's future. I was reared in a hard school, and even today my family and I are more comfortably situated than were my parents in my childhood days. Though my own Government has temporarily bereft me of my freedom, I visualise an ultimately brighter and better future.

6 June, 1942

It's lovely warm weather and we work also during the afternoon to get the full day's pay – one shilling. This is the place where twelve pennies make a shilling, and the shillings, a pound.

7 June, 1942

Rev. Doehler's sermon is on Dives and Lazarus. The Commandant's call-up of a number to attend in the Mess hut at 11 o'clock tomorrow arouses much speculation. I notify the Orderly Room of my desire to see the Eye Specialist.

I get two letters from home, one of which is from Bert dated 1 June:

Dear Dad,

Well, here we are back home again. Everybody is asking how you are, and what things are like up there. I told Wilf that I had handed the Underberg Bitters in, and he is keen to hear whether you received them. Trudi was round at Theo Geyer's for a ladies' choir practice this evening, and when I called for her, everybody wanted to know how you were keeping. I told them we thought you were looking well. I also told them how we felt when we had to see our own father being marched away, followed by a guard with fixed bayonet. And believe me, many others feel the same way. Only this evening I was speaking to a man who said: 'I wrote to Minister Forde the other day, using my position in local affairs, to see whether he cannot do anything in the matter of your dad's release.' I wished him better luck than I have had so far. Things are gradually reaching that stage now, when they border upon the ridiculous.

We spent quite a busy time over the weekend. But, believe me, we slept mighty soundly after our visit to Loveday. Saturday found us busy in the vegie garden. I had the job of taking out stinging nettles – quite a tricky job, believe me. But it's just like the women-folk to leave all the difficult jobs to us menfolk. Even though a few panes of glass are broken in the glasshouse, I have decided to try my luck with a tomato plant which sprang up on its own account somewhere in the garden. It didn't seem to be doing too well, on account of the cold, I guess, so I'll give it a try under glass.

Poor old Fritz Schulz has been having a pretty bad spin of late. I believe they took him to a city hospital today for further observation. They think his gall-bladder is causing all the bother. It was at first feared that the trouble might be cancer. He looks terribly ill; you wouldn't know him now as the robust miller he always was.

Marie is certainly a wonderful traveller. She stood the trip to and from Loveday marvellously. We got home in quite good time, arriving at Nuri. at about 6.15p.m. We had a lunch stop en route. Ted was very interested in your 'Koffer Tisch' (small occasional table), but I couldn't unpack everything that night, so showed it to him when they were down for El's birthday party on Saturday evening. He, too, was very much taken up with it. And, believe me, it will be very acceptable as an occasional table in our living room.

Tomorrow (Tuesday) I am going to the city per rail. There are lots of things in connection with the business which have to be attended to. One gets down to the city so seldom these days. I may even have to stay down for two days – I hope not.

When we visited you, I forgot to enquire; have you received the one pound ten shillings I forwarded to your Camp Commandant on the 23rd May?

Another matter I failed to question you on: Can you obtain hot water, or have you access to a fire at any time, say for supper or so? Give us an idea please just how things are. Whatever you would like, just ask for it. It is rather hard for us to imagine things as they perhaps are, so please let us know. Winter is coming on, and you have every right to be comfortable.

Last Saturday we had a little celebration at the office. In May 1900 Chris started at the Printing Office. That means he has served the firm for 42 years. The occasion could not be allowed to pass without some recognition, so (I know I acted as you would have) on behalf of the firm I got up a gilt-framed address, suitably embellished in watercolours by Trudi, worded as follows: 'Presented to G. Christian Obst by the Proprietors of Auricht's Printing Office in appreciation of 42 years of faithful service. Tanunda, May 1942.'

Now, I have seen many a man taken by surprise, and so, no doubt, have you; but you cannot imagine just what this meant to Chris. He was literally speechless. He just kept on saying thank you! Thank you! And through me, he thanks you most heartily, and wishes you all the best. El supplied some 'business expenses' in the form of biscuits; I brought some 'business expenses' in the form of a bottle of Purple Para for that occasion. I trust the proprietor will not question the expenditure on these two items.

Until next time
Love, Bert

8 June, 1942

Only a half a day's work owing to rain.

9 June, 1942

Half a day's work with Mills carrying foundation studs. Half an hour to go and six studs to be carried about one and a half chains. The foreman (Boss) arrives on the scene, looks over the job and announces, 'Boys, you'll have to make the job last half an hour!'

10 June, 1942

An ideal warm day. It is a pleasure to work out in the open.

11 June, 1942

The Estonian asks me to give him a hand wiring up the new huts for lighting. It is easy work and under cover. I am only getting a shilling a day. I don't work myself into a lather of sweat, but I am giving more than one shilling's worth of labour in the service of my country.

I have another severe attack of bladder trouble, due, no doubt, to a cold.

12 June, 1942

While the other workers must stay 'at home' owing to rain, we 'electrical' workers can go on under cover.

13 June, 1942

Just eighteen months interned!

14 June, 1942

Pastor Steiniger has the Sunday Service.

Pastor Doehler and Nitzulas, known as Sandy, take a morning walk around the Camp. Sandy tells us how he likes to stroll about with a gun shooting birds. Doehler expostulates with him. It is wrong to shoot birds. The Pastor shoots cats only. He remembers shooting nine cats. Sandy is shocked at that: Every cat having nine lives, that means quite a lot of destroyed lives. 'You won't bl—dy well go to heaven,' he avers.

15 June, 1942

We finish wiring the first Italian hut. I had a very easy day and doubt if I even earned my shilling! But the staff is eager to keep 'Dad' on. At times it almost makes me sad to be called 'old Dad'. I would like to be as young as I sometimes feel. There is so much work ahead of us!

16 June, 1942

More rain during the night, but an ideal sunny day. The open window has brought on another cold.

17 June, 1942

I have a brush on rising with Lindeman re open windows. We come near to blows upon L. veiledly classing me amongst 'the Nazi's who are all against me.' He explains that he did not include me.

I watch a fresh batch of internees pass through the 'One Way Traffic' gate. It is 8p.m. A vehicle laden with the luggage of the internees and drawn by two draught horses heads the cortege. The internees, after a day and a night in the train, wearily plod along behind. The numberless spotlights in this and the adjoining Japanese Compound occasionally throw the procession into lurid relief. 'Abandon hope all ye who enter here,' the silent night seems to breathe.

The hut leader, Schmidt, has a brush with my neighbour over the removal of a protection across the upper part of his window. Deutsch wins the bout.

18 June, 1942

I had built a protection around the head of my bed to shield me against the night wind. L. considerably closes the window which he had protested in the morning must remain open.

Bert sends me my Pitman Shorthand Dictionary.

19 June, 1942

A cold day. I start to brush up my Shorthand.

20 June, 1942

Intensely cold today. The men working on the huts keep a fire going to keep themselves warm.

21 June, 1942

Pastor Materne is preacher today. The weather is still cold but seems to be improving.

22 – 24 June, 1942

I return to work on the hut and enjoy myself in delightful weather. I work in conjunction with Grisar occasionally who tells me that his old grandmother used to tell him: 'Paul, es geht nirgends so verricht zu, wie auf der Welt.' (The people of the world are crazy.) His demonstration of German wrestlers entering the lists and their introduction to the audience is comical in the extreme.

25 June, 1942

I get a parcel of three packets of Capstan Cigarette tobacco – just in time. I continue work on the hut.

26 June, 1942

Cold wind on hut work, excavating for stump piles. Limestone rock has to be chipped away bit by bit. Mat M is good at the crowbar. Ross advises occasional geological studies.

27 June, 1942

I receive a letter from Else and one from Bert and Gert dated 14 June – just on two weeks en route from Tanunda to Loveday! Bert writes:

> *Dear Dad,*
>
> *Trudi and I have just come back from a little outing, looking for mushrooms. Yes, we've got to go out looking for them now! The patch by the carob hedge, which stood by us so well last year, has let us down badly. Maybe we will be more fortunate later in the season (we had mushrooms till October last year) but I don't hold out great hopes. However, I am looking forward to our tea tonight, and I only wish you could be with us to help enjoy it.*
>
> *The time is a quarter to five and Trudi is just getting tea ready. You might wonder, why so early? Well, as a matter of fact, we intend going to church at Tabor Church tonight. Rather a special occasion, so we want to be there in good time. Pastor Gerry Obst has been fortunate in securing the Lutheran Army Chaplain with one of the American Camps to be guest speaker this evening. What a fine thing that will be for our Church. I expect the church to be crowded out, so we are leaving home early. The Americans, from what we have seen of them, are quite good fellows. Three of them were in church at Rev. Hebart's this morning.*

Fred. Richter told me yesterday that his son Vernon had now received his third stripe. He seems to be doing quite well.

You won't forget, will you, that in my last letter I enquired whether you were able to get hold of hot water whenever you wished, or whether you would be able to use a little spirit stove in your Camp. I thought you might sometimes of a cold night feel like a cup of beef tea or soup or something. These items we can easily get for you. Please let me know what your position is in this respect.

While we were out this afternoon, I noticed that the olives down the flat are ripening. You mentioned something last year about pickling them, but I'm afraid I didn't follow the recipe accurately. You might be able to get a simple recipe somewhere. If so, let me know, and I'll have another try.

We've had a terrific amount of rain lately. Too much for most folk I'm told.

Yesterday was first day for clothes ration coupon books, and do you think there was a crowd up at the courthouse to collect them! I had to wait almost an hour for our lot. How does this rationing affect you? Let me know what your position is.

Love from Bert and Gert

I didn't quite finish my letter before. Or rather: I had finished it, but had not posted it. So, I'm carrying on. I feel I must tell you about the service held by the U.S. Army Chaplain. The church was absolutely crowded out, with the porch way under the tower filled with a standing audience. He didn't give us so much of a sermon as a survey of Lutheranism in America and his work as an Army Chaplain. He made a wonderful impression, and everyone hopes we shall be privileged to hear him on future occasions in the various churches.

Today is Monday, King's Birthday holiday, and just before lunch we received a phone call from cousin Ern Bruhn, who is in camp in Adelaide. He has a few days leave, and asked whether he might spend them with us. So, we have a visitor. He came up by car with Ralph Eckermann, who is in the same camp. El has gone to pictures with him tonight. He tells us Aunty Polly is fairly well, but Uncle Carl is rather shaky, which is not to be wondered at, as he is getting up in years.

Am forwarding Pitman Shorthand Dictionary under separate cover. I suppose El has mentioned she intends seeing the Secretary of the Institute Library about some reading matter.

Jack Lindner sends greetings. He said a friend of his at Barmera had told him you were at Loveday, which I confirmed when Jack asked me the other day.

Keep smiling
Bert.

A parcel of writing material: paper, ink, pencils, rulers, etc. has arrived in the Camp for distribution. Sender: The Australian Christian Students' Association. A notice, 'Am schwarzen Brett,' (on the bulletin board) says they will be handed out 'nach den bewahrten Grundsatzen von Schiebung, Korruption und Protection (according to the tested principles of graft, corruption and protection). Nuff said!

28 June, 1942

Sunny but cold. Zinnbauer has today's service.

29 June, 1942

Mat and I dig the hole for an electric light pole, four feet six inches in depth – some job. How fortunate we are to get the good rations as we get just now and have a good cook. This morning we had A1 raw ham!

30 June, 1942

We have to change our four good blankets for inferior ones, but there are enough to keep us warm.

1 July, 1942

More finger printing during the day. The cook Sehl goes to the bunker in protest.

When hut-building, I notice men on the large garden plot – at least I think they are moving. A man on top of the building looking towards the plot, soliloquises: 'They don't appear to move.' After a pause: 'Yes, they are our men.' Mat and I sink an electric light pole hole, four feet six inches in depth and later erect the pole.

2 July, 1942

The cook returns from the bunker. There is very serious news from Libya and the Mediterranean. The many friendly greetings from friends of my hometown help keep my spirits up. The Arandora Star survivors remember this day two years ago.

3 July, 1942

I commence work but stop halfway through the forenoon because of the piercing cold wind. My throat does not want to recover.

4 July, 1942

An exceedingly bleak day and I do not go to work. A further one hundred and sixteen Italians are due to arrive in the Camp today.

5 July, 1942

The newcomers include many German Queenslanders from the north, and New Guinea people who travelled overland to Port Moresby. In 'Life Magazine' I see the startling caption, 'America makes Australia it's 49th State!'

6 July, 1942

A first-class sunny day, ideal for work. My eyes are tested and I am listed for new glasses at an early date.

7 July, 1942

There's a change to cold, bleak weather. I have to get my Burgandy overcoat from Hartle to wear it at work. The good news is, I receive a letter from Bert dated 26 June:

> *Dear Dad,*
>
> *I hope you have received the parcel of six ounces Capstan Fine Cut and one dozen cubes of Chicken Stock. I had enquired in one of my previous letters as to whether you had access to hot water whenever you might desire it. I haven't heard whether you can or can't*

obtain it; anyhow you should be able to use the chicken cubes even at meal times.

I am going to the city on Monday next in connection with a little Devotional Booklet we will probably be printing for the Church. You can well imagine that any jobs of that type are very acceptable in these hard times.

Chris. Obst and Alfred are felling the last of the sugar gums up at the printing office. They had been annoying Dr. Juttner (the trees, I mean). I believe he draws his fresh water supply from tanks just under these trees, and the gum leaves, bark, etc. used to make a fair mess of his tanks, so he says. Well, the men are quite glad to take them down for the wood, so everybody is happy.

It seems such a shame that all the land at the rear of the Office should be lying idle. The place certainly looks very forlorn. I have my hands full with looking after the Office, but sometimes I think it might be a good idea to plough up the whole of the land and turn it into garden plots – vegetables, or anything that's going. And it certainly is good soil. You will remember the time Mrs. Auricht used to spend in the gardens during her time. But there you are, it's the same old story, unless a man can do it himself, there's not much in such a side-line. No, times are not easy.

What sort of weather have you been having? We have had about three fine days during the last three weeks, and tomorrow, the 27th, is 'Siebenschläfer' (Seven Sleepers' Day). So, if we are to put up with a further seven weeks of this weather, things won't be too happy.

How is your pipe tobacco supply? Should be getting pretty low, I guess. Well, I'll see that I get some more of the good old mixture for you when I get to the City.

Love from everybody in the home town, and especially,
Bert and Gert

8 July, 1942

Parcel from home with foodstuffs. How well provided for I am. In addition, Pastor E. Stolz visits and in addition to his usual bag of oranges, he brings a parcel of cheer from the Light's Pass Ladies Guild, which we, Doehler, Mat, Zinnbauer, Steinig, and I share with the New Guinea folk.

I get a tin of Perfection Cigarette Tobacco with a card in the tin:

> *Greetings from W. Koop, Light's Pass, S.A.,' a booklet, Daily Light on the Daily Path, inscribed: 'To whom it may concern – from Mrs. B. Ruediger, Truro, Sth. Australia, Austr*

What a thrill these mementos give! My thanks float across the air to these kind donors. Also, to those who, un-named, have provided my tin of honey, the lovely biscuits and the lead pencil with which I now write.

I send a letter home, written on an air letter which includes instructions for its use in three languages: German, Italian, and English:

> *Dear Bert,*
>
> *Your letter of the 26th reached me yesterday. The receipt of the six ounces Capstan and the chick. cubes I think I have already acknowledged in my last letter to El. Since then the tobacco mixture has reached me and today the parcel: Ham, two Mettwurste, cocoa, two tobaccos. On top of this the pastor from Berri who visits several of us once a month and usually brings a parcel of oranges today brought in addition a case of good things packed by the Light's Pass Ladies Guild (I believe). What a red-letter week. Please thank the party responsible for this case of cheer. We need not go hungry here, sometimes having served more at meals than we can eat.*
>
> *But besides this evidence of good-will, it is wonderful now and then to rummage in your own larder and partake of something from home. Thank you everybody. I can guess that you have your*

business worries. You might have a plough turn over a plot at the back of the printery and try some potatoes or cabbages. Before long you will be busy on the Almanac which should be welcome work. This part of the country is experiencing the best season for many a year. Would to God the world were soon at peace!
    Dad

9 July, 1942

A strenuous day trying to break through rock formations for the eighty-four holes that take the stumps for each hut to house fifty-six people. We get a shilling per day. The Tribunal Committee that sits in judgement on us, gets seventeen guineas = three hundred and fifty-seven shillings!

10 July, 1942

Pay day. I collect nine shillings for a fortnight's work! It rained heavily overnight. We started work but the rain stopped us.

11 July, 1942

I get a letter from Else which disturbs me very much. It tells of Margaret being ill and she is apparently somewhere in Adelaide. I write and ask for details immediately.

12 July, 1942

Steiniger takes the Service: 'Tater sein, nicht Hörer allein'. (Be doers, not only hearers.) Our weather seems to be improving today.

13 July, 1942

Good weather so on with the hut-building.

14 – 15 July, 1942

I get a letter from Ted which took nearly three weeks to reach me. It tells of Margaret's illness.

16 July, 1942

I get my new job of Time-Keeper and Caretaker of tools. I am devoutly thankful for this though it has its unpleasantness.

17 July, 1942

I find my bearings in my new job.

18 July, 1942

Full day at work.

19 July, 1942

There is a rush to peg claims in the first half of the first hut built by us. I am just in time with my trunk to peg my corner.

20 July, 1942

Cold weather, but I have a secure 'posi' in my office. Buffalo Bill gives us a circus exhibition.

21 July, 1942

It is more tragic than comical to notice some of the Persian refugees at carpentry.

22 July, 1942

A constant number have their Appeal heard daily. Much confident hope not realised. We celebrate Mat's Birthday in the Missionaries tent.

23 – 24 July, 1942

Much rain from Thursday to Friday. The Tribunals continue.

25 July, 1942

I am promised my file for sharpening the saws used in hut-building. Today is Else's Wedding Day.

26 July, 1942

Boettger takes the Service and tells of work among New Guinea natives.
   I write a Business letter to Bert:

> *Dear Bert,*
>
> *From El's letter and the 'News' I have noted the particulars of Miss Auricht's sale. Selling furniture and her other belongings is, of course, her own affair, but the letting of the premises is a different matter. This at best, I think could only be done by her after consultation with me or you. She has not apprised me of her intention to do so. Have a look at the particular documents and, if necessary, have them interpreted for you. The premises would need repair and painting. If Miss A has let them without your consent, she will have to attend to this work herself, or it must be paid for out of rent. No buildings on the premises dare be removed, particularly the galvanised iron sheds at the rear. If Riedel has got his finger in the pie, give him nothing to get a leg in. The whole property is ours and we cannot allow anybody to monkey with it. This business has disturbed me not a little. Write me immediately who the new tenant is. In future do not put P.O.W. on your address. Just write No.3077 etc. This may facilitate transit. Trusting that everybody is in good health. Dad*

27 – 29 July, 1942

Ideal days for hut work. On Wednesday I move into position No.1 in Hut No.1 in which I had a hand in building.

30 July, 1942

An ideal spring day. The energy in hut-building has somewhat abated. The second hut should be ready by the weekend.

31 July, 1942

Life in the second hut. New 'tenants' moving in. There's likely to be bother.

1 August, 1942

Another week ended. Time passes quickly for me.

2 August, 1942

Rev. Zinnbauer takes today's Service. I remind him of his wrong pronunciation of 'bow' and 'category'.

3 August, 1942

Wonders will never cease! Eime, with ten others, are dismissed from the garden workers! Eime was probably found lecturing to an Italian audience.

4 August, 1942

Feeling runs high. Tables, walls, etc. in the Mess Hall are found decorated with Judenschwein, Heil Hitler and numerous swastikas. The decorations were done in red paint, still wet. The Officers in charge of the Inspection squad handled the early threatening situation very tactfully. The Commandant, Major Hill, visited the Mess Hall after breakfast. Developments are awaited!

5 August, 1942

Eime got hell at the meeting last night and probably deserved most of what he got. The worst feature was that he hadn't the guts to attend.

6 August, 1942

Together with seven others, we walk right past Camp 10 for dental ('mental' somebody understood) treatment. My tooth is replaced back in position and we then have a slow trot back to Camp.

7 August, 1942

Pay Day! For the first time I draw for a full fortnight inclusive Saturday afternoons = twelve shillings! I feel happy and proud! Tobacco in the main is supplied from home, so the one shilling a day that I can earn buys biscuits, condensed milk, matches, toothpaste etc. Boss Walker raises a loan from me. 'Can you lend me a penny?' he enquires. I did, with marginal observations. I also receive a parcel of tobacco from home.

8 August, 1942

Gris, who now works in the kitchen, retires temporarily owing to 'Muskel – Verrenkung'! (muscle sprain/dislocation). 'In the jawbone, no doubt,' somebody remarks. I receive a cake and two mettwurst from home!
I am reading an article in The Advertiser on page 6, dated today, titled 'The Unrationed', and write down what I consider are some very relevant points:

> The more the world is devastated by enmities, the more we value the friendships which shine the brighter because of the environing darkness. The more we share the rationed commodities the richer we shall be in the unrationable commodities. It is indeed one of life's strangest paradoxes that so many of our most precious commodities are 'without money and without prices'. They are free to all, they require neither cash nor coupons. The enjoyment of natural beauty cannot be rationed. The roseate hues of dawn and sunset, the silent majesty of the starry skies, the loveliness of the almond blossom, the glory of the golden wattle are ours without asking. God rations our years in this world, but he does not ration

the pleasures we may find in it; nothing is required for their enjoyment, but eyes to see and ears to hear, and minds to appreciate. The harmonies of nature are undisturbed by the discords of men. The rainbow in the clouds is the token of an everlasting covenant. While the earth remaineth, seedtime and harvest, cold and heat, summer and winter, day and night shall not cease. The enjoyment of nature is far from being the only unrationed and unrationable commodity. The Government can ration newsprint or even ration news, but it cannot ration thought. With unrationable faith we shall live through unrationed days. Courage cannot be rationed; we shall need all that we can muster. Ours it is to match our courage with the crisis of the world's destiny. Garfield, American President, once spoke these words, worthy to be remembered.

9 August, 1942

Missionary Zischler gives an inspiring sermon on the theme: Give account of your life – every day, every hour.

10 August, 1942

Bitterly cold and showery weather.

11 August, 1942

It's amusing to listen to the jargon of the men on the building job – i.e., 'This blasted winkel (corner/angle) isn't schqware, and the planes are no good for hobeling! (planeing)

12 August, 1942

Squally weather. A sudden burst of wind carries Buffalo Bill's tent over him. He returns to the Mess hut with bag and baggage.

13 August, 1942

Bob Nielsen objects to having epithets written on his private square. He accuses me of writing on it. I have it out with him.

14 August, 1942

Half a sheet of galvanised iron is missing from one of the hut walls. I suggest waiting. Somebody might come along to borrow our tin snips. Sure enough, at about 10 a.m. Drejer, who is building a private hut of bricks made by himself, asks for the loan of our tin snips.

I follow him and discover our lost half sheet, already flattened out and shaped as a chimney for the fireplace of the hut. During lunch time I rescue a parcel of flooring timber from a marauding Italian!

15 August, 1942

From my workshop window I watch about two hundred and fifty Japanese from 'C' Compound stacking their luggage at the gate. They comprise the exchange party for Australian civil internees in Japan. Quite a few of them, so report has it, reluctantly return to their homeland.

When will the gates open for me?!

16 August, 1942

Warmest day since winter. I have been approached to give English lessons. The suggestion has given me much food for thought.

17 August, 1942

I watch the Inspection Staff move into the Japanese Compound 'C' and compare the deferential attitude of the Japanese with some of the lousy, loutish behaviour of some of the men in our Compound, who fail to realise that the withholding of respect to others entails the loss of self-respect.

18 August, 1942

On enquiry today from the Commandant, Major Hill, I learn that my communication to the Intelligence Department months ago had been handed by him to Major Martin, upon whose advice he had sent it 'officially' per post.

19 August, 1942

Terrific dust-storms.

20 August, 1942

We get a taste of what dust-storms can do at Loveday! Today the Italians oblige with a concert. Some very illuminating remarks are made by a party of guards in attendance.

21 August, 1942

The Camp indulges in pig-killing. The chase after the pig at large in the Compound provides humorous episodes. Buffalo Bill comes to the rescue.

The wind is again blowing a gale. The large area, after weeks of careful preparation, is now ready to be sown and planted with vegetable seeds and plants, some of it already under crop, is moving in swirling clouds of dust into the adjoining bush. From my office window I get occasional glimpses of the workmen, at one shilling a day, leaning against the gale and moving phantom-like among the hopeless mess.

22 August, 1942

Cold and wintry. We have an amplified gramophone record concert with pork sausage and coffee. I give a rendition of 'Mary's little lamb'!

23 August, 1942

A glorious spring day and the night is delightfully cool.

24 August, 1942

The New Guinea contingent get word of transference to another Camp, presumably Tatura 1. Today we can buy sausages. It's a perfect day. I almost feel ashamed to claim my one shilling per day sitting in my office the greater part of the day watching other members of the building gang at work with saw, hammer, crowbar and shovel.

I have cut an article from today's paper, 'The News', which reads as follows:

ALL INTERNMENTS TO BE REVIEWED

Speeding Up Appeals.

Canberra.

All internments are to be re-examined, and appeals by internees are to be expedited. The courts have been clogged up by these cases for months.

The Commonwealth takes the view that appeals are too expensive for both the Commonwealth and the internees at present, and it is possible that the whole system will be revised.

The Attorney-General (Dr. Evatt) is known to be concerned at the cost of an appeal for appellants, particularly in view of the decision to release five of the seven members of the Australia First Movement.

He has already given a broad hint of what he considers the position of other still interned members by declaring that it was a pity that they had refused to go on with their appeals, as there was reason to believe that some of the appeals might have succeeded.

The Australia First members' successful appeals have shown that there are people in internment camps, who should not be there.

> *Dr. Evatt also believes that where an Australian's personal liberty is at stake, he should be given every possible facility to secure a hearing, and this is the motive which will lead him to examine the whole appeal system.*

25 August, 1942

New Guinea men to leave Camp this afternoon. 'Get interned and see Australia,' somebody suggests. One internee in Hut 1 has, to date, been transported to seven different places for detention.

26 August, 1942

We watch the Japanese and New Guinea men leave. We know not their destination, but conjure up visions of the day when we will pack.

27 August, 1942

Two of our hut are called before the Tribunal. How different from the day when I appeared and my Appeal was heard! Now it is all just considered a huge joke!

28 – 29 August, 1942

Extraordinary winter conditions.

30 August, 1942

Twenty-five internees are ordered to pack for elsewhere, presumably Tatura 2. Vacancies are created in various offices. I am offered the position of works and wages. I accept, relinquishing the cushiest job in the Camp. But I enjoy work and hope to cope with a full-time job. Dr. Graffunda, the man who was in charge before me, initiates me.

31 August, 1942

My first day in my new office. My head is in a whirl over the multitude of figures, and I wrestle with the typewriter. My knowledge of the keyboard, since operating the linotype, is almost nil, but after an hour or two I manage to make appreciable headway. I go to bed with a sore head and wonder what induced me to leave my old job.

My name is one of those on a list who were asked to come to the Orderly Room re an answer to their Appeal.

Today I receive a letter from Bert dated 23 August:

> Dear Dad,
>
> You will doubtless be waiting to hear from me how matters are going at the Office. I had hoped to discuss things in general with you in person, but am still waiting for an opportunity to come up. I had hoped, sometime back to be able to make the trip, but couldn't. I am surprised that you knew nothing of Miss A's arrangements with the mission authorities, as she twice asked El for your address. She has definitely never spoken to me about her intention to let the place to the mission committee. Your agreement with her says that she is to have 'the use' of the house during her lifetime. Now, what is one to understand by 'the use'? Does it extend to permitting her to

let the place – and that without the knowledge and consent of yourself? You might well write to her for her version of the matter.

You think she may have borrowed money from Riedel. Perhaps, although it would surprise me, for I should imagine he would want some security, which as far as I can see she couldn't produce.

The extension phone to the dwelling I have removed, as the ladies there have no use for it, and it was an added expense to the phone account. And expenses there are enough nowadays, as you can well imagine.

In the last letter I wrote you, (quite a while ago, I am ashamed to have to admit) I mentioned that Chris and Alf were taking down the last of the sugar gums down near Dr. Juttner's sheds. They tried for half a day, this way and that, but when the giant finally fell, it crashed right over what used to be Mrs. Auricht's actual fowl shed and the horse stable. If the sheds in question had been taken down before-hand we would have saved ourselves several sheets of iron, now rather badly crushed and also some of the timber, which naturally was split and damaged. Poor old Chris.! You can picture his face after the tragedy. They will have to take down the sheds and knock out the bent sheets. Fortunately, these were the two old sheds. The two newer ones were untouched. All the ground behind a line drawn from Juttner's fence to Polly Kleemann's on a level with the old Mangelschuppen (old storage shed), is not being used. If it is possible, I thought it would be a good idea to run a fence along this line and put a plough through the whole lot. Then fruit trees could go in, or vegetables in bulk lots. (But whoever is to do the work. I don't know!) It wouldn't really matter what it is, as the land is absolutely idle at present.

Your glasshouse has been put somewhat more ship-shape now. I put in quite a fair lot of lettuce plants some time back, also planting some in the outdoor garden. And you should see the difference. The terrific rains we had of course knocked everything back, but now the glasshouse plants look beautiful. We had a few seed potatoes lying *about, so Trudi put those in too – also in the glasshouse, by way of an experiment. Next, we intend trying tomatoes.*

Some cruel person has been laying poison in our neighbourhood. In the last three days, I have had to shoot and bury three cats; one belonging to us, and two strangers that had managed to crawl into our place. One wishes that such an animal poisoner could see the look of agony in the cats' eyes. It might frighten him.

El wrote you today also. Did she mention that Mrs. Tremel is in the Angaston Hospital? She broke her leg last Thursday, and the poor old soul is not too good at all, I hear.

The Chev. is being registered as from the first of September. I thought it time to give the old bus another spell on the road. It will be a lot better for Mum, as the Singer is somewhat small when all of us go out – especially to church.

Pastor Hebart is still not at all well. His attack this time seems to have been much more severe, and keeps him very weak.

Mum, Trudi, and I visited Tante Anna last Sunday. She isn't at all well, either, and has been in bed for some time. I took out a choir book and Trudi and I sang her a number of songs. She said she often thinks of you, and wonders how you are faring.

Mum got a letter from Auntie Maggie today. Uncle Paul has a good steady job at the Mt. Gambier Flax Mill.

With kindest regards from all in Tanunda, especially from E.G.H.

With love from
Trudi and Bert

1 September, 1942

My second day in my new job. I feel much happier and can see daylight today in what seemed just a maze of figures yesterday. The Corporal in charge tells me a day or two will put me right. If only I had not the dozens of Italian names to wrestle with.

Good news! I am told to be ready to receive visitors tomorrow.

2 September, 1942

A glorious day in more respects than one – weather conditions and a visit from Mum, Bert and Else.

3 – 4 September, 1942

I work my way right into my new job and now feel confident of being able to give satisfaction. My fortnightly wages now amount to fourteen shillings. Hurrah! The counting of my 'sheep' after each muster is a problem often. 'I must not lose one of the ninety and nine'!

5 September, 1942

All sorts of rumours filter through the camp re reviews of internees' cases, but we despair of receiving favourable news.

6 September, 1942

We go for our first route march – about fifty of us. It was a novelty, the weather is perfect and we return back tired but happy.

7 September, 1942

May Dr. Evatt proceed with the good work he has undertaken.

8 September, 1942

Summer makes itself felt, but the nights are definitely crisp. Somebody suggests an Association – the badge to be of barbed wire.

9 – 10 September, 1942

It was not an easy job but I was able to get out my first fortnightly pay sheet on time, and correctly.

11 - 13 September, 1942

Much changeable weather. The summer makes a cautious attempt at approach only to be ousted by the severest winter conditions.

14 – 19 September, 1942

The days and weeks pass quickly with continued work at day and a game of Skat at night. On the 15th I draft a letter to The Official Visitor:

> *Sir,*
>
> *The attached is a copy of a letter handed by me to the Camp Commandant for transmission to its address. It was handed in on May 16th. The Commandant assured me about four weeks ago*

that the letter had been forwarded. To date I have had no reply to it. I would thank you for information as to whether the letter has reached its address, and if it has, am I to be given an opportunity of appearing before the Advisory Committee a second time.

Thanking you in anticipation.
Yours Respectfully
J.F.W. Schulz. 3077

I receive a letter from Bert dated 16th September:

Dear Dad,

By way of a change I'm writing from the Office and on Office stationery. We are just laying the foundations for the Almanac, so to speak. The paper position now is really serious, and we have informed the Almanac people that the issue for this year should be reduced by thirty-two pages, that is, one sheet, at least. We have suggested to the Editor that the reading matter, which was usually set in 10 point, could very well be set in 8 point. If this were done, the actual loss of reading matter would not be great at all.

Miss Auricht was in the Office yesterday morning. She says she has been on sick leave for some time. She went over to Mrs. Daly at the Hotel at Freeling with Bert Teusner yesterday afternoon and intends returning early next week. I don't know when she has to sign on again. She tells me that she wrote to you a week or so ago.

How is your tobacco store? El intended getting you some of your special mixture from the City when she got back. She hasn't let us know whether she was able to get it or not, but I assume that she got it or she would have let me know.

20 September, 1942

Another route March. Work prevents me from taking part. Tomorrow is 'Atonement Day' for a certain Jewish group in the Camp. I feel a humorous vein in me tinkling at the 'preparations' being made for the 'fast day' tomorrow.

21 September, 1942

Wood arrives in the Camp for one hundred beds – almost six months after my arrival here. I feel loathe to change from my o/s bush bed. Doehler has a visit from his brother John and hears 'that he has not put in an Appeal.'

22 September, 1942

The worst dust storm ever experienced by myself. The works office building seems right out of alignment, the door refuses to close.

23 September, 1942

Owing to a reduction in the number of men to be paid for work inside the Camp, all men working, with the exception of the Kitchen staff, go on strike. Conveyances for lifting garbage tins and the man with the wood, return through the gates, the latter to unload himself outside the Compound. I sincerely hope the affair will be speedily and satisfactorily settled.

24 September, 1942

With give and take, camp routine promises to settle down to normal conditions. At work I type out a list of the number of nationalities of Internees in Camp 14D:
British 30
Naturalised German 20
Ditto Italian 73
Austrian 9
German 99
Italian 393
Danish 1
Polish 3
Albanian 5
Finnish 17
Hungarian 3
Swede 1
Rumanian 1
Norwegian 2
Dutch 2
Yugo-Slav 1
Estonian 2
French 1
Czechoslovak 2
Singapore: German 11, Hungarian 1
Palestine: German 1, Austrian 1
Iran: German 18, Austrian 3
New Caledonia: Italian 3

Nineteen Nationalities with the Nationalities again divided into political factions.

25 September, 1942

I am on my second bi-monthly pay sheets. Owing to less men on pay, the amount earned for the fortnight will be less than during the first. Hope Mr. C's 100m will be a success.

26 September, 1942

The pay sheet is causing problems owing to the alteration. I hope the chief will allow the full pay – one extra day. If not, much extra work is needed to affect alteration.

27 September, 1942

One of the best days climatically to date. W.H. arrived in Camp last night.

28 September, 1942

The pay sheets have to be altered to exclude the two days included in the last pay sheet. Today more men are called in to expedite the work in hut-building.

    A lengthy list is read calling men into the Orderly Room after tea. They are advised that their detention is to continue. This reminds many of us of the days and days of agony.

29 September, 1942

There is a call for extra men to finish more huts to give us recreation rooms and workshops.

30 September, 1942

Tonight, the entire Kitchen staff persists in walking out. That we might be without cooked meals tomorrow is hardly taken seriously.

1 October, 1942

New men, at least a skeleton staff, will be ready to provide porridge and coffee in the morning. Buffalo Bill is the new stoker and was blowing off steam as early as 4 a.m. A call for a further five men for the Kitchen at breakfast time was announced by dinner-time. Chagrin and regret is noticeable on the faces of a number of retired staff.

2 October, 1942

The Kitchen is almost fully staffed again. Boss Walker leaves for Melbourne this morning. I wish him luck. May he not return here. He deserves well, unless my knowledge of his past actions is entirely at fault.

3 October, 1942

A letter from Ted, who is holidaying at O's, heartens me. May God protect and keep them all.

4 October, 1942

A complete change in the weather. After the storm and dust of yesterday, calm and rain sets in.

5 October, 1942

The Camp leader, Graf, announces, under instructions from the Commandant, that within two days all tents have to be evacuated; the inmates to fill the completed huts. There appears to be no great hurry on the part of the tent lodgers.

6 October, 1942

Cold night, warm day.

7 – 9 October, 1942

Busy days getting the pay sheets out, but the work runs more smoothly now.

10 – 11 October, 1942

Summer is gradually making its presence felt.

12 – 13 October, 1942

I hand in my spectacles frame and mention Stevenson's! Later, I was called on by the Official Visitor. My letter to the Intelligence Department, Adelaide, dated 15 May this year, did not reach its address. I make another attempt to get the ear of the powers that be:

> Sir,
>
> *In June of last year, I was transferred from Wayville, S.A., to Tatura Vic. Internment camp. It soon became evident to me that the internees in this camp, were, with few exceptions, Nazis. I approached the Official Visitor and asked him, if the internees who remained in Camp 1. Tatura were considered Nazis. He gave me no satisfactory answer. On February 19 of this year, when Darwin was bombed for the first time the inmates of Camp 1 rejoiced and proclaimed: 'The Japs are coming and will get us out of here.' On that date I wrote the following short note to the Intelligence Dept. Vic.: 'The midday broadcast announces that Darwin has been bombed by Japan. Camp inmates here assure one another that Japan will soon get us out of here. I don't want Japan to liberate me. I am almost 60 years of age and want to place what strength I still possess at the disposal of the country of my birth, Australia. I make a final appeal for my release.'*
>
> *To this letter I received no reply. A few weeks later I again wrote to the Intelligence Dept. Vic. (I regret having mislaid the copy of this letter). In effect I asked that if the Military Authorities recognised Tatura Camp 1. as a Nazi camp, and if my staying in that camp automatically lined me up as a Nazi also, I respectfully requested that I be transferred, preferably, to a South Australian camp. I received no reply, but on April 20 last I was sent to Camp 14D, Loveday.*
>
> *Sir, I ask that I be permitted to appear before the Advisory Committee a second time. I desire to give further evidence,*

supplement some of the evidence given on the occasion of my appeal, and to correct some of the evidence as recorded on the twenty odd sheets transcribed from shorthand taken down at the appeal. This evidence, by the way, was never presented to me for perusal or signature. My solicitors later secured a duplicate copy for me.

If this request cannot be granted, can I not be given some work on parole? Everybody's help is needed, we are told. I am not disloyal to my country, and I sincerely desire to help.
Yours respectfully
J.F.W. Schulz. No. 3077

14 – 15 October, 1942

Summer is approaching in earnest. Today I write to the Official Visitor, W.V. Ray S.M., at the Local Court in Adelaide:

Sir,

I beg to advise that I have this day handed to the Commandant of this Camp, Major Hill, a letter addressed: The Deputy Director for Security, Box 1429J, Adelaide, and, as arranged, am advising you of this fact.
Yours respectfully
J.F.W. Schulz. 3077

16 October, 1942

Real summer weather is with us.

17 – 18 October, 1942

Rumours of transference are continually with us.

19 October, 1942

Five men leave for their Tribunals at Melbourne and Sydney. O. Morschke, C. Enchelmair, Laun, and Liddle go to freedom. One day I also will be free.

20 October, 1942

A remarkable change in the weather – back to Winter. A two-horse Trolley bolt ends without serious mishap. The fortunate crash into a gate prevents a catastrophe. An announcement is made after lunch: 'All who know something about tobacco growing to come to the Office and have their names entered.' I have my name entered.

21 – 22 October, 1942

Cool and windy weather. Rumours of our transfer to another Camp have once more proved groundless. It is the end of another pay period.

23 October, 1942

Internee G. Schreiber intends to end his internment term by committing suicide by cutting arteries in his arm. He is hurried to Hospital.

24 October, 1942

The pay sheets cause me some worry as the total fails to tally by one shilling! It took me several hours to trace the discrepancy.

25 October, 1942

A warm day. It takes me all day to get out the new Time Sheets for all the working parties.

26 October, 1942

I get a wonderful parcel of good things from home including this copy of a letter Bert has written to Dr. Evatt, date 19 October:

> *Honourable Sir:*
>
> *Twelve months ago I made representations to the Minister for the Army, the Honourable F.M. Forde, through the Honourable Minister for the Navy, the Honourable N.J.O. Makin, on behalf of my father, Mr. J.F.W. Schulz, who is at present held in internment at Loveday, S.A.*
>
> *At that time I pointed out that at my father's appeal we had engaged a King's Counsel to represent him. After the hearing, the K.C. was definitely of the opinion that upon the evidence given at the hearing, no British subject could be detained. I further mentioned, that the fact that my father's detention continued, left us with no other conclusion to arrive at than that he was being held on a charge or charges, against which he had never had the opportunity, surely due to him in common justice, of defending himself. The Honourable Minister for the Army, however, replied*

that he could see no reason for reversing the decision arrived at by his predecessor, Mr. Spender, namely, that my father's detention should continue.

We at home have been afforded fresh hope by recent newspaper reports of your personal attention to the whole question of internments. We know that your aim is to see that justice is done, and we thank God for it. Why shall a man suffer internment, and why shall his spirit be broken, when his whole home district vouches for his integrity? Can nothing be done to right this wrong?

Respectfully yours,
W.B. Schulz

The Sergeant Major accuses me of having smuggled out a letter to the Deputy Director of Security. I resent his imputation and ask him to call on me when he has proof. All my dealings in the Camp have been above board.

27 October, 1942

Wind is blowing and dust is flying in clouds.

28 – 29 October, 1942

An order to wear burgundy pants or at least a patch of that colour on ordinary pants, brings to light some amusing designs.

30 – 31 October, 1942

The official announcement that Tuesday next, three hundred Italians are due to arrive on our side of the Camp, causes consternation and apprehension. We await developments.

1 November, 1942

Some tangle-foot in the Compound causes unpleasant diversions. Michael Brice stages a showdown on big Pahuke. An inmate of Compartment 'B' of our hut, who had apparently come from the fountain-head, indulges in blasphemy, invective and foul language, the like of which I have never heard before. He spoke and sang in German. God preserve us from the domination of a people who suffer such creatures.

2 November, 1942

Tents are being erected in haste to shelter the three hundred Italians due to arrive tomorrow. Our office moves from Mess 2 to Hut 3. We are comfortably quartered. Work in connection with the new arrivals cuts out outside work for the afternoon. Men returning from 'work' are taking exercises in weight lifting etc. This amuses me.

3 November, 1942

At about dusk, lorry loads of the announced fresh Italians with their luggage arrive outside. By and by they are drafted into the lane between ours and the Japanese Compound. Even in the failing light they appear forlorn and travel weary. In due course they are marched into the Compound, firstly to be fed and then to be searched. The searching takes place opposite my hut. I fall asleep about eleven o'clock and sleep without a break until the morning.

4 November, 1942

The Compound is now one thousand strong – over eight hundred Italians. Yesterday's arrivals are settling down. A huge pile of luggage is still out in the lane with a row of sanitary pans keeping silent sentry. Let us hope that we succeed to live amicably together behind barbed wire.

5 November, 1942

A number of internees are called to see the Deputy Director of Security re their Appeals. When were they heard? Have they heard the result? Koch and Boss Walker, who have just returned from Melbourne, are also called in.

6 November, 1942

The recent Italian arrivals appear outspoken Fascists. Let us hope we may be permitted to live in amity alongside one another. I finish the Pay Sheets in record time.

7 November, 1942

A delightful day after the changeable weather.

8 November, 1942

Summer makes its presence felt.

9 November, 1942

The hottest day so far. I write a letter to Bert:

Dear Bert,

Your letter and Else's both reached me Saturday. With all the work you have at the present time I am looking to you for letters, since I know that letters from Mum, Else and Nuri will provide me with the family news. I am, of course, pleased to hear, that you might be enabled to secure the necessary paper to bring out the most urgent publications. Please convey to the workmen my thanks for their co-operation in these difficult times. I am so thankful that Else is at home to lend a helping hand, especially since you have taken on so much additional work in the garden. Is Miss Auricht still in employment elsewhere? I do not know whether you are paying her any money weekly, but she is hardly entitled to any unless she does her share of work (other than 50% of the profits, if any, at the end of the year). I am pleased that you have written a letter to headquarters. Be sure to let me know the nature of the reply, whatever it may be.

My health is good and with steady work throughout the week, time is passing quickly. Just now we are having some hot days. A hot cup of tea with orange or lemon juice is a good thirst-quencher. Trusting that both you and Trudi are well.
Dad.

10 November, 1942

I have been reading the following books:
    Looking for Trouble by Virginia Combs
    The Road to Bordeaux by Cooper and Freeman
    All interesting and informative.

11 – 12 November, 1942

About twenty Italians are moved from the Camp at short notice. Allegedly they are Fascists.

13 November, 1942

Carl V. feels sore that someone is beating him for cigar and cigarette bumpers outside.

14 November, 1942

Salami at night.

15 November, 1942

The Works Corporal is not coming in today and I have an entire free day – first one for weeks.

16 November, 1942

With the summer days on us, shorts are becoming the custom of the day – long shorts, half mast, and short shorts. Men of three score years and ten with the Constitutional Bowlers Corporation give rise to humorous comment and good-natured banter when parading in tight fitting burgundy coloured half-masts.

    Little Margolies had a smelly trick played on him when a hut mate mischievously used his ancient helmet as a bed pan during the night!

17 – 22 November, 1942

Days of unrest. A death by violence is reported from Camp 'A' across the fence. Report has it that the recent Italian arrivals are determined to clear our camp of all but Italians. Then again, a list of names mentioning men from among us who are reported to be urging the Italians on, is disclosed. The names on this list are men who are to be transferred to another Camp shortly. Let's hope for the best.

23 – 25 November, 1942

The transfer of thirteen to Camp 10 has taken place. It includes two men who have been doing persistent maligning and fostering distrust and discontent. The Camp is well rid of them.

26 November, 1942

Schmidt and Mills return from Melbourne. In the Orderly Room I sign up for 'work outside under restrictions.' What rate of pay and what nature these restrictions might be is not specified.

27 – 30 November, 1942

Time is fleeting. Boss Walker is to be further detained. He is much upset. So were many before him. Still, sooner or later, the hour of liberation will come for all of us.

1 December, 1942

After a few warmer days we have winter with us again.

2 – 6 December, 1942

I finish Pay Day work in good time. Extraordinary weather! The temperature drops from 98 degrees F to 60 degrees F in twenty-four hours. Today is a real mid-winter Sunday.

7 – 8 December, 1942

Owing to the altered time of passing the men through the gates half an hour earlier, something akin to a strike has developed among work gangs. I am a disinterested spectator.

106.   Appendix D

I make a bed for myself

Appendix F

Digging holes

Back to Work

111.   Appendix I

Erecting the electric light poles

Electric Light Poles

Cook for the Work Party

Appendix E

Sowing seeds

NICHT HIER SCHREIBEN
VIETATO DI SCRIVERE QUI
DO NOT WRITE HERE

English

NUR DIE ADRESSE AUF DIESER SEITE SCHREIBEN
L'INDIRIZZO SOLTANTO SU QUESTA PARTE!
THE ADDRESS ONLY ON THIS SIDE

Mr. W. B. Schulz
Box 83.
Tanunda

PASSED BY CENSOR

No. 3077
Name: J. W. Schulz
No. 14D CAMP
4th MILITARY DISTRICT
SOUTH AUSTRALIA.

1942

NICHT HIER SCHREIBEN
VIETATO DI SCRIVERE QUI
DO NOT WRITE HERE

NICHT HIER SCHREIBEN
VIETATO DI SCRIVERE QUI
DO NOT WRITE HERE

SCHREIBEN QUI HERE

Letter (front)

NICHT ZWISCHEN DIE ZEILEN SCHREIBEN!
NON SCRIVERE TRA LE RIGHE!
DO NOT WRITE BETWEEN THE LINES

Loveday 8/7/41 ← 1942

Dear Bert, — Your letter of the 26th reached me yesterday. The receipt of the 6 ozs Capstan and the chick cubes I think I have already acknowledged in my last letter to Eb. Since then the tobacco mixture has reached me and today the parcel: Ham, 2 Mettwurste, cocoa, 2 tobaccos. On top of this the pastor from Berri who visits several of us once a month and usually brings a parcel of oranges today brought in addition a case of good things packed by the Lights Pass Ladies' Guild (I believe). What a red-letter week. Please thank the party responsible for this case of cheer. We need not go hungry here, sometimes having served more at meals than we can eat. But besides this evidence of good-will, it is wonderful now and then to rummage in your own larder and partake of something from home. Thank you everybody. — I can guess that you have your business worries. You might have a plough turn over a plot at the back of the printery and try some potatoes or cabbages. Before long you will be busy on the almanac which should be welcome work. This part of the country is experiencing the best season for many a year. Would to God the world were soon at peace! — Dad

(JWSchulz)

Letter (back)

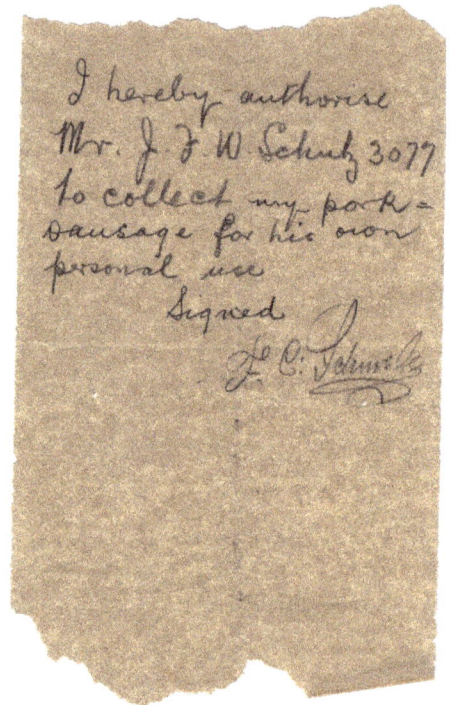

Pork Sausage

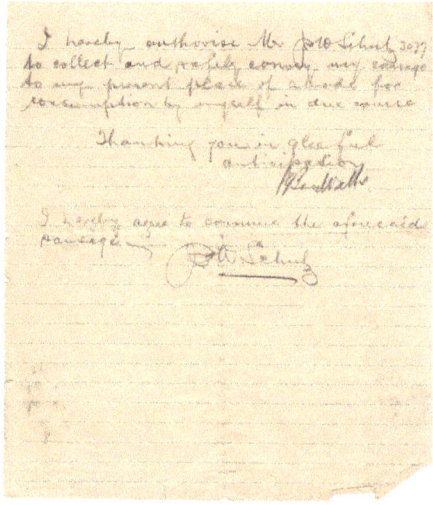

Sausage Collection

Why all this trouble?

13

9 – 16 December, 1942

On the thirteenth I was interned two long, short years. On that date I wrote to Dr. Evatt. My draft of the letter reads as follows:

> *Dear Sir,*
>
> *Two years ago today the Military Authorities took me from my home at Tanunda, S.A. Since then I have been detained in turn: from Dec. 13, 1940 to June 2, 1941 at Wayville, S.A., till April 20, 1942 at Tatura Camp 1, Vic., and since then at Loveday 14D, S.A. I appeared before the Advisory Committee in Adelaide towards the end of February 1941, and though informed by my solicitors that the Committee's recommendation was favourable, it was not until September, that I was officially informed that my detention was to continue.*
>
> *Twenty-six typed foolscap sheets of evidence were taken down at my appeal. A stenographer took down the evidence which was never read to me for verification after having been transcribed. A copy was later supplied to me by my solicitors. There were errors and omissions. Soon after my transference to Tatura I wrote to The Chief of the Intelligence Dept., Melbourne asking that I might be permitted to appear before a tribunal a second time, as I desired to correct inaccuracies in the recorded evidence and tender additional evidence supporting my appeal for release. To this letter I received a*

reply that my application could not be granted, since I had supplied no fresh evidence. This evidence I intended to give at the appeal I was seeking. When early in this year Japan bombed Darwin, and the Nazi inmates of Tatura Camp were rejoicing: 'Japan will get us out of here,' I again wrote to the Intelligence Dept., Vic, stating that I desired my own country, Australia, to release me, not Japan, and that I was ready to serve in any capacity that my age permitted. I received no reply.

Early in March, I think, I again wrote to the authorities stating if Tatura Camp 1 was officially recognised as a Nazi camp, and if my staying in that Camp automatically lined me up as a Nazi also, I asked to be transferred to another camp, preferably to S.A. since I was born in that State and my family lived there. I received no reply, but was sent to Loveday, S.A. on April 20 of this year.

About the end of May I addressed a letter to the Chief of the Intelligence Dept., Adelaide, seeking a second hearing before the Advisory Committee. Having received no reply, I sought an interview with the Official Visitor in September, and asked him to ascertain if my letter of May had reached its address. On his visit in October the O.V. informed me that my letter had not been received by the Intelligence Dept., Adelaide. He asked me to send a copy of the letter in question to the Deputy Director of Security at G.P.O., Adelaide. This I did. I have no advice that this letter reached its destination.

Sir, rehearsing in my mind the evidence given before the Advisory Com., I made a statement which may have been incorrect. Asked if the Returned Soldier who accompanied Count Luckner on his itinerary in S.A. was dressed in uniform I replied 'yes.' Prior to appearing before the Committee, I had spent two months under military guard – uniformed men. On reflection now, the Captain who accompanied Luckner may have been dressed in civilian clothes.

Filming was my hobby. Film paraphernalia and films cost money. In order to recoup myself a little I had to look for subjects of general interest. From a showman's point of view pure and simple I seized upon Luckner's visit to S.A. Since the outbreak of the war I showed only for patriotic bodies and helped raise just on two hundred pounds.

True, I attended a meeting of Nazis in Adelaide, having been offered a ride to the city by Dr. Becker. This happened at a time when rapprochement appeared likely between England and Germany. Public statements made by politicians and business men returned from trips abroad gave rise to the hope that a more complete understanding between the two peoples would soon be brought about. I have in mind an address given in Tanunda Memorial Hall by the late C. Hawker M.H.R.

At my hearing the solicitor for the Intelligence D. asked me, did I remember ever discussing the personnel of the staff in the Tanunda election booth on the occasion of the last Federal Elections, and did I then say, referring to the staff: 'They are all bloody Returned Soldiers.' I denied this. I desire to state emphatically again that any report to the Intelligence Dep., that I did say this is not a mere mis-statement, but a wicked lie, uttered with malice aforethought. I can distinctly recall the conversation I had with the local postmaster (the head of the election staff). We were discussing the election of the following day. I asked him who would be assisting him. He told me. My reply: 'All Returned Soldiers,' and my demeanour could leave no doubt in the others mind that I was delighted to learn that Returned Soldiers had exclusively been engaged. I respect no-one more than the man in uniform. Whether the soldiers dies fighting, returns wounded or safely, or does duty in non-combatant areas, the moment he dons the King's uniform, he offers his life's blood, he is 'all-in.' How could I, how dare I make the remark attributed to me!

During the present war, when trainees would come home weekends, and there being no train from Tanunda on Sundays, I have collected these men and driven them 18 miles to Gawler, the nearest station. On one occasion a group of West Australian men who had trained on in S.A. had come to Tanunda when on leave. They were at a loose end. I collected six of them in my car and took them through the large Seppeltsfield winery, six miles from my town. I have secretly handed cash to needy men, who had come home on their final leave. I find pleasure now in recording these facts. How could I refer to Soldiers as 'bloody.' Sir, if you have time to peruse the evidence given before the Advisory C. in my behalf (there were included 6 Justices of the Peace), I beg of you, would I be capable of the statement attributed to me!

Several months before my internment I visited the Intelligence Officer (Major Sharland, I think) with reference to my son, who was desirous of fitting in three months military training, when work at our printing works was slackest. I journeyed to Adelaide, where I met a Mr, Wilson, a former resident of Tanunda, now licensee of the Commercial Hotel, Gawler Place. I told him that I was on my way to Major Sharland. He gave me a letter of introduction to the Major, offered also to ring up the Dept. and arrange the interview. I first had an appointment with Mr. Edmunds, President of the S.A. Red Cross, with whom I discussed Red Cross and Trench Comforts work. I told Mr. Edmunds where I was going. He said: 'Mention my name, and your work with me.' Arrived at Major Sharland's room I was plied with questions about incidents and people of my town. The subject I desired to discuss received scant reference.

At this time enrolment for military service was not compulsory, but my son was desirous of fitting himself for work when the necessity arose. I mentioned nothing of the above incident before the Advisory C., trusting that in fairness to me it would be recorded in my favour. Can you ascertain, Sir, if this was done?

I am not a man of means, and I was forced to work my printing business on a bank overdraft. Yet I have supported all war efforts to my utmost. My wife, my two children and myself invested one hundred pounds in War Savings Certificates. I was instrumental in forming several War Savings Groups in my town. I raised close on two hundred pounds by film shows. On the occasion of a Penny Drive in my town I drew five pounds in pennies from the bank and distributed these among the organisers along the street. My wife and children spent all their savings – two hundred pounds, engaging a K.C. for my appeal.

My entry as a Labor Candidate at the last State elections was prompted by the honest belief, that our fighting forces, the men who are 'all-in' would now and later find more ready support from a Labor than any other form of government.

In the Tatura camp I busied myself with handicraft. When I arrived in Loveday the internees were quartered in tents and mess huts. There was no manpower available for hut-building. I was one of the first half-dozen who volunteered to erect huts and helped sinking holes for foundation posts until my hands blistered. Later when the gang numbered more than a score of workers, I was appointed time-keeper and tools supervisor. At present I am in charge of the Camps Works Office recording the time daily worked by men engaged in work inside and outside of the camp, and preparing the fortnightly wage sheets.

Believe me, Sir, there were never ulterior motives underlying my actions or public statements. I love the country of my birth, Australia. If it is believed that I have influence outside, I will in the future, as I did in the past, use it for good and not for evil. I have today been interned two years. I have had much time for reflection. I recall past activities of which I am not proud, my association with a betting shop for instance. But I sincerely desire to lend a hand. Beside my own I have a complete command of the

German language. Can I not be of assistance somewhere, rather than vegetate behind barbed wire?

Thanking you for a review of my case,
I am,
Yours respectfully,
(signed) J.F.W. Schulz 3077

Below this, in pencil, I have written: '*Handed to Commandant on 14/12/42. J.F.W.S.*'

On the 14th the Official Visitor came. He was with Graf, our Camp Leader, for quite a while, but the latter had no news for me.

17 – 24 December, 1942

What a burst of heat we have had and what a change to date, with the promise of rain. Tonight is Christmas Eve.

25 December, 1942

We had quite an enjoyable Christmas Eve. Our Mess hut quite tastefully decorated with about one hundred large candles burning in among green pine boughs and twigs, and round a large wreath of pine in the centre of the Mess hut. Coffee and well-baked cake was served, and over a loud speaker a gramophone recorded Christmas songs and carols, also Beethoven's 5th Symphony.

On reflection now, the eternal truth of the birth of Christ obtrudes. It overshadows all events, even the Armaggedon of today. May Christ's entry into the world, His atonement for our sins, be an accepted truth by erring and suffering mankind. Good-will towards men will bring peace on earth.

It rained a little during the night and heavily at breakfast this morning. I am hoping for a fine day tomorrow for the trip of my people here. Trudi's letter brought pleasant news.

Lutheran Christmas service in the Italian Mess hut tonight. Christmas tree with suitable decorations, and candles among greenery along half a dozen tables. Electric lights out. Yes, I felt again the truth and the power of the birth of Christ.

26 December, 1942

My children come to see me. Margaret, little Marie, Else and Steve. Steve's appearance in uniform makes me both proud and sad – proud that a member of the family is wearing the King's uniform, sad that he comes to visit me in an Internment Camp. But I feel content that the day will come when I will prove that I have been unjustly interned, that my children will be able to answer my traducers, assured of the fact that their father neither did nor said anything disloyal to the country that gave him birth.

Old Arnold, who celebrated his 70th Birthday a month ago, is being released today. I am not concerned about Arnold's politics for the moment, but I feel comforted in the thought that the powers that are, are allowing an old man to go to his home, whatever might be the restrictions.

After much delay we received our Christmas beer tonight. One pint each free of all charge. The evening is hot and it is asking much to make the pint hold through possibly another twelve months.

27 December, 1942

A sultry day. Zinnbauer has the day's Service. I regret that he perhaps quite unintentionally makes use of his turn as a practice half hour in the study of the English language.

I write a letter to Trudi.

Dear Trudi,

Thank you ever so much for your letter and the good news that it contained. I pray that you may be kept in health and that at some future date we may all celebrate a happy reunion. The visitors yesterday cheered me up a lot. It is now over two years ago that I am away from home. I live and work so that upon my return I will have proved that even during the term of my internment I have done and said nothing that can be construed as disloyal to my country. Some day we may learn what it was all about.

Yesterday Else, during her visit here said something about Ian Seppelt having approached Bert about some films, but she was unable to give me further particulars. On reflection I think I have found what he wanted. I had approached Mr. Wally Seppelt for assistance to enable me to buy films to film the Tanunda Baby Show for Patriotic purposes. He gave me a cheque for ten pounds. In return I promised him the 'Seppeltsfield' film: grape wagons at Seppeltsfield ranging up the hill, wagons waiting at the weighbridge, etc. etc. Try the film out on Rensche's projector and give it to Ian Seppelt. If they wish they may have the film titled at Kodaks.

I wish all of you a blessed New Year. Dad

The Camp Leader's office hands me the following note today:

14D Internment Camp Loveday

26 December, 1942

German Compound Leader,

> Please have the undermentioned Internees advised that their letters to the Attorney-General have been received.
> --- 3077 Schulz, J.F.W.
> Lt./Adjt.
> 14D Internment camp.

There is no signature to the document. The same ambiguity. Who has received my letter addressed to Dr. Evatt? The note does not say that it has been received by the Federal Attorney-General. It appears to be the end to this chapter again.

28 – 31 December, 1942

The Commandant marched a squad of garrison men into the Compound on the 28th and searched Hut 8 of the Italian section. Under the Hut, so report has it, a complete distilling outfit was discovered, besides a large sum of money in chits. A patient taken to the hospital in the morning was found to be under the influence. He came from Hut 8.

On the 29th, Boss Walker gets his release. I am glad. Boss appeared a genuine fellow. With him went three Italians including old Bernadario. At first, so I am told, he did not know what to do with his 'Freedom Ticket'. I would! Owing to lack of travelling facilities, so we are told, the party only left on the morning of the 31st.

I had a disturbed night on the 31st. In Compartment 2 of our Hut, Helbriegel was apparently attacked by acute appendicitis. The ambulance arrived and took him to the Hospital.

1 January, 1943

The beginning of a New Year! What has it in store for the individual, for all of us, for the nation? May God so guide the hearts and minds of the men that guide our destinies that Peace on earth and good-will towards men reign again.

2 – 3 January, 1943

In the Works Office, five of us enjoyed a supper deluxe last night; eggs, tomatoes, cucumbers and lettuce, prepared by Cerrato, our Chief Cook. Apart from it being a festive occasion, the break from our regular simple fare was a welcome change. Weather-wise, after a hot spell we are enjoying the cool change.

4 January, 1943

I am settling down to routine work in the Works Office, and enjoying the work. There are further searches for Stills in the Italian quarter. The best haul was apparently under the stage in the Mess hut.

5 January, 1943

The cleaning up process in the Italian section continues. Following a find in a shack alongside one of the huts, the entire shacks are being demolished today. Good riddance in the interest of the entire Compound.

6 – 7 January, 1943

On the 7th I go to Camp 10 to the Dentist and have one of my teeth put back for the fourth time. The Dentist did his job well. I see the humorous side of this. I was fortunate to recover my tooth after having spat it into the sand on the way to the Dentist. I run back and clean it under the tap.

8 January, 1943

I get a large case of good things from home and feel quite happy. Two Italians in Mess hut 'B' engaged in some bloodletting immediately after tea. Both combatants went into the bunker. The face of one looked like a jigsaw puzzle.

9 January, 1943

What a day! The morning broke tolerably fine. About midday the wind rose. Soon it increased in force. The Compound was enveloped in dust – fine dust, coarser bursts that stung. Though doors and windows of the huts were closed, any exposed part of the face or body reacted as though rubbed with sandpaper. Various were the interpretations why the Military Authorities had selected Loveday for an Internment Camp!

10 – 11 January, 1943

A fine day following the inferno of yesterday. Rills of sand piled along in regular formation indicated the sandstorm's wild display of twenty-four hours ago. Beds, clothing, meal utensils, everything needed dusting. We have ample time.

12-16 January, 1943

Almost winter conditions. On the 15th I hand in a note for the Commandant: 'Some of us young fellows in the Camp desire to engage in cricket practice. Can you assist us with some gear? A bat or two to begin with would be appreciated.'

The Commandant made available four second-hand bats from the Garrison's kit. Our side of the Camp played the Italians this afternoon. The game ends in a draw; sixty-three runs all, after an interruption to retrieve the ball when it had been hit through the barbed wire enclosure. It was a keen match.

On the 15th, the Commandant hands me a copy of a letter received from the Chief Director of Security, Melbourne. It reads:

'With reference to the representations made by you in your letter to Dr. Evatt, I have to advise that arrangements are being made for a full investigation of your case. You will be advised of the result in due course.'

A little ray of hope.

17 – 19 January, 1943

Kohnke and a number more have gone to Adelaide before the Advisory Committee. I wish everyone a favourable result.

I bought a dozen eggs yesterday and Pastor K. and I had three Spiegeleier each for tea. The first fried eggs after two years! What a shock my innards must have received!

20 January, 1943

Some weeks back, signatures were solicited by the Commandant for possible work outside the Compound – possibly grape picking. During the last few days 'Dame Rumour' had it that this business was nearing fruition. Today the lying jade responds with 'definitely nothing doing.'

21 – 25 January, 1943

Changing to summer weather. Examinations as to physical fitness are underway in the Compound. It does seem as if some will go out grape picking.

Sunday's cricket match was easily won by the Italians. Schloss provided the humour, when, after having had his eye badly cut by a rising ball, and upon being urged to leave the field for medical attention, he, with blood running down his face, desired indignantly to know, 'who is playing this blooming game?'

I receive a letter from Bert, dated 21 January:

Dear Dad,

This time I have quite a lot to write you about, so take a comfortable seat, and consider my letter carefully.

When the girls and Marie and Steve were up to see you on Dec. 26, El mentioned a few things regarding the Office in general. Since then I have gone further into the matter of the Auricht home, having also had legal advice. Here then, is the position in a nutshell. Your agreement with Miss Auricht gives her 'free use and occupation' of the house, 'during her lifetime.' And legal opinion is that the free use and occupation includes a life-interest, which in effect allows Miss A. to enjoy any benefits from the house, this also allowing her to sub-let the place. I know of course, that this was never your intention, namely that you never intended Miss A. to be in a position to receive monetary benefit from the place, but only that she or her mother should be permitted to do what they liked with the place so long as they were the occupants. I pointed this out to legal opinion, but it makes no difference, and there we are, with the following position facing us: you paying all rates and taxes, and Miss A. having free use of the place, including any rents collected! Well, that is the legal position, and I guess we can't alter it, and believe me, we at home have been racking our brains for days to arrive at some arrangement whereby your eventual interest in the house can best be served.

As you know, the place is in a terrible state, and as you also know, Miss A. would hardly be in a position to affect the necessary alterations. So that, if she let the house, it would only be to the type of tenant who would assist in the rapid deterioration of the place. You can well imagine how we would be feeling all the while! So, after very lengthy consideration I have decided to approach Miss A. with this offer: Trudi and I to take the place at fifteen shillings a week for as long a term as we can get (I will try for a term of twenty years), and we to make the necessary alterations. In this way we would be protecting our eventual property and saving terrific repairs at some future date. Miss A. would still be getting the 'benefits from a life-interest' in the place, to which she is entitled by law. Actually, we think Miss A. wants somebody to come into the place who would agree to let her have the use of the kitchen and, perhaps, the bathroom. That would, of course, be quite impossible with us. You will say right away, 'If she has the right to sub-let it, then she should also effect any necessary repairs and alterations.' Quite so. But if she were in a position to do so, which I very much doubt, you may be sure we would hardly get first chance to go into the place, especially if she is looking for a chance to part-let it. The one point I want to make very clear to her when she comes up to Tanunda next time is that our rental of fifteen shillings would be certain, and she would not have to bother about expenses on the house. You can imagine what a fifteen shilling per week tenant of the usual type would do to the place, and the many little odd repairs that would be demanded. Anyhow, we here at home don't think that anyone, not even the fifteen shilling a week type, would go into the place without a fairly decent bathroom, which, as you know, doesn't exist in the place.

Now, another matter. El also mentioned the extra one pound per week which Miss A is getting. I had always been under the impression that this was according to the terms of the agreement. On checking up, however, I find that this is not so, it being as I presume, an arrangement between yourself and Miss A while she was still doing work at the Office. Now, of course, this payment will cease. I will point out this position to her also. Strange that she didn't mention something about it when she left for the City! As this coming weekend is pay day, I expect Miss A up at the Office, and I will then be able to discuss these various things with her. She will require time to consider her position in the light of my offer.

Placed in her position, a person would naturally think of a place in which to spend ones last years. That is, of course, her matter to decide, but while the Mission ladies were in her house, she was happy enough in the spare room which is part of the Printing Office. There is another room adjoining this one which at present houses paper, but which could well be done out and made quite comfy. These two rooms with a veranda added to the roof should be quite comfy, especially if she has been satisfied to have all her belongings in the one room and live in it. However, this is a suggestion which would have to come from her. I would never dream of making the suggestion – I might be 'trying to get her out of the place,' or something like that! (Although, as El has just reminded me, she once made these suggestions to El of her own accord.) Anyhow, after her sale she hasn't the furniture to equip her house completely. Nor have we for that matter, but we are struggling along towards that goal.

Otherwise we are still plodding along at the Office, and what spare time there is I usually spend in the gardens, yes gardens. One at home and the other at the rear of the Office. Anything you want to know about tomatoes I will be pleased to advise you upon. We have been picking several every now and then for about a fortnight, but the main crop has not come into bearing as yet. One time I thought a tomato was just a tomato. Now I know better. I have eight different varieties in my various plots! And Trudi has pickled several lots of gherkins from our own cucumbers. Mum has just told me not to forget to mention her cabbage plot; about the nicest heads she has ever grown. Yes, we are real gardeners now!

Alf Pfeiffer, Ted Knispel, Alwin Zerna and I had a bit of a blow-out out bush last weekend. We had all been in fairly strenuous harness for quite a few months, and the break did us a lot of good. Trudi has been keeping really remarkably well, a thing we are both very thankful for. I trust things will turn out just as well eventually. Regarding other news, you have been kept well-informed by Else, I imagine. As you will realise, I am very keen to hear your views on the suggestions I have enumerated in this letter, so I'll await your reply by return!

Love from Gert and Bert

26 January, 1943

A very important day. Captain Sexton called me into the Commandant's office. I am happy to appear before the Advisory Committee a second time – in about three weeks' time. It is to be an entirely new Hearing before an entirely new Appeal Board. Captain Sexton offers any assistance I might desire. 'Make no mistake, Mr. Schulz, I am going to fight like hell to keep you in and you want to fight like hell to get out.'

I write to Bert and ask him to engage Teusner. Captain Sexton gives his telephone number C2172: Bert or Teusner may contact him and collect further particulars.

Dear Bert,

Thanks for your long and informative letter. I mailed a letter to El yesterday and trust this one will reach you without much delay. I absolutely agree with your suggestion re the residence at the Printing Office. Ask Miss Auricht to let you have the house at as reasonable rental as possible. Payment of rent to commence only when you actually move in. You could then have the necessary repairs effected without undue hurry. In any case I take it that you would not desire to move for a few months. Whatever money Miss Auricht has drawn from the business weekly must be debited to her a/c just as you must debit my a/c with the money you draw for Mum every fortnight.

Please tell Miss Auricht that I did not reply to her last letter, as I felt that she would hear from me through my letters to you. Tell her please, that I am working continuously for one shilling per day; that I have asked for no money for many months and prefer to do without things that are not absolutely essential – as all of us must these times. But endeavour to secure the premises at all costs, if possible. The lemons you sent me recently are wonderful in these hot days: half a lemon in cold water filled into my thermos lasts me half a day. I am so glad that Trudi is feeling well, and hope Mum can get over these extremely hot days alright. If Miss Auricht is not agreeable, she should write me before letting. – Dad

27 – 31 January, 1943

I interview the Commandant who gives me all the possible assistance. He allows a copy of the letter to Dr. Evatt to go through to Mr. Richards, and helps with a telegram to Bert etc.

We are struggling through a sweltering heat wave for the best part of a week. In food and drink I do everything possible to keep up my health. I must be well for the job ahead of me. Practically every day the ambulance is called in and takes men to the Hospital. Sun stroke etc. has laid many low and the fare is not suited to the weather conditions.

I write a letter to Bert dated 27 January:

Business Letter

Dear Bert,

You no doubt have my letter of yesterday's date. I have had another opportunity of speaking to the Intelligence Officer (Capt. Sexton) this morning who left me in no doubt that the fight at the tribunal would be all out, but he gave me all possible assistance. I gave him Bert Teusner's name as that of my solicitor, who may contact Capt. Sexton at 4th Floor, Trustee Buildings, Grenfell Street, Adelaide, Telephone, Central 2172. Teusner may make an appointment with the Captain and discuss particulars of the hearing, when it will take place, when I might be expected in Adelaide etc. Maybe you can include a Returned Soldier among those who are prepared to testify for me. Last time it was suggested that I would not have my daughters married to an Englishman. I would like Else to appear for me as the wife of an Englishman and a corporal in the forces. El might also produce the letter I wrote to her when Steve left for service. You might produce for B. Teusner's perusal (confidentially) the evidence taken down at my first appeal. I am writing to Mr. Richards asking him to appear personally or supply evidence on affidavit why it was impossible to withdraw my candidature at the 1941 State Elections.

It may be desirable, if you think so, to ask F. Homburg to come as a J.P., if he will, and Teusner might seek his collaboration in preparing for the hearing. To all my friends you may say this: In spite of experiences during my two years' internment which often times have driven me right to despair, I have at no time done anything savouring of disloyalty to the country of my birth. When it became evident that Camp 1 Tatura was recognised by the authorities as a Nazi Camp I did not rest until I was transferred. At Loveday I have given my services, almost from the time of my arrival here, at one shilling a day, building huts etc. I shall endeavour to supply Mr. Teusner with a copy of the evidence I am preparing if not before, then when he visits me at Wayville before my hearing comes on.

I know you will all do what lies in your power to help me.
Your father
J.F.W. Schulz
NB: I need a few pairs of cashmere socks.

1 – 2 February, 1943

The weather breaks on the 2nd. Thank God for the change. Schloss also has news for a second Hearing. There appears to be a break in the darkness.

3 February, 1943

A very marked change in the weather – extreme heat to cold. I work studiously on notes for my upcoming case.

4 – 5 February, 1943

Not feeling well. The Kitchen is doing its best to please the palates of four hundred odd boarders, but with the supplies at their disposal they rarely succeed. Still, cooler weather will alter things.

6 – 23 February, 1943

A long interval. Preparing for my Hearing, these daily notes have been neglected. On the 9th I receive a reply-paid telegram from Bert: 'In your interest highly advisable to engage Harford also his fee very low we urge you to agree wire immediately.'

On the 12th I, with others, move through the gates en route for Adelaide. Schloss, Huppert, and Dr. Muggia are members of the party. Altogether twenty-nine eventually move on to Adelaide. The night from the 12th to the 13th was passed in the bunker.

The trip to Adelaide, commencing at 9 a.m. at Barmera Station via Renmark and Murray Bridge, lasted until 7.50.p.m. En route, girls in the hills wave to us. They did not see our red pants. At a hillside station one of our guards told a bystander not to converse with us or he 'would go along with them.' Them!!

At the Adelaide Station we had to wait approximately an hour before conveyances took us to Wayville.

On Sunday Bert, Else and Ted visit me.

On Monday, Teusner sees me and I am informed that it would be impossible for my case to be heard during the week. I would probably have to return to Loveday and come again the following week.

Tuesday was an extremely hot day – 111.1 degrees Fahrenheit in the shade. Overnight, conditions changed and rain set in and the temperature dropped to 69 degrees F.

On Wednesday 17th, the Intelligence Department brings me the news telephoned to Bert that a little daughter has been born him and Gert, on the 16th. How happy I feel!

On Thursday we were joined by thirty released Italians who had volunteered to do work under certain restrictions. Noticeable was the behaviour of some of the 'released' men against 'internees'. Altogether, our stay at Wayville was a pleasant one. Food good and plenty of it. Anything we needed was brought for us from the Canteen.

Today, the 18th, I write a letter to Bert:

Dear Bert,

You can hardly imagine how overjoyed I was to learn that a daughter had been born to you. I trust that Gert and the little one will return to the home safe and well. Marie is now not the 'one and only grandchild in all the world,' but one day she and I will both, God willing, stand and discuss admiringly the newcomer's little nose and eyes and chubby cheeks and then compare how big Marie now is and Uncle Bert's little daughter is so wee and small. God protect you all.

I am staying on here, probably over Sunday and until my appeal comes on for hearing. This is not meant as a summons to you to come and see me on Sunday, I am well and have brought clothing sufficient to meet the change in the weather.

Trusting that Mum and all of you are well and that Gert will soon return home restored to strength. I often thought of her and the little one during the extremely hot day following the baby's birth.

Dad

On Friday night a party of nineteen of us was informed of our return to Loveday the following (Saturday) morning. I had contracted a severe cold overnight and the return journey was a trying one for me. Before leaving Wayville, I sent a telegram to Bert: 'Returning Loveday today.' At around 7 o'clock on the 20th we were back in Loveday. I shall forever cherish the memory of acquaintances made at Wayville and friendships renewed. Corporal Thomas, associated with the Adelaide Girls Band which competed at Tanunda, G. Hayes, Riedel and Lambert. The sustaining friendship of these men is a guarantee that they bear no ill feeling towards me.

24 February, 1943

My cold is gradually shifting. Another thirty Italians are being released today for work outside. The ranks in the Compound are gradually thinning, the Manpower position outside being correspondingly improved with the recent releases of some internees.

25 – 28 February, 1943

The month has drawn to a close and I have not been called to Adelaide. The nights are cool though the summer prevails at daytime. I wonder how little Elizabeth Margaret is developing? How I would like to see her!

1 March, 1943

No further news as to when I am to go to Adelaide again.

6 March, 1943

The Western Australian Italians, evidently unwilling to join their Queensland countrymen, have had their tents removed from over their heads.

7 – 11 March, 1943

No word of when I am to go to Adelaide again to be heard. I am beginning to fear---! We shall see. A wireless has been installed in the Mess hut.

12 – 17 March, 1943

I have still heard nothing further regarding my second Appeal. Italians are being released in large numbers also, occasionally, some from our part of the Compound, including Stein and Penkfeld.

19 March, 1943

My 60th Birthday. The third Birthday spent behind barbed wires. I receive heartening letters, telegrams and parcels, including photos of Baby Elizabeth.

20 – 26 March, 1943

No further developments re my Hearing. It is eight weeks today (26th) since Captain Sexton told me that I was to have a second Hearing. Most of the men who went to Adelaide with me for a Hearing already have replies (mostly unfavourable), while mine has apparently been lost sight of. Luky, through Solicitor King, hears that he is to have a second Appeal.

28 March, 1943

Dental Inspection for all. The dentist's remark after inspecting my teeth, 'You want a bit of an overhaul, don't you?' He told his assistant to mark 'B' opposite my name.

29 – 31 March, 1943

Still warm and unpleasant days. For those at work on the Kit store, it was a disappointment that the foundation was built in the wrong place. Seventy bags were used. The building is now to be erected in the Garrison area.

On the 31st, I hand the following cover note and two articles written by me, to the Commandant for Captain Sexton:

> *Sir,*
>
> *While my appeal before the Advisory Committee is still pending permit me to present to you the attached notes for your kind perusal.*
> *Yours respectfully*
> *J.F.W. Schulz*
> *S/3077*

Written on my 60th Birthday.

My parents came to Australia about seventy-five years ago. Neither they, I, nor any of their children returned there. Though my parents were never well off, they were never in want of food and clothing. All I have I owe the country of my birth, Australia. It is my country; for it I have worked and it I desire to assist with all the means at my disposal in the future. It is my fervent wish that neither Germany nor Japan have a say in the government of this country. Our rising generation must be more diligently taught a love for its country and to say and believe: This is my country; for it I will work and fight! Every drop of sweat will save drops of blood. We must have an army with a country rather than a country with an army. Our men who have fought and died have not made the sacrifice for the world as it was and conditions as they were but for better future conditions. Our immediate rehabilitation and repatriation schemes must be mindful of the work done and the sacrifices made by these men who fought off the Japanese in the Bismark Sea. The Returned Soldier must receive our first and fullest consideration. He was all-in, and our efforts in his behalf must be wholehearted. All I have and am I pledge in support of the very great task confronting us when the war ends: which I pray must end in a victory for us.

Loveday, March 19, 1943
J.F.W. Schulz (The date of my 60th Birthday) 3077

Manpower Shortage.

On several occasions I have offered my services to the authorities – ready to serve in any capacity that my age and strength will permit. A few days ago, shortage of firewood is again referred to in 'The Advertiser.'

For seven months I have now been in charge of the Works Office in Compound 14D. In that capacity I have come to know the men in this compound, at any rate those who are at work inside and outside of the compound, about two hundred in number. I have had to take men off the pay sheet, and engage new men. Preparing the fortnightly pay sheet has also been part of my work. I believe I have been able to gain the confidence and respect of the men with whom I have come in contact, and make bold to say that a selected gang of men from this camp to cut firewood with myself as overseer and time-keeper would work harmoniously and help overcome the firewood problem. The gang would be composed of Italians, though I believe a few Australians could be induced to join.

It is understood, of course, that the men engaged be released to work under restrictions similar to the gangs already at work.

Kindly accept these suggestions as in earnest of my desire to be of help.

Loveday, March 26
J.F.W. Schulz. 3077

1 April, 1943

April Fool's Day joke: 'I am released.'

2 – 7 April, 1943

The examination of Italians continues, also Persians, for release to work. I want to join the Dental party to have a tooth extracted but the list is full. Bad luck!

8 – 13 April, 1943

On the latter day – 13th – I am advised by Captain Sexton that I am to proceed to Adelaide for a second time to appear before the Advisory Committee. When I told Captain Sexton that I would engage counsel to defend me, he said: 'I am going to fight like hell to keep you in.' Those present on this occasion were: Major Whitehill, Camp Commandant, Mr. Graf, Camp Leader, and the latter's assistant, Mr. Nofz.

14 – 16 April, 1943

On the 14th I write to Bert:

> *Dear Bert,*
>
> *I have just had advice that I am to proceed to Adelaide on Saturday 24 inst. for hearing before the Advisory Committee and have today wired you this information. Since my return here over eight weeks ago I have not had one scrap of information why this long delay. Now you must make the necessary arrangements with Mr. Teusner, so that I am not returned a second time without being heard. I am guessing I might be heard on Tuesday 27 inst. Maybe someone may be able to see me during the Easter holidays. From El's letters I learn that your little Elizabeth has been giving you and Trudi some anxiety. I do hope that she will recover and soon grow strong and well. With the work in the office, the renovating of the house and your probable moving into your new home, you sure have got your hands full. However, when we reflect how much hardship and suffering there is all around us, we cannot but be thankful that we have been spared the lot of thousands of our fellow creatures. May God grant that the sacrifices of our forces are not in vain, and may we never forget what we owe them.*
> *Your father.*
> *Bring me a few books to read.*

On the 16th I am vaccinated a second time since my stay in Tatura, the other occasion was about twelve months ago. It can only be for good even though, especially at my age, it causes some inconvenience. Buffalo

Bill provided the highlights. He was afraid of the vaccination and finally, barefooted, eluded capture.

17 – 21 April, 1943

I receive a letter from Else with the information that I am to be heard before the Advisory Committee on the 27th inst. On the 20th it is twelve months since my arrival at Loveday. On the 21st one hundred and fifty Italians are brought into the Camp.

24 April, 1943

A party of four from our part of the Camp and eighteen Italians leave for Adelaide to be heard before the Advisory Committee.

25 – 30 April, 1943

Together with a number of other internees I arrived in Adelaide for my second Hearing. Upon arrival there, Captain Sexton visited us at the Detention Barracks on the day before the cases came on for hearing. One of the internees asked Captain Sexton: 'Will our evidence be read to us at the conclusion of the Hearing?' Captain Sexton's reply: 'It will not.' 'Will we get a copy of the evidence?' Reply: 'You will not.' 'Can we engage someone to take down the evidence in our behalf?' Reply: 'Definitely not.'

At the commencement of my second Hearing, the charges against me were read. The first charge was that I had visited Germany shortly before the outbreak of the war. Now, I have never been out of Australia, with the exception of a twelve month stay in New Guinea in 1920.

In reply to questions by my Solicitor, I told the Advisory Committee this. Am I to take it that the Intelligence Department holds sworn declarations that I did visit Germany?

1 – 8 May, 1943

On the 3rd another full day before the Committee. I am happy about the two days hearings, feeling assured that whatever the result as to my future liberty might be, no evidence was proved during the course of the two days that can brand me a traitor to my country.

9 – 15 May, 1943

Wintry conditions have set in, but without rain. Rather than go to the fire to warm myself, I go out to the wood-heap daily splitting firewood for the Kitchen for an hour. This provides exercise I am badly in need of.

16 – 21 May, 1943

I receive three pounds from Bert. I need shoes and a hat and maybe a pyjamer suit may be procurable for that amount.

1 September, 1943

A long interval with no Diary notes while awaiting Tribunal's decision. I feel optimistic about the result.
 Today is the anniversary of my occupancy of the position as Works Supervisor in the Camp. During these twelve months I have faithfully

carried out the duties devolving on me. In particular, finding as much work as possible for inmates of the Camp willing to work at one shilling per day, at the same time endeavouring to conserve the interests of the Authorities who provide the work.

During leisure hours I have busied myself at the wood-heap for muscular exercise, keeping in good health as a consequence.

The Lancaster Bomber visiting Australia circled low over the Camp several times this morning. Its speed, bulk and general appearance impressed immensely and eliminated any inferiority complex under which we might have been labouring. It helped us move from a possible fearful defence to a fearless offence. With a fleet of Lancaster Bombers at our command, we need not hesitate in calling the Japanese bluff.

9 September, 1943

News over the radio of Italy's unconditional surrender! What news! Please God we have the end in sight. Ours then will be the task of creating a state of affairs making a Third World War an impossibility.

14 September, 1943

Visit from my family, including little Elizabeth who I have not seen as yet. I feel very happy and the bonny child's green eyes scintillating with laughter are ever before me. Yes, I have a lot to be thankful for. Whatever betides, nothing must make me step out of the great big picture. There is so much suffering in the world. Our resolve must be to shape the future so that our children are spared a repetition of the present Armageddon.

17 September, 1943

Thank God the sacrifices made by our men landed in Italy now appear not to have been made in vain. May we now win through here. The end would then appear in sight.

Splendid rain towards morning. Large pools of water everywhere in the Compound. Lo and behold, by lunchtime a gale is blowing and beyond fifty yards you can see nothing for dust!

20 September, 1943

The morning broke fine, but within a few hours wind sprang up and by noon had developed into a dust storm surpassing anything experienced in the Camp as yet. There was no escaping the dust. It found its way into the huts covering everything with a gritty surface. If you lay down to read, it soon made its presence felt in an irritating itch on your face. It formed a thin layer on your soup, and seemed to be felt and heard in wireless broadcasts.

The water in tubs set out for washing our Mess gear was soon a yellowish gritty substance, and on the way from the Mess Hall the still wet plate and pannikin was soon covered with moist dust and sand, while you found yourself forging ahead with bent head and cap pulled right down in an attempt to escape the driving, stinging pebbles of sand.

The place appears swept clean of everything, but still a dense cloud of dust seems to envelope everything, at times making it difficult to distinguish objects but a few yards distant. Working parties are cancelled for the afternoon because of the weather conditions.

14 October, 1943

During the week almost one hundred have been released from the Camp, almost exclusively Italians. Though I am still being held, I am glad to see men being placed in work rather than idle away their time, costing the country additional money. Furiously, some of the released were loath to leave!

28 October, 1943

Releases are lagging, but today two men from our side got their freedom. Report has it that they have volunteered for the Army. Good luck to them – Stier and Schmidt.

3 November, 1943

What a day! Following a night of thunder and rain, a westerly sprang up early in the morning. Defying the efforts of the downpour overnight to bind and hold the soil, the gale literally tore sand and pebbles from their beds to send swirling eddies across the Compound. One sinuous, sneaky, rainy cloud followed and overtook the other. Occasionally one dull yellow coloured mass appeared to bite back at the one immediately succeeding it, to continue its madcap career in full enjoyment of destruction and discomfort it had wrought.
'Love' – day: a first-class study in soil erosion.

26 November, 1943

Materne, Zinnbauer, and I were visited by Rev. J.J. Stolz today and he assured us that we are not forgotten either by the Church or by himself. He brought us up-to-date on Church matters, and also told us he has written to Dr. Evatt about our internment but, as yet, has had no reply.

7 December, 1943

I hand a letter in at the Orderly Room addressed to Dr. Evatt, reminding him of the letter I wrote him on Dec. 13th 1942, relative to matters concerning my internment. I was then promised that a full investigation was underway. I appeared before an Advisory Committee finally on May 3rd. To date I have not heard what was the Committee's recommendation! Will I spend my fourth Christmas behind barbed wires?

My letter reads as follows:

> *Sir,*
>
> *On Dec. 13th 1942 I wrote you relative to my internment. On Dec. 26th I was advised that you had received the letter and on January 15th of this year the Chief Director of Security advised that arrangements were being made for full investigation of my case. On January 26th Captain Sexton (S.A. Intelligence Dept.) informed me that I was to appear before the S.A. Advisory Committee a second time. For this purpose, I was taken to Adelaide on February 12th, but was returned to Loveday without being heard. It was not until May 3rd that I finally appeared before the Tribunal, notwithstanding that during the interim other internees from this camp were called to Adelaide.*
>
> *To date I have had no intimation as to the Advisory Committee's recommendation, nor of the Security Department's action in reference thereto.*
>
> *When this letter reaches you, sir, I will have been behind barbed wire three years and approaching my 61st birthday. Christmastide with its message of good-will towards all men will soon be with us again.*
>
> *May I look forward to spending Christmas with my family?*
>
> *Yours respectfully*

J.F.W. Schulz'
8 December, 1943

A day after my letter to Dr. Evatt, I receive word from the Deputy Director of Security, S.A., Ref. No. 13476 dated Dec. 3 and signed 'English' for Deputy Director of Security, advising me that the recommendation made by the S.A. National Security Advisory Committee that my detention be continued, has been approved. I was also informed that the Attorney-General has directed that my case be further reviewed in February, 1944. I acknowledge receipt to the Dep. Director S.A.

9 December, 1943

I write to Dr. Evatt, expressing the hope that the review in February be expeditiously dealt with. The draft of my letter to Dr. Evatt reads as follows:

> Sir,
>
> *Yesterday, the day following the dispatch of my letter to you dated 7th inst., I received advice from the Deputy Director of Security S.A. advising that my detention was to continue and that the Attorney-General has directed that my case be further reviewed in February, 1944.*
>
> *After nearly eight months of waiting since I appeared before the Advisory Committee I have now at long last received a reply and am looking forward confidently to favourable news in February next.*
>
> *In case the time mentioned for a review of my case has any connection with the S.A. State Elections, I desire to state that I had not intended to take part in the election in any form whatsoever. My home will be my castle, ever mindful of the debt of gratitude*

we owe our fighting forces who have preserved our homes intact. At my appearance before the Advisory Committee I resented nothing more than the imputation that I had made derogatory remarks with reference to returned soldiers. I honour and respect nobody more than our men in uniform, the men who are giving their lives that future generations may see and enjoy better conditions.

Trusting that I will be favoured with an early and favourable reply when my case again comes up for review.

I remain,
Yours respectfully,
J.F.W. Schulz.

I write a second letter today, this one to the Deputy Director of Security in Adelaide. My copy reads as follows:

Sir,

At the Camp Commandant's Office I was yesterday advised of your intimation that my detention was to continue and that the Attorney-General had directed that my case be again reviewed in February next.

In case the time mentioned for a review of my case has any connection with the impending S.A. elections I desire to state that it had not been my intention to take part in the elections in any form whatsoever.

Trusting that an early decision will be arrived at when my case is again reviewed,

I remain,
Yours respectfully.
J.F.W. Schulz'
12 December, 1943

Padre Davies conducted his second service in the Compound today. In an eloquent, inspiring sermon he outlined the fundamentals of true faith. A larger congregation than is usually in evidence on Sundays was present, and, I feel sure, left the service much cheered. We are promised a monthly service and I, for one, am looking forward to his next visit.

13 December. Third anniversary of my internment! Three years behind barbed wire! Two appearances before Advisory Committees, in each case having to wait eight months before receiving advice from the Security Department relative to the Advisory Committee's recommendations. What I have, at times, suffered, having testified before God that I was innocent of any act prejudicial to the safety of the Empire and the successful prosecution of the war, it is impossible to write down.

In the meantime, the numerical strength of Camp 14D has dwindled from close on one thousand to two hundred and fifty-five today, owing to like Exodus of Italians. And what class of man was included in the released? Outspoken Fascists, secretaries and presidents of Fascist organisations! Many left here against their wish and will! And many of us are still being held. Still, everything will come right in time.

I am today taking over supervision of the camp flower garden. I shall put my heart and soul into the work of sowing and tending God's creations for man's enjoyment.

16 December, 1943

Today I am a member of the Dental party. On the way to Headquarters, a hare that has strayed on to the netted main road causes excitement and amusement. What some people don't know about hare-hunting would fill an encyclopaedia! I have three teeth drawn and two filled. A bit gruelling for the moment. The Dentist did his job well. I feel much the better for the operation. Why were we not born with false teeth? And perhaps with a false liver and false corns!

20 December, 1943

I get much enjoyment out of work in the Garrison garden. Am making an attempt to restore a Bowling Rink to order.

22 December, 1943

Another one of our infamous sand storms. Throughout the morning it blew all out hot from the north, and half way through the afternoon, in repentant mood, it sought to repair the damage done earlier in the day by carrying through southern windows such dust and sand that had failed to gain ingress into the huts by northern doors and windows in the forenoon.

I obtain permission to show my films in Camp. Sergeant Richter phones Bert for me telling him what films to bring me. I am promised a visit for the 29th.

24 December, 1943

My fourth Christmas interned. We celebrate the occasion with a meeting in the suitably and tastefully decorated Messroom. A lavish display of pine tree branches and sprigs, and innumerable candles shedding subdued flickers of light. Christmas carols and music remind us of the day we celebrate the birth of Christ. The Camp leader, Mr. Graf, and myself, gave short addresses. I based my remarks on the dialogue between Scrooge and his nephew: 'A Merry Christmas.' All present received coffee, biscuits, apple tart, and cigarettes.

25 December, 1943

Church Service in the morning consisting mainly of the singing of Christmas hymns, and reading Scripture passages. Pastors Materne, Zinnbauer, and Doehler officiating.

In the evening we received our annual mug of beer! Six of us enjoy a special Christmas dinner. It included poultry! My first taste of poultry in three years!

26 December, 1943

At about 5.15 p.m. we experienced the worst dust storm yet. You could see nothing of the Compound save the hut you were in. On entering the Mess Hut it was impossible to distinguish who walked at the other end.

28 December, 1943

Continued releases of Italians had reduced their number from seven hundred to about one hundred, but today we received the first Contingent from Camp 9. These, however, are also to be released soon. All told, about two hundred and fifty are to arrive here by the 31st.

29 December, 1943

How could I omit this day! A visit from Bert, Ted, Margaret, Gert, Else, and the two dear grandchildren, Marie and Elizabeth. What a wonderful hour we spent, and what tokens of love and considerations they provided in the many gifts they brought. In gratitude, I will also ever remember the Hurst family. All this tangible evidence of good-will will sustain and help to cheer me on in the days ahead. I also receive a collection of seeds and bulbs for the Garrison gardens. Among the many gifts is a card with the wording: 'Christmas Greetings to Grandpa from Elizabeth' and six small photographs of her are inside. In four of them she is wearing her Christening gown, and in the last one, she is giving Grandpa a beautiful smile.

1 January, 1944

Abreast another milestone in the march of time. May God grant that the New Year bring peace on earth and relief to suffering humanity. The weather has eased somewhat with promise of a further fall of temperature. Ossie Schubert arrived here yesterday from Camp 9.

2 - 3 January, 1944

I receive word that I am to be released!!
    I show films in Camp on the 3rd. The Sergeant Major enjoys a joke about my censoring newspapers when I am released!

4 January, 1944

I sign a statement as follows:

> *Following my release from No. 14D Internment Camp, Barmera, South Australia, and en route to my proposed place of abode in South Australia, I, Johann Friedrich Wilhelm SCHULZ,*
> *HEREBY UNDERTAKE TO REPORT TO:*
> *The Deputy Director of Security for S.A., 4th Floor, Trustee Buildings, 22 Grenfell Street, ADELAIDE. at 9 A.M. on Thursday, 6th January 1944.*

DATED at Barmera, South Australia, this fourth day of January, 1944.
Signed: J.F.W. Schulz
Witnessed by: Lieut. Roesler

5 January, 1944

Homeward bound! First refreshments paid for at Allawoona. Sign: 'No Beer.' We, Drish and I have two Ports! At Karoonda: Beer! Eleven pence!

6 January, 1944

I sign another statement:

Following my release from Internment, I, J.F.W. SCHULZ, hereby undertake to report to the Deputy Director of Security for South Australia at 09.00 hours on Monday the 10th January, 1944.
Signature: J.F.W. Schulz
Witness: F.M. Styles
Dated at Adelaide South Australia this Sixth day of January, 1944.

- END -

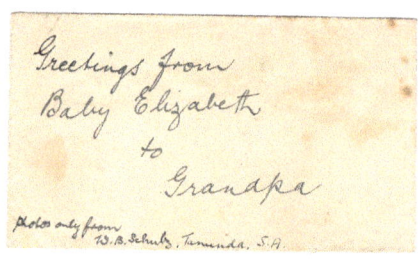

Greetings from Baby Elizabeth to Grandpa. Photos only from W.B. Schulz, Tanunda, S.A

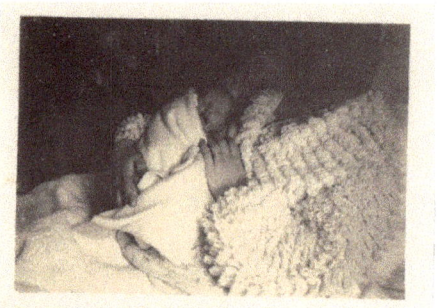

Trudi and baby Elizabeth in hospital, age – 6 days!

'Elizabeth, age 3 weeks'

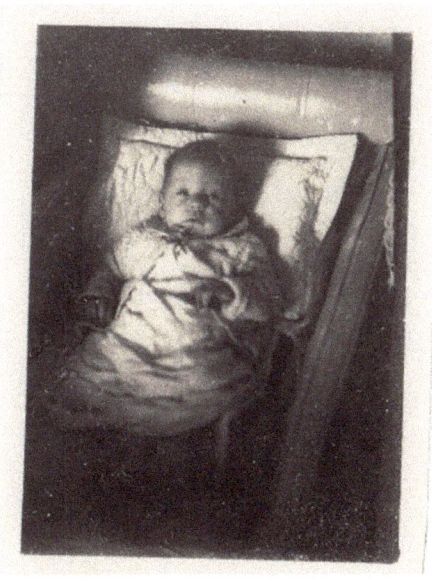

A special pose for Grandpa at 9 weeks

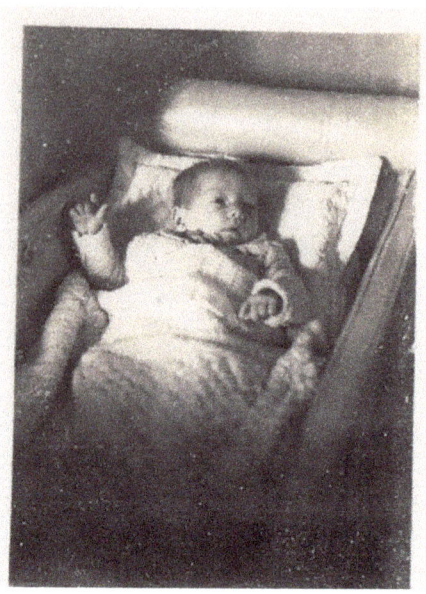

Elizabeth, aged 9 weeks.

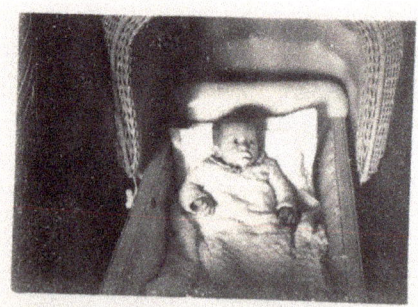

Smoke--oh at last!

Pop has to help too!

Programm

zum Heiligen Abend Weihnachten 1 9 4 3.

---

1) "Halleluja" aus dem "Messias" von Haendel.
2) B Sanctissima (Blasorchester)
3) A Christmas Carol (Ch.Dickens) vorgetr. von Herrn Schulz.
4) Ave Maria (Violinsolo) v. Schubert, gesp. von Herrn Dr.V.jhelyi.
5) Ansprache - A.Graf.
6) Oh Du Froehliche (R.Tauber).
7) Stille Nacht, Heilige Nacht.   Mitsingen erwuenscht.

Weihnachtsbescherung.

Kaffee u.Kuchen.

Unterhaltungsmusik.

1) Es leuchten die Sterne (R.Serrano)
2) Vagabond King (Orgelsolo)
3) Sweet Mystery of Life (R.Crooks).
4) Tosolli Serenade)Tauber)
5) Il Trovatore (J.Schmidt)
6) Man darf nicht so schwau seh'n (Val.Martens)
7) La Paloma (R.Serrano)
8) Carmen cita la gitana (R.Serrano)
9) Recuerdas tu ?
10) Violetta.
11) Wenn ich gross bin, liebe Mutter. (Gruendgens)
12) Nachtgebet (M.Thoma).

Programm (back)

1943
Dec. 20ᵗʰ - 25ᵗʰ

Weihnachts-Dinner
Menu

Hühner - Bouillon
Gefüllte Tomaten
Brathuhn, Erbsen
Filetsteak, Butterkartoffel, gem. Salat
Fruchtsalat
Obsttortelettes, Kaffee

Kalte Getränke

14 D
S.A.

Gemeindebücherei
Loveday

Christmas

Greetings

to

Grandpa

from

Elizabeth

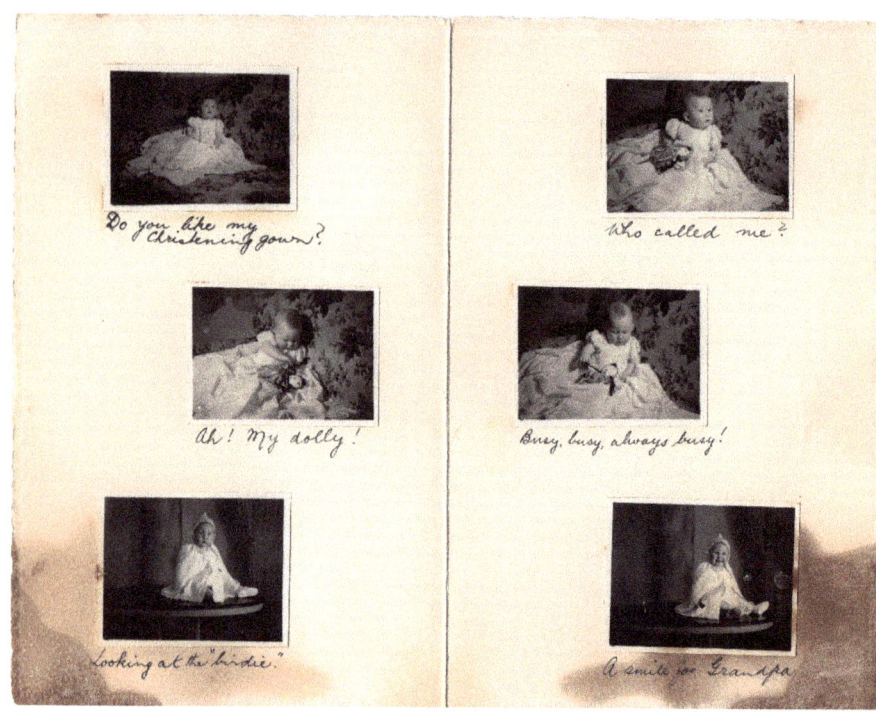

ABOUT THE AUTHOR

Liz Schulz by Maria Ames

Liz Schulz is an artist, educator, and author. The catalyst for the research that would become Prisoner Diaries and Guilty Till Proven Innocent was a request from Liz's mother more than 50 years ago. In 1970, on returning from living overseas for 10 years, her mother asked her to help research the Schulz family history. After she died 7 years later, the job of gathering together all the family documents fell to Liz. When she found the diaries, she knew they were an important part of not only her family, but Australia's social and wartime history.

As part of Liz's Bachelor of Education, she was encouraged by her professor, Margaret Allen, to research her grandfather's detention story. She researched the papers at the Australian Archives, and used content from her grandfather's diaries, family letters, and military documentation. After successful presentation and positive feedback, Liz sent copies to family members. Typed and bound, her copy languished on a bookshelf for decades.

When Liz retired in the mid-2000s, she chose the tranquillity of Andamooka in a semi-underground home built of local stone. She started sorting books and papers and came across the notebook where she had transcribed, in pencil, all his diary entries. Re-reading the papers provided her with the understanding that there was much more to tell.

Liz has wonderful memories of her grandfather and it feels like she is honouring him to tell his story and to share it as an example of detention, especially given Australia's current legislation.

Prisoner Diaries and Guilty Till Proven Innocent are dedicated to the memory of J.F.W. Schulz and Liz's twin sisters, Josie and Helen.

ABOUT THE BOOK

J.F.W Schulz was an Australian of German heritage who was born north of the Barossa Valley in Robertstown. He was the owner of Auricht's Printing Office, he had a keen interest in film, and was an aspiring politician. He was also a prisoner.

On 13 December 1940, Schulz was arrested and transported to the Wayville Army Barracks. No accusations were made at that time, but Schulz knew what the arrest meant; someone, somewhere, considered him a threat.

Despite an absence of evidence of his disloyalty to Australia, his country of birth, and without a fair trial, Schulz was detained for more than three years. Prisoner Diaries is a record of Schulz's internment during World War II and his relentless search for answers.

www.ingramcontent.com/pod-product-compliance
Lightning Source LLC
Chambersburg PA
CBHW051533010526
44107CB00064B/2714